T0148795

MEMOIRS OF A LOST WORLD

MEMOIRS OF A LOST WORLD

Lascelle Meserve de Basily

Stanford, California 1975
Distributed by Hoover Institution Press

International Standard Book Number: 0-9600928-1-1
Library of Congress Catalog Number: 75-29793

Table of Contents

Preface

These pages are an account of my journeys through a lost world, a world which today seems unreal, vanished in the mists of time.

Calderon de La Barca, the seventeenth century Spanish poet, wrote a drama entitled: *Life is a Dream.* Was my life a dream? Or was it reality? Who knows? Begun in the first part of the twentieth century, this existence has been one of travels, in Europe and to distant lands, Korea, Japan, China, and Imperial Russia, with my father H. Fessenden Meserve, and later to South America with my husband Nicolas de Basily. In spite of spacious homes on four continents, Fate always sent us forth on new adventures in a changing world.

Born in the United States, brought up in Paris, the magic thread of life led me through two wars, one in Korea, the other in Russia, and two revolutions in the latter.

When I married in 1919, my husband was Counselor of the Imperial Russian Embassy in Paris. I received Russian citizenship and a Russian passport, an immense fold of white paper whereon was written in French: "Madame Lascelle de Basily, épouse de Monsieur Nicolas de Basily, Conseiller de l'Ambassade de Russie à Paris, continue son séjour à l'étranger." My husband of course received the same document, stating that we "continued our stay abroad." This "stay abroad" lasted throughout life. We never returned to Russia. With the fall of the Empire and the Bolshevik administration, my husband, like all patriotic Russians, turned his back on the past. He died many years later, in exile, still mourning his beloved, lost fatherland.

Lascelle Meserve de Basily

New York
June 1975

Childhood

My Grandfather

I entered this world in my grandfather's house, and a few hours after my arrival he paid me a visit. Later, he swore that in the arms of the nurse, I turned my head and followed him with my eyes as he moved about the room, and that I recognized him. Such a phenomenal child had never before been seen and he adored me.

My grandfather was a stately man with a noble head and intellectual brow. Therefore his tall silk cylinder hat was of corresponding proportions.

One day when I was about two years of age, the family was united in the drawing room after a meal. I seized this occasion to fetch my grandfather's hat and, turning it upside down on the floor in the center of the family circle, lifted my petticoats and seated myself within the hat which fitted my small person perfectly. This is probably the most outstanding achievement of my career.

Thereafter my grandfather considered me a genius, and became my devoted slave. Gifts were showered upon me, a pink silk frock from Paris, upon which I promptly spilled ice cream, and a small band of emeralds and diamonds set in a ring, which I hastened to lose in a sand-pile.

After that I was no longer heard from for some time.

At evening when I was supposed to be asleep, my grandfather would come to me and speak to me of Europe, saying that I would go there some day, and I imagined a white-sailed ship nearing a green shore. My grandfather would sing to me a nostalgic song: "Listen to the Nightingale upon the Danube River." Thus he instilled in me the love of Europe.

1

At other times we would walk together, my small fat hand curled about his ample forefinger, and I felt that no power on earth could harm me under such protection.

My grandfather, Henry Gordon Struve, was of German origin. He came from a well-known Russian family of scientists and intellectuals, some members of which had settled in Germany. A Struve was a Russian minister to Frankfurt (I do not know in what year). My grandfather was born in Oldenburg. An uncle of his was Friedrich Wilhelm Struve, a famous astronomer at the Observatory of Dorpat, who wrote several important books on astronomy. Another uncle was Gustav Struve, a German patriot, president of the Oldenburg Diet during the 1848 revolution and member of the Frankfurter Parliament, fighting for the unification of the thirty-eight German principalities to form one state. When the Revolution of 1848 failed, Gustav Struve left Germany for the United States. He was the author of an erudite "Weltgeschichte," a history of the world in many volumes, written in German.

In 1849 my grandfather's father died, and he was living with an uncle on the family place near Oldenburg, a simple manor-house approached by a long avenue of trees on the estate, and surrounded by a moat with a drawbridge. That year my grandfather left Germany for the United States.

For years after his departure, his old uncle would leave the drawbridge down at evening. "Perhaps Heinrich will return tonight," he would say wistfully. Forty years passed before my grandfather retraced his steps to the homeland.

He sailed around the Horn to North America, and eventually reached California, then in full effervescence of the gold discovery, but that was no place for him. He continued north on the Pacific coast, to the then primitive Territory of Washington, at that time not yet a state. There he started a newspaper, a copy of which still exists, printed on cloth, as the publication appeared during the Civil War, when paper was scarce. He became a prominent, honored citizen of Washington, a lawyer, and a judge. Under President Grant he was made Territorial Secretary, and later was mayor of Seattle.

Photographs of Judge Struve and Mrs. Struve are in the Washington Historical Museum in Seattle.

His wife, born Lascelle Knighton, was a beautiful woman whose father was English. There were four children, Harry, Helen, Mary and Frederick.

My grandfather's sister, Marie Struve, was the Frau Oberin (Mother Superior) of the Diaconessenhaus, a Lutheran religious order in Eisenach, on the Wartburg, where Martin Luther had preached. Tante Marie, whom we never knew, was a very fine person. A photograph of her exists, with plastered down hair beneath a white coif, and a serene countenance. Her motto was: "Fest und treu durch Freud und Leid" (Fast and true in joy and sorrow), which my mother adopted as a guide in life. She possessed a small cup her father had given her, having belonged to Tante Marie, with the image of the Wartburg and her noble motto. My mother prized this cup greatly, but it has been lost in one of the many wars we have lived through in our sinister century, which has ruined and destroyed so much.

Coming from an intellectual family, my grandfather was himself a highly cultured man. Reading was his passion, and often his light burned until early morning. He never slept more than four hours.

My Aunt Mary told me that as a young girl she had few fancy dresses, but if one of the children wished to take lessons, to learn something, funds were always available. My grandfather became a fervent American, fervent perhaps as only men from other countries can be, fervent as converts to religion. He loved the great Northwest, its lakes, mountains and forests.

In 1848 a wind of revolution swept over Europe. France,

Italy, Austria and Germany were affected.

For decades Italian leaders of the Risorgimento had been agitating for a united democratic Italy, instead of a dozen states and duchies, one third of them under the Hapsburgs. Similarly in the thirty-eight states and principalities of the German Federation, a unifying nationalistic spirit was steadily growing, particularly among the students and the more aspiring members of the middle classes.

The news of the Paris revolt stirred an unprecedented spirit of insurgency in the backward principalities of Germany.

On March 31st, in Frankfurt, a hastily formed parliament called for an all German Constitutional Assembly to be chosen in the first popular election ever held on German soil. On May 18th, eight hundred and thirty elected dignitaries gathered in St. Paul's Church in Frankfurt to draw up a new liberal constitution for an, as yet, non-existent German Empire.[1]

Gustav Struve, my grandfather's uncle, a German patriot, was a member of the Parliament.

The Frankfurt Assembly's constitution was ignored, and the Assembly passed into history as a might-have-been, like the 1848 revolt itself. Although deliberating in a vacuum— the German princes were not amused—the Assembly had raised high hopes in Germany.

When the revolt failed, Gustav Struve left for the United States. At that time my grandfather also crossed the ocean to the new lands of America.

My Mother

When Helen, my mother, was a little girl, she protested against going to church on Sunday morning, in contrast to her sister Mary who was always ready an hour early, waiting

Helen Struve Meserve (Mammá)

solemnly in the entrance hall, her small white cotton-gloved hands clasping her prayer book. Helen rebelled. "Let her go with me into the woods," said my grandfather to his wife. "There she will learn to worship Nature and revere beauty." So together they went into the vast forests of fir trees, forming a vault overhead, and the child understood that some great power had made all this, and her heart was inspired. This love of Beauty she passed on to me, and it has been my refuge and solace in life.

My beautiful mother was high-spirited, intelligent and talented, with artistic ability and the highest ideals. She always reached for the stars. Of a delicate nature and strongly influenced by her father, she was imbued with the desire to study and to learn. At sixteen she made an unfortunate marriage and was desperately unhappy. The marriage ended in a divorce. I was her only child, and I adored her. Young as I was, I understood her anguish, and it became my own. Sensitive by nature this intensified my sensibility, which has followed me through life. I would have died to save her pain.

Immediately after her divorce, my mother went to Paris with her sister Mary and me. From then on our life was in Europe, and we never returned to the Pacific Northwest.

In Paris, Mammá took an apartment and studied painting under Baschet and Schommer, learning to paint well in oils. Her sister concentrated on French, of which she already had a certain knowledge, as well as of German. She had a gift for languages, and later learned Italian. She was of an angelic nature and we loved her dearly.

Mammá wore long, bell-shaped skirts, touching the ground, lined with taffetas and a little ruffle around the bottom, called a "balayeuse," which rustled delightfully when she moved. Often she placed a large bunch of Parma violets at her slender waist, which matched her violet-blue eyes.

School Days in Paris

I was placed in a private girl's school in Paris, where there were no other foreigners. The day of my arrival was dramatic. "Les demoiselles" gathered around, contemplating me in silence. Unable to say a word in French, I stood before them, my two long, blond braids of hair drooping dismally. Had such an apparition ever been seen before in heaven or on earth? "Qu'est-ce que c'est que cette machinette-là?" cried Jacqueline, her black eyes snapping. But it was she who eventually became my friend.

Clad in a long-sleeved black serge apron, covering me entirely, I sat on a tabouret in the class-room, listening to the different subjects taught—history, geography, mathematics and grammar. I heard nothing but French and, like a parrot, absorbed it with the air I breathed. Within a few months I was able to take my place in the classes with the other girls.

One of the teachers, Mademoiselle Mathilde, gave me private lessons. Mademoiselle Mathilde, a small, energetic person, wore a high-necked black wool frock down to her ankles, and stout little buttoned boots. Her pretty dark hair was drawn up into a chignon on top of her head, and her deep blue, thickly fringed eyes sparkled mischievously. I liked her, and my most contented hours were spent in her presence. We read together children's books, "Le tour de France par deux enfants," and of course the Bibliothèque Rose, "Les malheurs de Sophie," by the comtesse de Ségur, the food which nourished French childhood.

At recreation time the girls walked beneath the trees in the garden, surrounded by high ivy-clad walls, where a blue and white plaster Virgin kept watch over them.

For exercise we jumped rope. One girl held each end while a third skipped to the tune of a little song, three turns of the rope after each phrase

> "Alexandre le Grand," un, deux, trois,
> "Roi de Macedoine," un, deux, trois,
> "Avait un cheval," un, deux, trois,
> "Nommé Bucéphale," un, deux, trois

and many more turns until the skipper stopped for breath.

At four o'clock a dried-up little old maid, Mademoiselle Marthe, appeared with a huge basket of "petits pains" on her arm. Each pupil took one, and going to her locker, fetched a tablet of chocolate from the little stock she kept there. This was a longed-for hour of the goûter.

Meals were served in the large refectory, its long narrow tables covered with light brown oilcloth. Heaping plates of thickly sliced crusty French bread were placed at intervals along the center of the tables, with carafes of highly watered pink wine like sentinels between. We sat on narrow wooden benches without a back.

In a corner of the garden rose a small chapel where pupils gathered at seven o'clock each morning for prayers. Kneeling, they beat their meager little breasts, as their young voices murmured: "Sainte Marie, Mère de Dieu, priez pour nous. Vous êtes bénie entre toutes les femmes, et Jésus, le fruit de vos entrailles est béni."

Journeys with Mother

Social life never interested my mother. She always wished to achieve something, and ardently pursued her painting. In summer she went with her sister and me to Holland, and following an artist's life, lived with the peasants in the "gute Kammer," the best room, in their thatch-roofed cottage, which she found most amusing, and spent each day out of doors painting. The peasants were very sweet and kind. At times the "Vrouw" would invite us to "kaffee-trinken" with her family and we would sit together, they speaking only Dutch, of which we knew nothing, but we got on with German. By the time the "bal-le box" was passed, we were all laughing. "Bal-le" means candy in Dutch, a hard kind of barley sugar candy. They taught us to take a bal-le between our teeth, and drink coffee through it, in guise of sugar. The women were a picturesque sight with their winged lace caps and dark dresses.

One year my mother made a painting which was accepted by the Paris Salon. This was an honour then, and work had to be fairly good to be received, not just a pot of paint flung on a canvas which passes for Art today. The atmosphere of this painting was very Dutch, a sunset sky behind trees, an old woman picking up faggots, and a peasant house at the left with a light in the window, done with the deep feeling which characterized my mother.

We visited Amsterdam with its tranquil canals, overhanging trees, and barges. We haunted the Ryks Museum to view its countless treasures. We saw the dykes of Holland, and the island of Marken with peasants in costume, and often watched canal barges sailing unperturbed through fields where windmills waved their arms.

In Paris we frequented the Louvre and the Luxembourg continually, and thus I learned much history, biblical and other, as well as mythology. This was good, as schoolbooks at that time were unutterably dull. History comprised wars, coalitions, and kings with numbers. I often wondered where they wore them—on their chests or hung down their backs?

Paris itself was an occupation and we delighted in the beauty of this rare city. It was the day of the horse. The Champs-Elysées were wide, elegant and unencumbered. Omnibuses raced up and down, drawn by three horses abreast, like a Russian troïka. Fiacres trotted along, the jaded quadruped plodding conscientiously, and the coachman with a high oilcloth hat. Broad victorias drove toward the Arc de Triomphe, bearing lovely, beplumed ladies to the Bois de Boulogne. This was the Paris de la Belle Epoque, but I, behind my high walls, could know nothing of that. On Sundays Mammá would take me to a museum, to Notre Dame, the Conciergerie, or to Versailles, and at times, a trip on the Seine in a bateau-mouche. I wore my Sunday hat, black velvet, with two tiny black ostrich feathers standing erect in front, and felt very elegant.

Autumn afternoons were enchanting in the haze of twilight, with the heavenly odour of chestnuts roasting in braziers on the street corners, and little carts laden with violets which women offered to passersby. "Voyez mes violettes, deux sous la botte." Why do violets no longer play a role in life? Are they too modest for our blatant century?

Besides France and Holland, we traveled in Germany, Italy and Belgium, our hearts filled with the desire to see and learn, to discover the treasures of Europe.

We spent a winter in Italy. Italy, mistress of the world. Throughout the ages kings and plunderers have invaded this rich, siren land, and still what treasures of Art and Beauty remain.

Rome, the Coliseum, St. Peters, the Vatican, the Forum, the Pantheon, and a thousand other sights greeted our eyes. We passed hours studying these marvels, and our legs grew stiff mounting the miles of steep staircases in the museums. Somehow it was the Spanish steps with their myriad flower-booths blooming like fairy gardens, which enchanted me most, and left a memory of what seemed another world, and has lasted through life.

Florence, poetic Florence, with endless art treasures, and jewel-like monuments, enhanced by the bluish haze of distant hills, the landscape that Renaissance painters used as background for their canvases. Souvenirs and paintings of vanished Medicis and Savonarola and of the violence which disrupted their times. The Arno flowed between high quays, where young boys sold baskets of violets and freesias, whose fragrance still perfumes my memory.

Venice with its amazing canals, and the piazza San Marco like an open-air salon where all Venice gathered toward evening, wove their enchantment.

Then Pompeii, Naples and Vesuvius, and the beautiful bay of Parthenope, Capri and the Blue Grotto—what treasures Italy shared with us of her fatal beauty.

At that time all was calm and tranquil, no mobs tramping through museums and churches, no loud-mouthed automobiles encumbering the streets, no tourist buses. It seemed a private meeting with Beauty. We rode in dilapidated cabs like queens and the world was at our feet. Once in Naples I saw a flock of goats being driven up steep stairs inside a house, to be milked.

About this time I received a proposal of marriage which is worth recording.

My admirer was Isidore, aged nine, the son of our concierge in Paris. I was a year or two older. I seldom had occasion to see Isidore, but at times caught a glimpse of him coming from school clad in his black satinette school apron, with a flowing red bow tie.

One day the doorbell rang, and Isidore appeared asking to see my mother. She found him seated in the biggest chair he could find in the salon.

"Madame," said Isidore, "je viens demander la main de votre fille en mariage."*

"Mais, Isidore," replied my astonished mother, "qu'est que tu ferais de ma fille? Est-ce qu'elle serait concierge?"

"Non, Madame," responded Isidore solemnly, "elle serait la Reine."

"Et toi, Isidore, tu serais toujours concierge?"

"Non, Madame, je serais le Roi."

* * *

Later we went to Munich in beautiful Bavaria, where the people, so unlike the Prussians, charmed us, and we enjoyed the Gemütlichkeit of this lovely city. Frequently we attended the Opera, especially the Wagnerian evenings—Tristan and Isolde, Tannhaüser, Lohengrin, the Meistersingers and the Ring, and grew to know well these tremendous works. In the intervals we marveled at the spectators consuming beer and sausages at the buffet.

---

*"Madame," said Isidore, "I am coming to ask your daughter's hand in marriage."

"But, Isidore," replied my astonished mother, "what will you make of my daughter? Will she become a concierge?"

"No, Madame," responded Isidore solemnly, "she will be the Queen."

"And you, Isidore, will you always be a concierge?"

"No, Madame, I will be the King."

Mammá continued her studies of Art. This was the epoch
of Lenbach's fine portraits, of Herkommer, of Böcklin,
whose "Island of Death" was greatly acclaimed. Art
Nouveau was in the throes of birth. Böcklin was quite a
virtuoso with the wine-bottle, and is said to have once remarked that he liked to recline on the floor, because he could
lie there without falling off.

Again I was put in a private girl's school where I quickly
learned German, and soon even spoke it better than English,
having little occasion to practice the latter.

The Frau-Direktor of the school was an ample dame stuf-
fed into a black satin dress, with jet embroidery indignantly
quivering on her powerful bosom. A gold chain and locket
hung about her neck, and a lace cap with a purple bow
adorned her tightly drawn grey hair. Her quick eye spied
everything it should not see, and her strong voice made the
pupils shudder. At meals spinach soup was frequently
served. The girls heartily despised this dismal mixture, and
at times rejected it. Then it was brought back at each meal
until the last drop was consumed. "Grass soup," we called
it. Once several pupils including myself openly refused to
swallow it. We were instantly summoned to the Frau-
Direktor's office, and went, green with apprehension.

"What do you think you are doing?" she shouted, purple
as her cap ribbons, "What is the matter with the soup? It is
perfectly good. Your stomachs are what you hold most
holy."

We got away with our lives, but we never again attempted
open rebellion.

One summer we went to the country with my mother's
painting teacher, a small prickly man whose downtrodden
little wife always addressed him as "Schatz" (treasure), but
Schatz was far from deserving this tender appellation, and
apparently did not respond to her flame. The village,
Haimhausen, was in flat country, out in the wheat-fields

yellow with grain at that season and starred with scarlet poppies and blue bachelor buttons. Here and there fir forests made somber shadows in contrast to this flowering of Nature. A short distance from the village a small votive-chapel, dedicated to the Virgin, rose on an eminence in a wood, its walls covered with silver ex-votos, legs, hands, hearts, any member which the fervent prayers of believers had restored to health. While my mother painted, I sometimes walked to this chapel, and there, in the silence of the woods, lay down beneath the sighing fir trees, and dreamed the dreams of any young German Backfisch.

At evening the old diligence from a nearby railway station rolled down the road in the sunset, the driver on his high seat, sounding his horn to announce the arrival of the mail-coach, in the peace, quiet, and simplicity of the German countryside long years ago.

* * *

We visited Oldenburg where my grandfather was born, and met his brother, Karl, who resembled him, and Karl's wife, Frieda, a little lady with a black lace cap.

Aunt Frieda took us to see the family place, with a long avenue of trees leading to a simple old manor-house, with a moat and drawbridge, which had remained untouched since my grandfather's youth. After his departure for America, his uncle, who then occupied the house, left the drawbridge down at night, nostalgically hoping that "Heinrich" might return unannounced.

We walked in a charmille in the garden, decorated with classical statuary, and were greatly moved by this environment which had been the scene of my grandfather's youth, alas, how long ago, but it remains very vague in my memory.

We made the beautiful Rhine journey by boat, passing the legendary castles set high on the rocks above the river. The haunting melody of Heine's "Lorelei" rang in our ears, and we imagined the glamourous mermaid elegantly seated on a rock, combing her golden hair, and luring men to their doom by her siren song. This was still the romantic period.

We visited the castles of the mad king of Bavaria, Ludwig, in the Bavarian mountains, Hohenschwangau and, across the valley on a high solitary peak, Neuschwanstein, Ludwig's fantastic dream come to life, and made a reality in stone.

Near the castle of Linderhof is the grotto, the famous Venusberg, where Ludwig floated on a tiny lake in a swanboat, like Lohengrin. He was completely beneath the charm of Wagner's music. It was principally through him that Wagner could pursue his career.

We attended a representation of the Passion Play at Oberammergau, in the mountains, which was given each year by people of the village and surroundings, who are wood-carvers by profession. They take their role of biblical characters with great earnestness and consecration, and play very convincingly. Anton Lang was outstanding as Christ. We remained two days in this tiny village of the Bavarian mountains, and I always remember its simple, kindly people, and the riot of yellow crocuses painting the encircling fields.

My mother's life was a Quest for Beauty. Everywhere she went she created it, and she passed this longing on to me. From her I learned that the Beauty of Nature was a defense against the mediocre and commonplace, to be eagerly sought after, and preciously guarded, as a retreat in times of stress.

I always preferred dreams to reality, and lived in my own little world, writing descriptions of my surroundings, stories and bits of verse. The fate of these guileless imaginations was determined years later when en route for Russia, on the *Rotterdam*, between England and the Danish coast, my mother inquired if I had anything written with me. I had taken along my beloved scribblings, but fearing that in war-time any bit of written paper might be taken for a code, Mammá said I had better destroy them, so my youthful efforts were flung into the stormy waters of the North Sea, a sacrifice to the First Great War.

Always in search of beauty and poetry, we visited one summer the unspoiled, archaic town of Rothenburg an der Tauber, standing on a low hill encircled by a red wall, intact from the Middle Ages. Rothenburg was an enchantment with its high pointed roofs and towers, a living example of a medieval city come down through the centuries intact.

Mammá found many subjects to paint, and we spent days of pure delight wandering through this vision of centuries long-past. In the valley below, the gentle Tauber wound its way through the plain.

During the Thirty Years War, Tilly broke through the walls of Rothenburg and took the town, promising, however, to liberate the city if the Bürgermeister was able to swallow in one draught three "bayerische Schoppen" of beer, about three liters. The Bürgermeister nobly rose to the occasion and accomplished this remarkable feat, thus saving the town. This was the famous "Meistertrunk."

We lodged in an old Gasthaus adjacent to an ancient clock-tower, simple and gemütlich.

One night a stupendous storm broke, shaking town and valley. The sky became yellow, rain fell in torrents, thunder roared and streaks of lightning stabbed the sky like sabers. With a terrific impact, one flash struck the ancient tower, and our Gasthaus, adhering to it, reeled and shook with a mighty reverberation. Mammá and I clung together, thinking our last hour had come. Morning showed that, in spite of our wrecked nerves, the lovely tower had not been badly damaged.

With difficulty, we tore ourselves away from the sorcery of Rothenburg, which had cast a spell upon us. We had journeyed back into time, and this experience will always remain an imperishable memory of my childhood, a blessed escape from reality.

During those years that my mother gave herself up to painting, I frequently accompanied her when she went to sketch, either in the fields or in a picturesque spot of some village. Charmed by her work, I also attempted to draw. Alas, I did not inherit the skill of my talented mother, and my efforts were most dismal. Therefore, seated on a small stool beside her, a block of paper on my knees and a pencil in my hand, I began to write, endeavouring to put into words that which I was incapable of drawing. I made little pastiches of the scene before me, until describing what I saw became a pastime and a necessity, which I have pursued through life. The memories written here are the result of that impulse.

Nothing remains of my mother's paintings. I could never learn what she had done with them. Perhaps, dissatisfied with her work, she destroyed them. Often I implored her to give them to me, but she only laughed evasively.

Frequently after these sketching tours we would go to some clean farmhouse, and on a wooden table before her door, the Frau would serve us delicious black bread, creamy butter, and milk in a pale blue pottery pitcher. So simple was life in those faraway days of happy memory.

Korea, Land of Morning Calm

Arise and seek the hill-tops
Let your gaze embrace the skies,
For men who dwell in valleys
Cannot see the new moon rise.

Korean proverb translated by Lascelle

My mother married again, and in this second marriage found the tender affection and solicitude which had been so tragically lacking in the first. H. Fessenden Meserve was from an old family of the Island of Jersey, "les Sieurs de Gorey de Grouville," and was the eighth generation in the United States, an ancestor having come to this country in 1673 and settled in Portsmouth, New Hampshire. The motto on the family coat-of-arms was: "Au valeureux coeur rien impossible," and he observed it, facing the difficulties of life with unfailing courage and spirit. He loved my mother with the devotion of a rare soul. He adopted me, gave me his name, and became a real father to me. He graduated from Harvard University in 1888.

H. Fessenden Meserve ("Papinka")

I loved him with all my heart, for himself, and also in deep gratitude for having brought happiness to my mother, and restoring her broken faith in humanity. My mother had found a husband with the most noble qualities. She was a goddess to him and their marriage was ideal.

Mr. Meserve, a banker by profession, had an interlude in his career, during which for several years he was General Manager of the Oriental Consolidated Mining Company, a gold Concession of fifty square miles in Unsan Province, Northern Korea, which had been granted to an American company by the Emperor of Korea. It was a little kingdom over which my father had been called to preside. Besides the administration of the Concession, he ruled over the natives who brought to him their difficulties and disputes to settle, accepting his word as law. They grouped about him, sitting on their heels in native fashion. Behind his chair stood Kim, the interpreter, clad in a long white robe, hands and arms crossed and lost in the vast sleeves of his garment. My father was deeply respected and loved by all for his high moral character, and unfailing sense of justice. About one hundred white men were under his orders, several hundred Japanese, mostly carpenters, a large number of Chinese cart drivers, and several thousand Koreans who worked the mines.

In later years we were to make many journeys, and it is of these that I write. The most thrilling took us to Imperial Russia, but first, our destination was Korea, a primitive Oriental kingdom of which Europeans then knew little. Later Mr. Meserve returned to banking and as Vice-President of the First National City Bank, in Europe, went to Russia on loans by that bank to the Imperial Russian Government (1915–1917).

To reach the distant land of Korea, named "Chosen" in the native language, meaning "Land of Morning Calm," a month's travel by boat was necessary, through the Suez Canal, the Red Sea, the Indian Ocean, the China Sea to Japan, and from there to Korea. Every five days the ship stopped to coal, at Aden, Colombo, Penang, Singapore, Hong Kong then up the coast of China to Shanghai, and on to Nagasaki and Kobe.

At Genoa we embarked on a Nord Deutscher Lloyd liner to Port Said, where we arrived in tropical heat. At sunset our ship entered the Suez Canal. I stood at the bow to observe the great locks raising our vessel to a higher level. On one side was a strip of yellow earth. On the other, lowland stretched to the horizon. A group of tents lay white against the burning sands. In those days a ship required eighteen hours to pass through the canal. That night I dreamed of caravans camping beneath the glittering stars. Next morning cries from the shore drew my attention, and I beheld Arabs in long, loose robes and turbans leading camels laden with baskets of earth, and shouting as they worked.

At the far end of the canal is the town of Suez, where the ship again passed through great locks lowering it to the level of the Red Sea. We entered this incandescent, land-circled body of water, with Egypt and Ethiopia on the right, and Arabia on the left. The heat was overpowering. We rested at night in our chairs on deck, as our cabins were unbearable, sleep impossible. I gazed over the silent sea beneath the moon, until dawn flushed the sky. We moved into the Strait of Bab-el-Mandeb, and reached Aden on the southern extremity of burning Arabia.

Aden, great British outpost, barren in suffocating heat. Our ship paused to coal. We went ashore to avoid the dust. Half-naked natives swarmed onto the liner carrying baskets of coal on their shoulders, running feverishly up and down the ladders, while an overseer in a long black robe shouted orders. The intense heat prevented much exploration.

The Indian Ocean stretched out serene and blue. The weather was perfect in spite of the temperature. Autumn is the best season to make this journey, before the winter monsoons.

Days of delight were spent in contemplation of the sea. Exotic fish floated by. Flying-fish leaped out of the water, falling back with a gentle splash.

Colombo enchanted me, the tall palm-trees, the low native huts with palm-leaf roofs, and the gentle Singhalese people with enormous soft, dark eyes. We rode in rickshaws to Mount Lavinia for a splendid "tiffin" of curried prawns. There is so much I could write of the ports we visited, but it would take too long, and we must get on to Korea. We bought little silver boxes embossed with Hindu divinities, and handfuls of sapphires and rubies (without market value) which merchants offered us for a song. I will never forget that dream-day spent in enchanting Ceylon.

After Hong Kong we stopped in Shanghai, visited the old walled city, saw the famous Chinese junks with an eye on each side of the bow, for "No have eye, no can see." The floating population living in sampans fascinated me. We drove along the Bund (quay) lined with foreign banks, to the famous Nanking Road, and the Bubbling Well Road, the favorite promenade for Europeans.

Then Nagasaki with its beautiful almost land-locked harbour, a city of low tile-roofed houses, built on picturesque hills. We rode in rickshaws to a temple high above the town where, in the courtyard, stood the bronze statue of a horse amid a blaze of peonies.

From Nagasaki we passed through the Shimonoseki Straits into the exquisite Inland Sea lying between the three islands of Honshu, Kyushu and Shikoku. Conical islands covered with pine trees arose from the waters, and small grey fishing villages dotted the shores. We saw a temple set high above Seto Naikai (the Japanese name for this sea). It was sunset, and the scene so breathtaking in the evening light that I stood in rapt contemplation of such rare beauty.

I loved the vibrations of the ship as it cut through the waters on this journey, like a warm heart throbbing and carrying us forward into a new world.

In Kobe we boarded a small, primitive boat which was to bring us to Chemulpo, the port for Seoul, after crossing the Straits of Tsushima.

At last we reached the southern coast of Korea, and went north among the multitude of islands, purple in the golden twilight, our ancient craft shivering and shaking with every breath of the engine. On the mainland no habitation was visible. The country seemed as closed and impenetrable as its name, the "Hermit Kingdom." For many years Korea was a secret land, opened to the world only in 1876. Our first contact with this remote, secluded realm was Chemulpo. Our vessel anchored far from the shore as no quay for ships existed. A frail landing for small boats was crowded with white-clad natives and coolies, carrying on their backs large wooden racks called "jighis" on which immense burdens of every description were piled. The town was low, brown and primitive, partly built on hillsides where steps often replaced the road.

Chemulpo was the port for the capital, Seoul, twenty-five miles distant, and connected with it by the only railway in the country.

We did not go to Seoul but sailed farther north to Chinnampo, a tiny port where we abandoned our groaning craft. A small yacht belonging to the Concession carried us overnight on the Anshu River to Anshu, an ancient walled town destroyed during the Chinese-Japanese War in 1894. Here several mine superintendents met my father and journeyed with us.

From Anshu our way lay northward to the Concession, a distance of about three hundred miles to our ultimate destination, Unsan Province, near the Manchurian border. We traveled on horseback or in sedan chairs borne high on the shoulders of four coolies, as they stumbled over stony roads or waded through rushing torrents. A relay of four coolies ran beside each chair. The journey was slow on account of rough roads, and two days were necessary to accomplish it. Sturdy Korean ponies followed behind our cavalcade, laden with luggage, encouraged by the cries of their mafoos (drivers).

As we proceeded on our journey, we were impressed by the beauty of this northern country, of hills, valleys and streams. It was a primitive world we were entering. At times dwellings of mud-huts with straw roofs appeared, where wolfish dogs barked violently, and the white-clad inhabitants gazed curiously.

The American Concession stretched out over fifty square miles in Unsan Province, and was situated some thirty miles, in a direct line, from the Manchurian border, with four large gold mines, twenty miles apart. Our home was entirely separated from any mine and no vestiges of them were visible in our vicinity.

In a wide valley of this lovely mountainous region, my parents had made their home. Standing on an eminence in a grove of sacred pine trees where formerly natives had worshipped their gods or spirits, the house was a perfect example of a Chinese or Korean temple, with upturned grey tiled roofs of romantic aspect. Beneath the broad eaves small brass bells were suspended, tinkling gently with each vagrant breeze. The tongue of these bells was in the form of a fish which, according to Korean superstition, represented the element of water, thus preventing the building from perishing by fire. Another superstition took the form of tiny grotesque figures riding on the roof-edge, to protect our dwelling from evil spirits. The house was named "Sonamo," the Korean word for pines, and was situated five miles from the nearest mine.

A great valley stretched before the house, surrounded by mountains painted pink with wild azaleas in spring, and white with snow in winter. Remote ranges were blue in the distance. A small stream flowed at the foot of our hill, continuing through the fields. A road led south in the valley, which Mammá, in this northern fastness, called "The Road to the World." We were far from the civilized world we had always known.

Sonamo—Meserve home in Unsan Province

(Photographed by Helen Strave Meserve)

Two "devil-posts" guarded the entrance to Sonamo.
These large figures roughly carved in wood, representing
fierce warriors with hideous, grimacing faces, painted in
bright colours, and brandishing sticks, were destined to ter-
rify any evil spirits who might attack us. They were placed
before the gatehouse, an offering to my mother from a Korean who, having been ill, Mammá had sent to the Concession Hospital where he was cured of tuberculosis. In
gratitude he had presented to her these powerful devils, one,
the "Greatest Man in the North," the other, the "Greatest
Man in the World," to protect his benefactress from peril.
Another example of Korean kindness and generosity.

Often in this northern wilderness, devil-posts were placed
at the entrance of remote valleys to protect the inhabitants
from harm. The Koreans believed in shamanism* and each
hill, stream or tree was supposed to be inhabited by spirits,
sometimes good, often evil, which needed to be propitiated.
The earth, the very air and clouds were said to be the abode
of these malicious creatures.

A picturesque element of shamanism were the "mudangs," or witch doctors, usually women, who pretended to
cure the sick by sitting beside them on the floor, beating
gongs in order to frighten away the "Tiger," who represented the spirit of sickness, and making an infernal noise,
sufficient to kill any normal living being.

A person afflicted by illness or any other evil, paid a sum of
money to a mudang to catch the spirit. Then these women
would run over the hillsides with an empty bottle in one
hand, and a cork in the other, pursuing the spirit and, when
captured, quickly put it in the bottle which was sealed with
the cork, so that the spirit was no longer free to torment its

---

* "Shamanism is the worship of a large number of primitive North Asiatic tribes,
having no idols, except a few fetiches and some rude ancestral images, or representations of the spirits of the earth and air. These malignant beings are supposed to
populate the earth, the clouds and air and to be the cause of most of the ills suffered
by men" (Griffis).

victim, who kept the bottle in his possession. The length of time involved in this wild chase depended on the amount of money paid, long if much, short if little.

A remarkable feature of our home was the fact that my mother had made all the plans and erected it with only the help of a native constructor, Pak. She had studied painting and architecture in Europe, but how she mastered Oriental architecture I never understood. The building was perfect in every detail. Koreans as well as foreigners came from far and near to look and admire.

Pak, the Korean contractor, was honest and faithful, as Koreans can be. He was devoted to my father and hung a large sign in decorative Korean letters above his door saying that "A good and kind man named Meserve lives in this house." A small stream flowed beneath our garden, so Pak placed another sign over the entrance door: "Listen to the murmur of the water from this verandah," a delightful Oriental touch.

Fourteen servants maintained this household, a Chinese cook, a Korean houseboy, a second houseboy, a Japanese amah named Chio, a gate-keeper, his assistant, a general coolie for cleaning and carrying wood for fires, a gardener, a water-carrier, two Chinese mafoos (stable boys), an interpreter and two night-watchmen, as Chinese bandits sometimes came over the mountains from Manchuria. Later Mammá's French maid, Marie, brought our menage to fifteen.

The Chinese cook revered my mother, and she alone could manage him. Once when Mammá was ill in an hotel in Chemulpo, of his own will and without our knowledge, he slept on the bare floor of the corridor before her door, in order to be near, should she need something during the night. He was a good cook, but occasionally sent in some carelessly prepared food. Then Mammá would call him into the dining room, and say sternly: "Cook, if you ever do that again I will cut off your ears." After that he would pay

Servants at Sonamo
(Photographed by Helen Struve Meserve)

attention, but I doubt if the idea of losing his ears alarmed him.

Yi, the first houseboy, was clean, efficient and a rascal. Once at luncheon he served whiskey in wine glasses to some passing missionaries, creating panic among those worthies. We never knew if Yi really did not distinguish between wine and whiskey, or if he had done it maliciously.

The diminutive Japanese amah, Chio, padded about the house in her native costume, decorative with a flower in her hair, but not very efficient.

Two sturdy Chinese mafoos cared for our horses and brought them around at evening as we rode each day. Our way took us across fields of stubble, along dry river-beds or through villages where the inhabitants rushed to the doors of their mud huts to see us pass, always very friendly. At times an old woman would offer her pipe to Mammá to smoke, as women do here, or else she pulled from her tiny garden a carrot, which she offered in the generous spirit characteristic of the Korean people, who were very gentle and kind.

The gate-keeper, a lazy chap, spent all his time smoking a long, long Korean pipe, occasionally applying a cautious eye to a hole poked in the paper door of the gate-house, to see if any trespassers were about. Of course he needed an assistant for these arduous duties. Mammá discharged him every Saturday night, but took him back upon his tearful entreaties each Monday morning. She called him "Fizzle," as he was such a complete failure. "What does Fizzle mean in the American language?" he inquired. "Oh, Fizzle is a Number-One American name," she assured him. "Many, many thanks" he said, clasping his hands together as if in congratulation and bowing low.

At night two watchmen came to guard the house and protect us from Manchurian bandits, but, alas, they generally curled up on the verandah beneath our windows, and snored royally. One cold night, the snores were louder and more insistent than usual. Exasperated, my father arose and seizing a large pitcher of ice water emptied the contents upon the blissful sleepers, who, rudely awakened, filled the air with roars and recriminations.

The occupation of the water-carrier was to carry water exclusively as we only had one well and no running water in the house. He was called "Yebbo," in the Korean manner of addressing a person of low condition and literally meaning "You there."

When the house was finished, the Governor of the Province came to call. He sat in the drawing room drinking tea with my parents. Behind his chair stood an interpreter, his hands thrust into flowing sleeves. Kim, my father's interpreter, also stood behind my father, his crossed hands lost in the wide sleeves of his white robe.

The governor of Unsan Province with his bearers

"Pray tell his Excellency," said the Governor to the interpreter, "that this house is like heaven, but I never dreamed that I would go to heaven and get a cup of tea besides."

The Governor traveled in a closed sedan chair, hung with black cloth preceded by "Yamen"—runners (palace servants)—who cleared the way, proclaiming in a loud voice that the Governor of the Province was approaching and warning the people to keep indoors. Numerous gentlemen-in-waiting attended him and occasionally he was accompanied by dancing girls. He was a keen old man, a picturesque figure in flowing white robes and black horsehair hat, fan in hand.

Several times a year the Governor made a trip from his walled capital of Yeng-Ben to the American Concession. These visits were not purely disinterested as he always tried to "squeeze" my father, in Oriental fashion, but he obtained no satisfaction.

My father spoke some Korean, but the language is complicated by the fact that three manners of expression exist, one when addressing superiors, another for equals, and a third for the lower caste. My father spoke "coolie dialect," but he occasionally used a few "coolie" words to the magistrate which were well received. The difference is in the termination of the word.

Korean graves are usually simple grass-covered mounds, but necromancers are necessary to choose a propitious site, free from evil spirits. Treasures are buried with the dead and once the Governor opened a tomb and found an ancient Korean bowl of value which he presented to my mother. This bowl was of grey-brown glazed pottery, a type of work dating from ancient times.

Once the Governor of the Province lunched with us. It was a solemn occasion and while we attempted to converse with him, our lives were so far apart that a subject in common was difficult to find, and the two white-clad interpreters often stood silent behind the Governor's and my father's chairs. Yi, the head houseboy, was greatly excited to have the Governor at table, and rushed about nervously. At the end of a perfect meal, a bowl of American tinned peaches was passed as the Koreans thought no European repast complete and elegant without this last touch. When my turn came to be served, Yi, in his nervous state, let the bowl slip and the peaches with their sticky juice cascaded down the front of my pink silk frock to the floor. After the solemnity of the occasion it was a relief for my parents and me to laugh. We laughed immoderately while the Governor gazed upon us

with round, astonished eyes. Then he turned to his interpreter and said: "Tell His Excellency and his family that I
deeply appreciate their regard for me in this disaster." The
Governor, according to Oriental custom, had taken our bad
Occidental manners for exquisite politeness in making light
of this mishap in order not to distress him. This was Oriental
courtesy. We felt abashed.

In the nearby village of Puk Chin, an agglomeration of
straw-roofed mud-huts, market was held every five days.
Merchants spread their wares upon straw mats lining the
village street, presenting principally rice, millet, lamb's wool
for winter jackets, Korean white cotton materials for clothing, always padded for winter wear. Men's stiff black horsehair hats were also displayed. Just the necessities of life.
There were no luxuries in these faraway hills. On market day
people came to obtain their provisions, quietly, peacefully
arriving on foot or riding donkeys so small that their dangling
feet almost touched the ground, clad in long white coats and
black hats. Something biblical emanated from these still
white figures, coming from distant valleys, mounted on biblical donkeys, robed in biblical white garments. So it must
have been through centuries since time immemorial.

Here my parents lived for some years in spring, summer
and autumn, surrounded by books, riding horseback. In
winter they traveled to Europe, Paris and London where
they met friends, went to the play, Mammá in a black velvet
evening frock, with aigrettes in her hair, and a pearl dog-
collar around her throat. Each year I returned with them
from Paris, where I was studying and living with my Aunt
Mary, to this tranquil, archaic Land of Morning Calm I had
grown to love.

The Koreans were very quiet and good natured. There
was never any trouble with them. They esteemed my father
and obeyed him, living peacefully in their humble dwellings
and we, on our part, became very fond of these gentle
people.

Winter was long and severe in those northern mountains. The snow lasted for months. Summer was hot, but tempered for at least six weeks by torrential, tropical rains that fell in avalanches, a most trying season to endure. The rest of the year was pleasant. In autumn fresh winds blew down the valleys, the hills were bare and brown. Gourds and red peppers were laid to dry on the straw-roofed abodes, which seemed to nestle closer to the earth, in defense against the coming winter.

If Korea, "Chosen" in the Korean language, means Land of Morning Calm, it was not so named without reason. The mornings were usually sunny, windless and calm, but in the afternoon strong winds often arose, blowing down from Manchuria. White figures walking on the high-road bent their heads to weather this storm, and white garments fluttered madly. The little bells beneath the eaves of our room, silent in the morning, raised their voices, tinkling, tinkling without end.

In autumn and winter wild winds shrieked across the icy fields, like lost souls. When they ceased, the silence was so intense one could hear its anguish, another lost soul. Northern Korea was a cruel world during the winter.

When spring came, swallows darted into the bare, brown valleys. The hills were ablaze with wild pink azaleas. Myriad fruit trees bore delicate pink and white blossoms. Cánari (the Korean name for forsythia) were the first to appear, pushing their long, yellow flower laden branches through the snow.

In my memories of spring in Korea, one day stands forth. In the fifth moon, which usually falls in June, a day called "Swing Day" was set apart when young women and girls were permitted to leave their seclusion, as from the age of eight young girls were confined in inner rooms and courts, and forbidden to appear outside of them. This also applies to young married women. For a young girl to be seen by a man is a disgrace. Older women of the coolie class and peasants work in the fields and are always visible.

On "Swing Day," when the girls and women were free to roam about, all men were supposed to remain indoors. On that day the young girl put on her gayest raiment and went with her playmates and the women to the hillsides where for this occasion swings were hung from the branches of the pine trees. The hills behind Puk-Chin village seemed a garden with little maids in bright hued garments, rose-red jackets and cornflower-blue skirts, dresses white as the opium poppy, or yellow as lilies. Green frocks fluttered like leaves tossed in the wind.

Black eyes sparkling, these little recluses in their long-roped swings flew far out over the ravine then back again and up until they seemed lost in the branches above. Throughout the long warm day they frolicked, the cuckoos calling to them from the trees. Midnight found them still swinging in the light of the crescent moon.

Fruit Blossoms

> Spring comes to old Korea,
> Which has seen so many springs.
> Into the bare brown valleys
> Flits the blue of swallows' wings.
>
> Spring comes to old Korea,
> Paints blue the April skies,
> On twisted boughs of fruit-trees
> Flowers cling like butterflies.

Lascelle

*   *   *

In the Middle Ages a great wall existed in northern Korea running across the country from the Yellow Sea to the Sea of

Japan, resembling the Great Wall of China, but smaller. This wall was built in defense against wild barbarians from the North who made sudden raids on peaceful Korea. It was constructed in the eleventh century, "probably in 1033," Mr. H. B. Hulbert in his book *The Passing of Korea* writes, "Remains can still be seen in the vicinity of Yong-Byun (Yeng-Ben)."

The ancient walled town of Yeng-Ben is the capital of Unsan Province and the seat of the Governor.

Native Korean miners having once stolen gold and amalgam from the American mines, my father was obliged to confer with the Governor and decided to go to Yeng-Ben. He left one cold November morning, accompanied by Mammá and me. We traveled partly in sedan chairs carried by eight coolies, and partly on horseback. Kim, the interpreter, was at my father's side as usual on such expeditions. The Korean houseboy, Yi, the Chinese cook, and the small Japanese amah trotted behind on Korean ponies. Two mine superintendents journeyed with my father, each with his houseboy. We formed an imposing cavalcade, together with a cart for luggage, bedding and provisions.

The distance from the American Concession to Yeng-Ben was not far, nevertheless the journey required two days to reach our destination as roads in this primitive land were lamentable. We stumbled over rocks and ruts, forded rushing torrents. Northern Korea is a region of hills, valleys, and narrow streams and we delighted in its wild beauty.

On the evening of the second day we reached the entrance of a canyon through which Yeng-Ben is approached. On either side rose hills wooded with gnarled pine trees. The great Yeng-Ben Mountain looked down upon us.

Yeng-Ben is a walled town, but the wall did not closely encircle this simple agglomeration of mud-huts with straw roofs. It ran for miles along the crests of the surrounding hills, while the village was in the hollow below. Although

Gate to Yeng Ben, capital of Wusan Province
(Photographed by Helen Struve Meserve)

mostly in ruins, there were parts remaining of a certain grandeur, and several fine entrance gates piercing the stone enclosure.

A government house had been placed at my father's disposal, one-storied with a tile roof, built around a court. Our rooms were small with low ceilings. We entered by paper doors and sat upon the floor, beneath which a roaring fire had been made in the "kang."* We dined on little tables, and slept on camp beds we had brought with us. There was no furniture.

The Governor received us that evening in the low winter quarters, instead of the spacious summer apartments. Seated on the floor, clad in a long white silk robe and horsehair hat, his men-in-waiting and dancing girls grouped about him, lighted by a single candle in a tall holder on the floor, the

---

*Kangs were flues beneath the mud floors of dwellings to convey heat from a fire built just outside the hut.

Governor was most affable, and offered us each a large black cigar, expressing surprise when Mammá refused, for women here smoke the long tiny pipes of the country. It was a truly Oriental scene which greeted us, but no splendor, for Korea is a poor land, and there is no display of any kind.

The Governor then asked my father's age. "Thirty-eight" was the answer. This of course was only Oriental courtesy in deference to Age, and intended as a compliment, as he knew my father already. However, he exclaimed: "Impossible. I am sixty and you look much older than I."

His eyes fell on Mammá's diamond rings which dazzled him. Turning to Kim, the interpreter, he said: "Tell His Excellency that when he next goes to America I would greatly appreciate his bringing me a few precious jewels."

Conversation lagged, so the dancing girls performed a slow dance with a droning, monotonous song. After that we departed and went out into the starlit night.

The following day the trial took place of those native thieves who had stolen gold from the American Concession. The Governor wore an enormous pair of horn-rimmed spectacles, and a threatening frown. The thieves were prostrate on the ground, shivering with cold, not daring to raise their eyes to the Governor's face. This administrator of justice asked my father if he would like to have the men killed for their offense. This question was mere routine as the Koreans are a gentle people and have no barbaric customs. My father answered "No." The Governor then sentenced the thieves to a year's work on the roads. The principal culprit, however, was first stripped and laid down upon a board, that raw November day, while attendants gave him thirty lashes, provoking groans and cries.

After the trial a performance was given in my father's honour in a great hall of the summer apartments, where dancing girls in brightly colored robes went through complicated movements, scarcely moving the body but slowly waving their arms with long floating sleeves, accompanied by drums and cymbals.

Hyang-San Monastery

Among the high hills of northwestern Korea stands an ancient Buddhist monastery, one of a few of such institutions still existing in this country. Formerly Buddhism was the prevailing religion in Korea, but eventually it gave way to ancestor worship and shamanism, the cult of good and bad spirits who are supposed to inhabit hills and rivers, trees and the air.

The monastery was about a twenty-four hour journey from the American Concession by primitive means of locomotion, over terrible roads. Wishing to visit this ancient shrine, we started forth one June day, traveling as usual in sedan chairs and on horseback, alternating from one to the other, followed by two mine superintendents, Kim the interpreter, the cook and several house servants with food and bedding.

We went north. The valleys grew broader, the scenery wilder as we penetrated into high mountains. The lowlands were enameled by the tender green of young rice fields. Flocks of white herons flew over these verdant expanses, and once an ibis soared by on pale pink wings.

We traveled all day and we traveled all night to avoid the heat, a full moon lighting our way. Fireflies flashed their tiny lanterns, and one of them journeyed with me throughout the night, seated on a pole of my sedan chair. Wild roses perfumed the air and the rush of turbulent streams was the only sound in those long, still hours.

Towards morning we reached a narrow gorge between high, apparently impenetrable mountains, but a foot path led through the gorge and beyond rose the grey roofs of Hyang-San, set beside a tempestuous stream, and shaded by pine and willow trees. About thirty small temples composed this monastery. We were greeted by monks who expected us, and led to a temple which we were to occupy as sleeping quarters. Upon entering, a huge Buddha seated on the altar gazed upon us, amazed by our rude invasion of his solitary retreat.

Exhausted by our journey and before the servants could unpack our camp beds, we fell upon the floor and slept in the holy sanctuary of the god.

Later an aged monk did the honours and with him we visited the temples. Some were simple, others quite elaborate with projecting roofs of curved grey tiles. Beneath the eaves the rafters were richly decorated in soft colours, a feature of Korean temples. On the main portal of one of these, a white dragon was portrayed, also the Buddhist emblem of purity, the immortal lotus flower. Within the temples were numbers of life-sized gilt images of Buddha. Often at their feet a small bowl of water was placed for the god to drink. In the courtyard of one temple rose a pagoda shaped monument symbolical of the learning of the monks. "Line upon line, precept upon precept, till perfection is attained."

Fish are painted and carved in many of the temples. "Fish live in water" the old monk said, "therefore their image in the temples prevents them from perishing by fire."

The monks told us that the most ancient temple was a thousand years old, but a "thousand" is a classical Oriental figure. The temple looked very old but no date is really accurate in Korea, that we could find.

Bright sunlight flooded the scene. Peonies grew in our courtyard. A feeling of peace pervaded the air and over the grey-roofed temples lay the hush of world-old dreams.

We visited the burial ground of the monks. The graves were marked by egg-shaped stones, five feet high, their inscriptions now indistinct and covered with moss.

In one temple a ceremony was taking place in memory of some departed brother. Sacrifices of food are made yearly on the anniversary of his death. On the altar were mounds of snow-white rice in shining brass bowls, dishes of seaweed, pea-cake, beans and piles of dough-like cakes. Earthenware jars contained "sool" (native whiskey). The monks chanted and droned their prayers clad in grasscloth coats. When the ceremony was over, I dare say they consumed the food.

We paid a visit to the head monk, the Superior, in his dwelling and found him seated on the floor. In one hand he held a paper fan, in the other a rosary. A decoration from the Emperor of Korea was flung over his grass-cloth coat. He was a good-looking man, about fifty years of age, with brown eyes and a thin black beard. For refreshment he offered us sweetened water and green leaves fried in oil.

In another temple a large gong was beaten all day and prayers were said for the soul of the Emperor. A young monk sat beside it, telling his rosary of a thousand beads, for each bead a stroke of the gong and a prayer. When he had finished another monk took his place, for the prayers must never cease.

While we were exploring the monastery, a crowd of at least fifty country people, peasants and farmers, had gathered in our compound, having come from far and near to see the white strangers, undoubtedly the first specimens of our race they had ever contemplated. They were gentle folk and timidly touched our garments, while the women gazed with wonder at the roses on Mammá's hat.

The sonorous tone of a great bronze bell marked the hour of sunset, and was echoed in all the temples, calling the monks to evening prayer. Each time a small brass bell was heard they raised their hands to their heads, then clasped them slowly before the breast, prostrating themselves at the altar where a great gilt Buddha was enshrined. Again and again they bowed, chanting softly, grey robes sweeping around them, shaven heads touching the floor. The tasks of the day were ended. In silence the black night fell.

The Russo-Japanese War

One winter we remained in northern Korea. The cold was intense. Deep snow covered the valley and surrounding hills, where in spring pink azaleas glowed. Now it was a cruel white world. Silence reigned except when wild winds swept down from Manchuria, howling mournfully. It was the winter of 1904, the first year of the Russo-Japanese War.

Unsan Province, on the border of Manchuria, was vulnerable and might become a theatre of war. The situation was dangerous. From Seoul, the United States Minister, Dr. Allen, telegraphed my father that far-reaching hostilities were imminent near us, urging us and all the white women and children in the American Concession to leave for Seoul, offering to send a United States warship to our rescue in Chinnampo, the nearest port. Alas, Chinnampo was far away and, due to the snow, a journey of several days was necessary to reach this port.

We started off through ice, snow and bitter wind in an antiquated, open vehicle called a "buckboard," drawn by sturdy mules, with a Chinese driver. Sedan chairs or horseback would have been out of the question in deep untrodden snow, over roads primitive at best. We formed a formidable caravan with servants, luggage, camp beds, mattresses and food supplies, and the people from the camps in wagons or Chinese carts.

Each day we ploughed for hours through unbeaten snow, in a temperature far below zero, sleeping in Korean huts, and giving battle all night to every species of insect that infest these dwellings. At our first night's stop we were informed by our interpreter Kim that Anshu, our next halt, was held by the Russians. The Japanese headquarters were only sixty miles distant. An encounter was expected daily. We were between the two forces.

We passed Yeng-Ben, where we were joined by Korean General Hyon Yung Tak, the Unsan magistrate who continued his journey with us, traveling in a sedan chair, heaven alone knows how, accompanied by numerous attendants and guards, running along beside his chair through the snow.

I have forgotten the details of this perilous journey, but refer to an article written at the time by my mother and printed in "Colliers' Weekly."

The Russians were installed in Anshu when we reached that old walled town that night, the second spent on the road. Their camp was adjacent to ours, but we heard nothing from them. The following morning as we were departing, we encountered a detachment of the first Russian Cossack scouting party in Korea. As the frightened natives had told us that the Cossacks ate raw pigs we feared that they might be a bit crude, but they were most courteous and well-mannered. We conversed with them through a Chinese interpreter and they offered us their protection, but we were somewhat apprehensive as the Japanese lines were near. We were between two fires.

The Cossacks remained with us most of the day, often galloping off to search villages where spies might be hidden. The next day they took leave and we parted in a friendly manner but not unwillingly, as we were approaching the old walled city of Pyengyang, held by the Japanese.

As we drew near we beheld a lone horseman riding toward us, holding above his head an American flag. He was a missionary and had been sent to escort us, as no strangers were permitted to enter the city. Japanese sentries were clearly visible at their posts on the wall, and would have fired on us, thinking that our cavalcade was the commissariat of the Russian army.

The Japanese soldiers were most polite, and gave us red-white-and-blue badges to identify us during our stay of two days in Pyengyang, guests of hospitable missionaries.

Throughout our journey from Unsan, we often saw pitiful,

poor Koreans and their families, with household effects laden on their backs, fleeing before the invading armies. The Koreans have always been a persecuted race.

Pyengyang was the capital of Kija Province, which was named for a Chinese who, after the fall of the Shang dynasty in China, invaded Korea with five thousand followers in 1122 B.C. This is considered to be the first authentic date in Korean history. The rest are legends we are told.

Kija was a wise and just ruler. His grave is still shown in Pyengyang guarded by beasts carved from stone. Ruins of the fortified wall he constructed are also visible today.

Pyengyang is built in the shape of a ship, enclosed within a wall. Outside are two tall monoliths, the anchors of the ship. Within the city no wells may be dug for fear of sinking the vessel. Each morning very early, coolies go to wells outside the walls to fill the large receptacles they carry swinging from both shoulders. Thus the town is furnished with water.

After leaving Pyengyang the cold increased, and the wild winds became almost unbearable. Despite extremely warm clothing we were literally congealed.

Through mountains and valleys we struggled desperately, crossing frozen rivers where the mules often slipped. Once these poor animals sank into a half-melted stream, and were dragged across with ropes, while we were conveyed in sedan chairs held high above the rapid current by coolies. Snow fell and the fierce Arctic winds howled among the ice fields. Between Pyengyang and Chinnampo, we remained two days in a dismal native hut waiting for the storm to abate and permit us to proceed on our way.

Chinnampo was occupied by the Japanese and we came into their lines, but we were known and expected and they did not bother us in any manner. They knew we were refugees.

The ice in the river was barely broken, therefore for several days we were obliged to await the arrival of the United States warship the Minister had sent to rescue us.

At last one morning the U.S.S. *Cincinnati* appeared, approaching majestically, white and shining, with the American flag floating abaft. How beautiful were the Stars and Stripes.

Moved and happy to end our journey from Unsan through a war zone, and warmly welcomed by the officers of this United States warship, we returned to Chemulpo, traveling from there to Seoul by train, a distance of twenty-five miles, the only railroad in the country.

Seoul, situated on the Han River, was a large town whose low, straw- or tile-roofed mud houses lined the unpaved streets. Occasionally a foreign legation lifted its head above the agglomeration. The palace itself was a low building. Remnants of an ancient city wall remained, with one or two entrance gates. Coolies carried loads on their backs on racks, called "jighis," and bullocks were used to transport heavy merchandise. White-robed gentlemen with horsehair hats moved along leisurely, fan in hand in hot weather. Few women were seen on the streets and these wore bright green silk coats which fell about them from the crown of their heads, well drawn over their faces, with only one eye visible to guide them. All was archaic and to me profoundly romantic.

My father was received by the Emperor, but retained no special impression of that audience. The Emperor was the last of a long dynasty which had weakened toward the end, the Yi dynasty (1392–1910).

Life in the legations was agreeable and we rode horseback every day. There were various foreign war correspondents awaiting news from Manchuria.

We lived in a large European house, an appendix of the palace, where the Emperor lodged guests of distinction who came to Korea on official visits. The house was kept by a matronly Swiss lady. Everything was done in strict European style, delicious food and perfect service. This imposing lady, Mademoiselle Sontag, was a character and a power in the community. She was a distant relative of the wife of the Russian minister in Seoul.

In town a Chinese kept a general store where all foreign goods were available, from food to dress materials and pink ribbons, and the foreigners traded with him, including Mademoiselle Sontag, who had attained what is politely called "a certain age." The Chinese shopkeeper, imbued with Chinese reverence for Age, once sent a bill to her addressed to "Old Woman Esquire, Mother of the Russian Minister."

We were cordially received by the United States Minister to Seoul and Mrs. Allen in the charming Legation to which Korean chests and other objects of the country lent much character. The house was always filled with flowers— forsythia in early spring and flowering branches of peach, pear and plum trees later in the season.

We rode horseback on mounts lent us by the Minister of a foreign legation, galloping out to the Great White Buddha carved on a wall of stone, a sacred spot to the people. We also rode to the gates of the East Palace, whose entrance was guarded by stone lions and, dismounting, walked in the palace gardens, a retreat of peace and poetry. I recall the white herons perched in the blue cedars, the lily pond where pale lotus floated, and a small pleasure house overlooking the pond. Several picturesque pavilions were placed here and there, but no large palace. This had been destroyed during some war and Korean Queen Min, a fierce opponent of the Japanese, was murdered by them in one of the pavilions of these poetic gardens in 1895.

The Japanese finally conquered this poor weak little country which had always been a prey to both Japan and China. The sorrow of the Koreans was heartrending. In 1910 it became a Japanese Protectorate. In despair, a Korean general, a friend of my father's, committed suicide.

Unsan had not been a theatre of war after all. The battles had taken place farther north in Manchuria.

I will never forget Korea, Land of Morning Calm, that archaic country and its gentle, kindly people. These memories are very dear to me. It was an oasis in life, far from the so-called "World," where one could forget and dream.

Of the aspect and customs of Korea at that epoch, I have written elsewhere in my little book entitled, "Korea, Land of Morning Calm," added to this volume as an appendix.

This northern wilderness formed my youth. The beauty of the hills surrounding Sonamo, the low, straw-roofed mud-huts, the biblical white-clad natives astride donkeys, the wind in the bells tinkling beneath the eaves, and the nights when ten thousand stars stood in the heavens, and only the chirp of the crickets broke the silence, all made a deep impression on me and I grew to love it. The simplicity of this archaic world gave each thing a significance and to simplify is to intensity. It inspired in me an appreciation of beauty and poetry that has lasted throughout life, making of me a dreamer.

In the East Palace Gardens, Seoul, Korea

In an ancient eastern land
Age-old palace gardens stand.
On the lily-pond's deep breast
Pale-faced holy lotus rest.

Gleaming in dawn's coral light,
Paling in the amber night,
Jade-white cups of lotus-flowers,
Close and open with the hours.

Buddhist sign of purity,
And of immortality,
Lying on the lily-pond
Dreaming of a life beyond.

In nirvana, blessed, at ease,
Buddha rests on lotus leaves.

Lascelle

Egypt and the Sudan (Before World War I)

Each year we traveled to and from Korea to Europe, at times taking the Trans-Siberian Railway through vast regions of Siberia where people clad in coarse fur jackets and caps came from their distant habitations, squatting on the platform of the tiny stations where the train halted a few minutes, to gaze in wonder at the Siberian Express which passed only once a fortnight in this wilderness. At the frontier between Asia and Europe, our convoy halted, and we bought quantities of caviar fresh from the Volga. Here a pole was planted, as a line of demarcation between the two, with a sign "Asia" on one side, and "Europe" on the other.

On one journey Colonel Mannerheim was on our train, and we became acquainted with this great soldier—tall, stern and handsome—who later became President of Finland.

At other times we went by ship through the Indian Ocean, Red Sea, and Suez Canal. Once we broke the journey in Egypt.

An American friend of my father, a great promoter, had created a large cotton plantation in the Sudan, which we were to visit.

We stopped at the famous Shepard's Hotel in Cairo. It was December. In stifling heat we went about the city with a dragoman, viewed the mosques, entered the large columned court of the ancient El Azhar University where students, clad in Egyptian striped robes, were seated on the pavement, studying their lessons. In shops we found silks, tissues and the national red fez, also silverware.

The people we passed on the streets aroused our interest. A few veiled women and many men, tall, powerful Arabs, in long striped native robes, coiffed with a fez. These men frightened Mammá and me. They came so close to us and gazed with their bold, piercing black eyes into our faces. My father endeavoured to drive them away, but they were very persistent, unaccustomed perhaps to unveiled women.

In a broad victoria we drove to the pyramids at Ghizeh, a few miles from Cairo, and lunched at Mena House. Like Napoléon, we contemplated the formidable pyramid of Cheops and the fabulous Sphinx, seated majestically in the burning desert, her face half obliterated by wind-swept sands.

On the road to the Pyramids, our carriage passed strings of camels burdened with merchandise, led by Arabs in native costume and red fez. These camels were a delight to me with their small aristocratic heads held high and their slow undulating stride. They glanced at us disdainfully and apparently despised us.

We went by train to Luxor where the fantastic ruins of the Karnak temples with their lotus and papyrus columns burst upon our entranced vision. Crossing the Nile to Thebes we raced on donkeys across the hot sands, ostensibly to visit tombs which never materialized. That wild gallop enchanted me, a flock of Arab boys running beside me beating the donkey to an ever faster pace. In the sand lay bits of coloured pottery which the donkey drivers attempted to sell to us for much lucre, stating that they dated from the time of Christ.

Our host, Mr. H-, had left Cairo on his dahabijeh before our arrival. We were to join him at Assuan and continue the journey with him to the second cataract at Wadi-Halfa, where we crossed the Nile in a felucca to the cotton plantation in the Sudan. We traveled from Cairo to Assuan on a boat plying the river. I had expected to find the Nile of a pale green hue, but to my dismay beheld only a muddy stream flowing between low flat banks. A strip of bright green cultivated land on either side lay like embroidery on the limitless desert. Flying sand and alluvion had painted the river a tawny brown. Later the green embroidery disappeared and only desert surrounded us.

At sunset the ship reached Assuan and we went on board the dahabijeh, a luxurious floating palace, characteristic of the Nile. Several distinguished English guests whose names I have forgotten were on deck with Mr. H- to greet us.

Fading day revealed the island of Philae rising out of the river, crowned by the famous temple, square in shape and surrounded by columns, its classical, harmonious silhouette a fantastic vision in this wilderness.

After dinner the dragoman led our party to Philae. In Egyptian darkness we penetrated into the temple by the light of a magnesium taper held in his hand, passing from one chamber to another. Startled bats, aroused from their slumber, flew about in frenzy, ugly and frightening. We trembled lest they become entangled in our hair. This visit by night to a temple of ancient Egypt was amazing and through the years comes back to me like a dream.

The following morning the dahabijeh moved south to Wadi-Halfa. No habitations were visible, only sand, endless sand. The primitive austerity of this vast waste was awe inspiring. Hills appeared, hills of arid rock, bordering the desert.

At last we reached Abu-Simbel on the right bank, the famous rock temple of Ramses II, hewn from the tawny cliff, set high above the Nile, approached from the river by a hill of sand. The dahabijeh stopped at the foot of the cliff. The heat was almost intolerable. Going ashore, beneath an incandescent sun, we scrambled up the hill of burning sand to the temple and found ourselves face to face with four colossal statues of Ramses seated immutably, hands on knees, coiffed with the superb Egyptian royal head dress. These colossi ornamented the façade of the temple, cut from the living rock, the temple that the great Pharoah had built to his own glory. At his feet were tiny statues of his wife.

To our bewildered eyes this temple seemed unreal, but there it was, and we ourselves standing before the lord of ancient Egypt so many thousands of years ago—a personal encounter.

We reached Wadi-Halfa at sunset. We had entered Nubia.
Leaving the dahabijeh we spent the night in a small hotel
whose garden walls were covered with purple bougainvillea,
a strange contrast to the desert. We walked to a nearby
village of earthen huts beside the Nile. At the river's edge
were Nubian women drawing water. Clad in long, dismal
black robes, a black veil covering their heads and faces, the
eyes alone remained visible, large, dark and luminous, giving
promise of a beautiful countenance. Alas, one or two unveiled proved the contrary. Proud and erect they passed with
splendid bearing, a bucket of water on their heads. We
smiled at them and they gave us friendly glances.

Next morning we left Wadi-Halfa by train, the railway to
Khartoum. Descending at a small station we embarked in a
felucca, a small boat with a triangular sail, familiar to the
Nile, and a puff of wind blew us to the opposite bank of the
river, to the Sudan.

The plantation house stood in the midst of the cotton
fields, a large square two story building, encircled on the first
floor by a covered verandah, onto which the living rooms and
sleeping apartments opened, the latter with no inner windows. This verandah was the boulevard where everyone
passed. The ground floor was given over to the servants.

Plump little dourah birds fed in the millet-fields (dourah)
and green parakeets screamed in the yellow acacia trees.
Beyond the plantation the silent immensity of the desert
unfolded.

By day we did not venture forth in the scorching sun. One
morning we made an early tour of the property but the heat
was overpowering and Mammá suffered a slight sunstroke,
although we had returned to the house by nine o'clock.

At evening donkeys were brought around. In the red sunset we rode into the desert. The beating of tomtoms in native
villages sounded monotonously and jackals howled in the
low brush as we rode by. Later the full moon stood in the

heavens and brilliant stars seemed near enough to touch with an outstretched hand.

Throughout the night the noise of the "saghias" broke the silence, the mournful squeak of a wooden wheel raising water from the Nile, turned by a patient donkey circling endlessly around and round, a typical Egyptian wail.

The great adventure of this fabulous journey for me was a camel ride. I was placed aboard one of these "desert ships" which knelt at evening below the verandah steps. Perilously seated on the back of the beast which turned his head and stared at me contemptuously, I clung to the saddle while he rose to his feet with several violent jerks and started to stride along causing a volcanic upheaval that shook me to my innermost being and made me very ill. I implored his driver running beside us to let me descend from those dizzy heights. Accordingly the camel bumped to earth, first on his forefeet, then on his hind legs, folding up neatly, thus releasing me from my misery. The animal was as pleased to be rid of me as I of him and we parted without further ceremony.

A few days later we returned to Cairo from Wadi-Halfa by an excellent train coming from Khartoum, the carriages painted white in order not to show the dust and desert sand which filtered through and piled up in our cabins. The Egyptian adventure had ended, but left an imperishable memory.

The plantation was eventually sold to a British company headed by Lord Lovatt.

Memories of Imperial Russia
and of Two Revolutions, 1915–1917

In September 1915, in the second year of the Great War, my father, H. Fessenden Meserve, then Vice President of the National City Bank of New York in Europe, was sent to Russia on a mission for loans which that bank proposed to make to the Imperial Russian Goverment. My mother and I accompanied him as well as his secretary, Mr. Rodney Deane.

At that time Mr. Frank Vanderlip was President of the National City Bank. His keen mind and brilliant abilities made working with him a privilege, and the atmosphere of friendly collaboration which he created in that great institution was inspiring. It was said that he brought heart to Wall Street. My father admired his fine qualities and was devoted to him. Another dear friend in the bank was Mr. George Roberts, who wrote an excellent financial and political survey of the world, published weekly. Backed by this warm atmosphere my father set forth with confidence and interest on his mission to Russia.

The following spring, in 1916, two loans were made by him to the Imperial Russian Government. Mr. Peter Bark, a very able and charming man, was the Russian Finance Minister and my father was pleased to work with him.

My own feelings upon undertaking this journey were indescribably tumultuous. I had always had a passionate interest in this mysterious land. In some vague way I seemed to have known it before. Now Russia was to be mine and I vibrated on the threshold of a marvelous experience.

A journey to Russia in wartime was a difficult enterprise. The famous Nord-Express from Paris to St. Petersburg had ceased to function immediately after hostilities began. Instead of an easy forty-eight hour trip in a comfortable train, via Berlin, it was necessary to proceed by boat from England to the Hague, Hamburg, Warnemünde, Copenhagen, and Stockholm. From there we traveled by rail through northern Sweden to Haparanda, the Swedish-Russian frontier.

In New York my parents had taken a Dutch ship, the *Rotterdam*, and I met them in Falmouth, chaperoned by an English lady, having come from Paris where I had visited my aunt Mary Struve. Quivering with excitement, I crossed the British Channel on a ferry accompanied by two boats to detect mines. Overhead, escorting us to the English coast, floated a silver plane, gleaming in the sunset. I literally danced on to the *Rotterdam*, clasping in my arms a new Paris sealskin coat, and electrified my mother by my enthusiasm.

After leaving Falmouth, the *Rotterdam* plunged through the heavily mined North Sea patrolled by the British Navy. Standing on deck looking out over the vast expanse of stormy grey waters, we suddenly perceived a torpedo boat flying the Union Jack racing towards us. It rushed alongside while the sailors manning it shouted to our captain: "Turn about, mines ahead!" Our vessel veered from its course. Thus the vigilant British patrol saved us from German mines and prevented an early end to our Russian adventure.

We spent several days in Stockholm; then, after a long journey through northern Sweden, we finally reached Haparanda, the terminus of the Swedish railway. There the Torne River forms a natural boundary between Sweden and Finland, the latter at that time being part of the Russian Empire.

Across the narrow stream from Haparanda lies the Finnish hamlet of Tornio, a lone outpost in flat desolate country. A few wooden houses on both shores were the only signs of human habitation. A small boat ferried passengers across.

An exchange of war prisoners had taken place that day. We witnessed the moving spectacle of Red Cross trains bearing away German prisoners while others repatriated wounded Russian soldiers. In Haparanda the latter were put on the ferry to cross the Torne River. Some lay on stretchers; others walked with difficulty, leaning on canes and supported by Sisters of Charity whose white caps fluttered in the breeze. Shouts of welcome arose from the impatient crowd awaiting them on the Russian shore, while the national anthem, "God Save the Tsar" (Bozhe Tsaria Khrani), rang from eager throats. Russia, the motherland, received her mutilated sons and took them again to her broad breast.

Later we also crossed the Torne River on the same boat, thus entering the vast Slav Empire. In Tornio a Russian train awaited the passengers for St. Petersburg.

It was a crucial moment. I had always longed to see Russia. Now it lay before me and I wondered excitedly what images and secrets it held. Fate made of it a turning point in my existence and from it depended my future life.

Our train ran through Finland past tidy farms, lakes, fir forests and white stemmed birch trees. Thirty hours later we reached Beloostrov, the frontier between Finland and Russia, and were obliged to leave the train for customs and passport formalities.

Upon entering the dim station, our eyes fell upon large gold icons, revealed by the soft light of candles burning before them. Not knowing the Russian custom of placing icons in railway stations, I gazed with amazement at their mystic presence. Orthodox travelers crossed themselves and made genuflections, invoking the protection of the saints.

The starlit sky without, the glowing sacred images within, moved and enchanted me. This was indeed a royal entrance into Holy Russia.

Another hour's journey brought us to St. Petersburg. We drove to the Hotel d'Europe on the Nevsky Prospect where

we were to spend two thrilling years and live through a
revolution.

We occupied a suite on the first floor of the hotel, the
"belétage," as the Russians called it. The large salon had
two windows giving on the Mikhailovskaia, a fireplace and
green plush furniture.

In the "perednaia" (entrance hall) heavy winter coats and
snowshoes were removed, and officers unbuckled their
swords before entering the salon.

A timid chambermaid named Hilda from the Baltic provinces attended us. She spoke German, fortunately, as we
knew no Russian. The revolution metamorphosed this simple girl and under the bolshevik régime she became rampant.

Life in St. Petersburg

Russia, mysterious, mystic Russia! Infinite charm
prevailed—streets covered with deep snow in winter,
sledges silently gliding over the white surface, shop windows
filled with fresh flowers, opera, ballet, people, all were a
source of wonder. We drove through the city and on the great
granite quays of the Neva lined with palaces where the
immense red mass of the Winter Palace rose; down the
Nevsky Prospect to the Alexander Nevsky Monastery, and
across the Neva to the Islands, the fashionable promenade
facing the Gulf of Finland.

St. Isaac's Cathedral and the Kazan, the two principal
churches, offered nothing typically Russian on the exterior,
but were rich with golden icons within. I liked the Church of
the Saviour with its bulbous domes, and often walked there.
Nearby Emperor Alexander II, the Liberator, was killed in
1881 by a nihilist bomb. We visited the Alexander III
Museum (the Hermitage was closed during the war).

Near St. Isaac's was the Admiralty, with a slender golden spire gleaming in the grey light of winter. On the quay stood a huge bronze statue of Peter the Great on a rearing horse, by the French sculptor Falconet, erected by the Empress Catherine II in memory of the great Tsar who in 1703 founded St. Petersburg on the marshlands of the north, to the distress of the ancient Moscow Slavophiles, thus dividing the country between Peter's new order toward Europe and the established Slavophile order of Old Russia. St. Petersburg is an eighteenth century city and presents no aspect of typically Russian architecture.

We attended the opera and the ballet, falling beneath the sorcery of the latter, and the exquisite art of the dancers.

When we reached St. Petersburg in 1915, Imperial Russia was entering the last phase of its existence, but of course no one could know this. The two years we spent there were the swan song of the majestic Empire, which at that time presented a facade of perfect stability, riches and power, and seemed immutable as the universe.

It was an entrancing world. Russia had been at war with Germany for over a year, and the former brilliant life of the capital was suspended. Still, enough remained to make it the most alluring place on earth. Nicholas II, autocrat of All the Russias, sat on the throne of an absolute monarchy and the mere idea that he could fall would have appeared impossible. If there were cracks in the edifice, they were not visible to the outsider.

Frequently we attended Orthodox religious services in gilded churches hung with precious icons. The eyes of the stranger were dazzled by the rich gold iconostases (altar screens) and sacred images, his ears intoxicated by the strains of celestial music sung by choirs without accompaniment. No organ is used in Orthodox places of worship and the soulful voices rise like a heavenly host. Long-

bearded priests in glittering brocade robes and mitres officiated. At the end of the service prayers were offered for
the Imperial family in deep sonorous tones like bells.

Formerly in winter, fresh flowers were sent daily by train
from the French Riviera to St. Petersburg. The war ended
this, but even when the mercury was far below zero, tender
blossoms appeared in florists' windows behind frozen panes.

The Russian upper classes were highly educated, with
great charm of manner. An ease, an elegance and amiability
prevailed which I have not seen elsewhere. Life was
exhilarating. Due to the war, few receptions if any were
given in private houses, although formerly entertaining had
been on a lavish scale. The main distractions were the opera,
and the ballet. The latter had attained a high degree of art,
and the Russians were connoisseurs. They could spend
hours comparing the respective merits of first ballerinas,
such as Pavlova, Karsavina or Kshessinskaia. The ballet
was an occasion for elegant Petersburg society to show
itself. Loges and stalls were filled. Many fauteuils were
reserved for a lifetime by the same person and passed as
heirlooms from father to son. Smart officers in uniform and
lovely Russian ladies made a brilliant spectacle in the famous
Marinsky Theatre with its pale blue draperies.

In spite of a little gaiety, the war was taken very seriously
and ladies worked for the soldiers at the front. In innumerable ouvroirs they knitted, sewed and made bandages. In
Tsarskoe Selo, where the sovereigns resided, the Empress
Alexandra had her own hospital and she herself cared for the
wounded with her two elder daughters, the Grand Duchesses Olga and Tatiana. Throughout the war they were always
dressed in nurse's costumes. Military uniforms were seen
everywhere, and there was much coming and going between
the Army General Headquarters, the "Stavka," at Mogilev
and the capital.

The revolution of 1917 sent this brilliant world crashing to the ground with a reverberation which shook the globe.

From the beginning we heard much about the evil "starets," Rasputin, a Siberian peasant who professed to be a monk. This depraved creature had been introduced to the Emperor and Empress by the Montenegrin wives of two of the Russian grand dukes, as a holy man possessing the power of healing and who might be helpful to the Tsarevich Alexei Nicholaevich stricken by the terrible malady of haemophilia. When an attack occurred, the Imperial couple would summon this so-called holy man to the bedside of their son, and the flow of blood would cease, miraculously, perhaps by hypnotism. The young Crown Prince would recover temporarily. No wonder that when all else failed, the afflicted parents had recourse to this impostor who eventually became the evil genius of Russia, and one of the principal causes of its downfall. To the sovereigns he was a "Holy Man," and they could believe no evil of him.

Russia. At that time what magic dwelt in the name. Russia was not merely a country, it was a world. To the newly arrived foreigner, unable to understand the language or to decipher street names and shop signs, Russia was like a blow on the head, leaving him utterly bewildered. He eventually recovered, and soon the irresistible charm of this strange land swept over the visitor like a torrent. The brilliance, grace and erudition of the nobility, the endearing gentleness and simplicity of the people, the kindness and generosity of all, the lavishness of their fêtes, the perfection of their music and ballet, the darkness of winter days, the whiteness of summer nights, soon wove a magic spell which held the stranger enthralled. Even after leaving Russia, neither time nor distance could diminish the enchantment, and he always remembered the Giant of the North with tenderness and regret.

Upon arrival our first care was to procure some means of locomotion. All automobiles had been requisitioned by the army, therefore we resorted to a closed carriage, painted dark green, and drawn by a pair of fast black horses. The fresh-faced young coachman, smothered in a curly blond beard, was named Kyril, an amiable youth who wore a square-topped black hat with a rolled up brim and a green cloth coat. After the manner of Russian coachmen in winter, this coat was so thickly padded that Kyril's waistline attained an incredible circumference, and he appeared to weigh several hundred pounds. Later we experienced how indispensable these garments were to protect coachmen against the intense cold of winter in Russia, but Kyril's young bearded face and small twinkling eyes above his rotund figure always made me laugh.

Immediately I began to acquire an elementary notion of the Russian alphabet. A whole world hides behind these unknown letters jealously guarding their secret. I found a key to unlock the enigma. A Russian lady and I battled with the thirty-six letters of the alphabet. At first they appeared like small insects. Laboriously I unwound the puzzle, "fly, ant, mosquito, spider." Soon the shop signs ceased to defy me. I could even read a bit and was able to give orders to Kyril without assistance from the hotel porter, but Mammá doubted my accuracy. "Are you quite sure he understood?" she queried. When Kyril answered, "Da, da, baryshnia" (Yes, yes, Miss) and arrived at the appointed hour, I would look at Mammá proudly.

My father's first visitor was Mr. Protopopov, former vice president of the Imperial Duma, who was announced soon after our arrival. Slender, black eyes, grey hair and moustache, with suave, affable manners, but in spite of this simplicity one felt intense intrigue. Mammá and I conversed with him a moment before leaving him with my father. He spoke excellent French and English, and his conversation was agreeable. Immediately after his departure, two enormous bouquets of flowers were brought to Mammá and me. These floral offerings were indicative of this lavish people who do everything on a big scale. Just before the fall of Imperial Russia, Protopopov was named Minister of the Interior on the demand of Rasputin, the fatal power behind the throne. In this position he developed "la folie des grandeurs," and eventually went quite off his head.

Mr. George Marye was United States Ambassador to Russia. We liked this cultured gentleman and the handsome Ambassadress. An ouvroir had been organized at the American Embassy in the Sergeevskaia, where ladies of the American colony sewed and knitted for the soldiers. Mammá and I joined, helping to make bandages. The American colony also supported a small lazaret for wounded soldiers, as well as a crêche for war orphans under the patronage of the Grand Duchess Tatiana, the Emperor's second daughter. Mrs. Marye was president of the Tatiana Committee. A year later, when she left Russia, Mammá became president and was deeply interested in this work, loving the children. We went frequently to visit them in the orphanage on the Kamenny Ostrov Prospect. Mrs. Noble, mother-in-law of Captain Sherman Miles, Military Attaché at the American Embassy, was also very active in this organization. Near the end Mammá received a Tatiana medal, a dark blue enamel shield with the initials of the Grand Duchess in diamonds, in appreciation of her services.

Several delightful people were in the Embassy besides Captain and Mrs. Miles; the Counselor of Embassy Butler Wright and Mrs. Wright; Assistant Military Attaché Francis Riggs and Embassy Second Secretary Norman Armour; Admiral Nelson McCully was Naval Attaché. We were devoted to this great gentleman whose warm heart and gift of friendship made him universally liked. He spoke Russian fluently. North Winship was American Consul.

Another dear friend was Ivan Charlier, Belgian Consul, whose sterling character and high courage in adversity after the revolution, when he lost all, have always been a source of inspiration to me. The cock was his emblem and his motto was "Toujours le jabot en l'air" (Always keep your chest out). Gallant Charlier. The Counselor of the Belgian Embassy was Bernard de l'Escaille, whose friendship I valued highly. Handsome Comte Jacques de Lalaing, another Belgian diplomat, was most popular. Monsieur Paléologue was French Ambassador, and his memoirs of that period are historical. Brilliant Charles de Chambrun and Francois Gentil were in the French Embassy.

Russian General Count Gregoire Nostitz, with a great fortune and a high position, was most kind to me, dear "diadia Grisha" whose memory I cherish. He and his handsome American wife, Lili, received in their home on the Sergeevskaia. The jewels of the Countess were fabulous—rubies, emeralds and diamonds—from the Nostitz family, which she never wore during the hostilities. One memorable night in their loge during a ballet in the Marinsky Theatre, I met a tall, dark Russian diplomat just back on leave from the "Stavka" (Russian Headquarters at Mogilev) where he was Vice Director of the Diplomatic Chancellery of the Emperor (Division of the Foreign Office at Headquarters). He was the most handsome man I had ever seen and his name was Nicolas de Basily. I married him some years later in Paris.

There were several American ladies, wives of Russians in St. Petersburg. One was the beautiful, gracious Princess Michel Cantacuzene (a granddaughter of President Grant), whom I always greatly admired. Another was auburn-haired Madame Artsimovich, wife of Vladimir Artsimovich, a distinguished member of the Russian Foreign Office. Her daughter Miriam eventually married Boris de Yonine, a dashing Cossack officer in his "cherkeska" with cartouches spread across the breast, a "kinzhal" (dagger), a revolver and a sword at his slender waist, a tall astrakhan cap and untold charm.

I met him in a loge at the ballet at a time when ladies still wore décolleté dresses. He sat behind me and I saw him looking at me. In the entr'acte I turned around, thinking that perhaps he would make some graceful remark. Not at all.

He merely said, "You are an American?"

"Yes."

"I thought so," he replied, "You have a well-scrubbed Anglo-Saxon back."

After that we laughed and became good friends.

I was bewitched by this colourful world. The Russians had a most flattering way of making one feel welcome, as if one were something very special. In this warm atmosphere I trod on air most of the time. They accepted me simply, calling me "Baby," as my family did. Young, full of life and enthusiasm, I was entranced by Russia and this pleased them.

Mammá had a loge at the Marinsky Theatre for the opera. We attended performances of Glinka's famous opera, *A Life for the Tsar*, also Tchaikovsky's *Eugen Onegin*, a gem of Russian music based on Pushkin's famous poem. *Boris Godunov* was also given, with Chaliapin resplendent in the title role, and many others. Often I went in Charlier's loge at the Marinsky Theatre to see favorite ballets; *The Hunchback Horse*, *The Sleeping Beauty*, *Les Sylphides*, *La Fille Malgardée*, *Le Chevalier à la Rose*, etc., all executed with such perfection of technique and stage setting that the performances were an enchantment. Beautiful, ethereal Madame Karsavina was an exquisite ballerina. Madame Kshessinskaia was also a remarkable artiste. This high expression of art transported one into another world.

In winter French plays given in the Theatre Michel by troupes of the best actors from Paris were an elegant rendezvous for smart society.

Against this brilliant background, a figure stands out in my memory, an Imperial Highness, Grand Duke Boris Vladimirovich, cousin of the Emperor Nicholas II, pleasure-loving, often badly surrounded, but simple, attractive and kindhearted. We became good friends and he was always extremely nice to me. We danced the tango together in Petersburg or skied in Finland while on house parties in Terijoki on the Gulf of Finland. He skied beautifully, but I usually got my feet crossed and fell hopelessly entangled in the snow. Then all the party came to my rescue and pulled me up. What happy memories of days spent in great white stretches with snow sparkling in the sunshine on green fir and birch trees. What purity, what silence, but also what cold. How happy we were to run to the waiting sleighs, filled with heavy fur robes. With jingling bells and flying hoofs we raced back to the warm villa. One night I was so penetrated by cold that I ran into the house wringing my hands and literally crying.

Another image I recall is that of Duke Alexander of Leuchtenberg, a handsome man, elegant of figure, gesture and bearing. With his khaki army tunic, decorations and high patent leather boots, he was the perfect aristocrat. He had blue eyes and a blond moustache which he stroked frequently, for he was a bit shy. I liked him very much and we became good friends. He received rarely but one night he invited us to a dinner party in his palace on the Angliiskaia Naberezhnaia. I had never before seen hot "zakuski" (hors d'oeuvres) and was surprised at the display of silver vessels on the buffet, containing hot appetizers, accompanied by vodka. It was an entire supper, but presently the doors of another dining room were thrown open revealing a long table set with glittering silver. A full menu was served to which the copious "zakuskis" had been but a prelude.

Another day, taking tea with the Duke, he led us into the garden to see his automobile which he used at the front, an enormous car containing a full-length bed, writing table, kitchenette and bath. Quite the last word in ducal transportation. As we passed through the garden, a soldier on guard whom I had not noticed in the twilight suddenly exclaimed in a loud voice: "Rad starat'sia Vashe Vysochestvo" (Glad to serve Your Highness). These words used by soldiers to their superior officer meant "at your orders." This strong voice coming so unexpectedly out of the night almost made me faint.

Each day we drove out with Kyril, in winter on the Neva quays, in summer in the park on the Islands, the fashionable promenade overlooking the Gulf of Finland, with Kronstadt outlined in the distance.

I frequently attended vespers in a chapel of the great Alexander Nevsky Monastery, seat of the Metropolitan. Before the icons hung small oil lamps of coloured glass, their wicks flickering feebly. One candle on the reading desk revealed black-robed priests whose sonorous chants broke the silence, deep and full of feeling. Without, snow was falling gently.

Once I went to the Finland Station to see the weekly exchange of war prisoners coming from German camps. The Grand Duchess Kyril met the repatriated Russian wounded with her suite. Food and money were given them, but they looked unutterably sad as they lay on their stretchers with the Cross of St. George, the highest military decoration, and other high orders on their breasts. The sight of these sacrificed lives made my heart ache. How brutal is war, how useless.

One night towards spring, 1916, Mammá and my father gave a big dinner in a private dining room of the Hotel d'Europe where we lived, inviting various people who had been kind to us. The Grand Duke Boris was present, also Duke Alexander of Leuchtenberg, General and Countess Nostitz, and a number of Russian and foreign diplomats. The American Ambassador and Mrs. Marye were also present. It was a gay, lively party, and at the end speeches were made and the health drunk of everyone. The best speech was by the United States Ambassador who, when called upon, rose and, holding aloft his champagne glass, said concisely in French:

"Un bon diplomat—n'ouvre la bouche—que—pour boire."

(A good diplomat—only opens his mouth—to drink.)

While I amused myself, my father was meeting all the principal bankers, Russian and foreign, as well as the people in the Finance Ministry. Before going to Russia, several persons had told him that he would not be able to do business with the Russians without giving "pots de vin" (graft). "Then I will not make the loans," he replied. The truth is that never at any moment did such a situation arise. The Finance Ministry put forth every effort to facilitate his task, and my father made many friends among the officials. The Finance Minister, Mr. Peter Bark, was not only an intelligent and agreeable man, but an eager and efficient collaborator, and my father enjoyed the negotiations. On looking back, I wish I had been less frivolous and had followed his work closely, for it was very interesting.

Besides putting through the loans, my father also opened a branch of the National City Bank in St. Petersburg. For this purpose he chose the former Turkish Embassy, a handsome building on the Neva quays, belonging to a Russian friend, Mr. Ratkov Razhnov. He also opened a branch of the bank in Moscow the following year, but the revolution of 1917 put an end to his activities.

In this golden age, the fashionable promenade was on the Neva quays lined with handsome buildings and palaces. Here the beau monde drove in carriages and autos, or went on foot. Here the red mass of the Imperial Winter Palace rose, surmounted by statues. The Emperor Nicholas II and his family no longer resided in this palace, having retired years before to Tsarskoe Selo, about fifteen miles from St. Petersburg where, according to their taste, they lived very quietly, only coming to town on special state occasions, such as the blessing of the Neva waters on January 6th. They took little part in the life of the capital. During the war the Winter Palace was used as a hospital where fifteen hundred wounded soldiers were cared for.

Nearby the Florentine palace of the Grand Duke Vladimir was inhabited by his widow, Marie Pavlovna, a German born princess whose salon, in the absence of the sovereigns, formed the nucleus of court society. On the quay also soared the Marble Palace, residence of the Grand Duke Constantin who, under the name of Constantin Romanov, had won fame as a poet. The British and French embassies were likewise situated on this promenade.

Frequently we walked or drove on these massive quays, admiring the scene before our eyes. When autumn came, fierce winds blew down from Lake Ladoga. The Neva waters froze and boats ceased to ply. Heavy barges, having delivered their load of birch and fir to heat the capital, lay motionless beside the quays, imprisoned in ice. The Neva bore the weight of pedestrians and sledges moving constantly between the mainland and the Vasili-Ostrov and the Kamenny-Ostrov. Soldiers drilled on the river's frozen breast.

With winter the cold became intense. Open sledges glided over the snow covered streets, their drivers clad in dark coloured cloth coats, made with a fitted waist and long full skirts, so thickly padded that even the most slender man appeared monumental. How they ever raised themselves to their high seats in these garments remained a mystery. Occasionally a small clock was fastened to the back of the belt encircling their huge girth. The town sledges were very small, accommodating only two persons, and generally had no back, so the gentleman placed his arm around his lady's waist to prevent her from falling out in case the horse made a sudden movement. Often unsuspecting foreigners tumbled over backwards and found themselves seated in the snow, while the sledge proceeded on its way.

During winter nights coachmen waited for hours in the snowy streets while their masters attended the ballet or dined out. On leaving a friend's house at a late hour, a striking picture presented itself—a group of coachmen gathered round braziers they had lighted in the middle of the street, endeavouring to keep warm during their long vigil, dark figures hovering around a bright fire flaming in the snow.

Winter in Russia was long, cruel and terrible. For months snow lay packed thick on the streets and the cold cut like a knife. Noses ached and fingers tingled. Fortunately, felt snow boots were worn by all to prevent the feet from freezing. The houses were well heated and had double windows. Between these two panes, thick pads of cotton wool were laid, and paper was pasted over the cracks. Lightweight clothing only was worn indoors, but people donned heavy fur-lined coats and boots on the streets. Ladies wore "botiki," grey or black felt fur-trimmed snow boots, an indispensable precaution. We saw a few beautiful fur coats, but usually fur served as lining for dark cloth coats called "shubas," which assured greater warmth and were adorned with immense fur collars. Men also wore this type of garment.

With intense cold without, the Russians made a delightful life within. They were hospitable, and friends went to their houses at all hours, even late at night, after the theatre or ballet to drink tea and talk. Even if the master and mistress were absent, the houses were open, servants brought hot tea and friends made themselves at home. Cozy people, they gathered around the steaming samovar, drinking innumerable glasses of thin tea with lemon and talking with great volubility. They loved to discuss abstract subjects. "If God exists or not," they called it and these conversations extended far into the night.

At Easter we witnessed solemn ceremonies in the Orthodox churches. Easter in Russia is even a more important occasion than Christmas. Easter, the resurrection, when light comes again to a darkened world, the time of hope renewed, joyous, luminous Easter.

"Khristos voskres" (Christ is risen), the glad tidings ran from mouth to mouth, in the church services, and as a greeting from friend to friend. "Khristos voskres," they said, and the answer was "Voistinu voskres" (Truly he is risen).

Easter services were solemn, sumptuous and the midnight rituals in the big churches the night before Easter were especially magnificent.

In 1916 we attended the midnight mass in St. Isaac's Cathedral, the largest church in St. Petersburg. The vast edifice was crowded with worshippers standing, each one holding a burning taper in his hand. Hundreds of little lights created a mystical atmosphere, and the choir of voices rose in heavenly Easter music, pure and joyous. The clergy, clad in gold and silver robes with jewel-studded gold mitres, officiated before great gold iconostases with all the intricacy of the Orthodox rites. At midnight the priests chanted "Khristos voskres," and the people answered "Voistinu voskres," and kissed each other three times on the cheek. "Khristos voskres, Khristos voskres, Voistinu voskres."

Outside, the church bells were ringing. In solemn procession the gilded clergy left the cathedral carrying the holy icons and, chanting, circled three times around the edifice before entering agin. "Khristos voskres, Voistinu voskres," truly he is risen. Ah, memories of Easter night so long ago when the Christian faith still reigned on Russian soil.

Elaborate preparations were made to celebrate Easter. Usually a supper was served in private houses after the midnight mass. There were two kinds of special Easter cake, one named "paska" was composed of hardened sour cream,

another, called "kulich," a plain sweet cake, accompanied
it. These were served throughout Easter week, as were the
famous "bliny" with "smetana" (pancakes with sour
cream) and caviar.

Many gifts were given at Easter, but the favorites were
eggs made of delicately coloured enamels, of all sizes down
to tiny ones which ladies wore as bangles, assembled on gold
bracelets. Fabergé, court jeweler, renowned for his exquisite enamels, incrusted with jewels, used them for photograph
frames, clocks, cigarette cases, Easter eggs, etc. A Fabergé
enamel was a most valuable gift, highly appreciated. Semi-
precious stones from the Ural Mountains were also
employed for these same objects, such as amethysts, lapis,
pink and green quartz, jade, etc. A delightful custom was to
present a small fat elephant carved from one of these stones.
Seven elephants, all voluntary gifts from friends, were supposed to assure happiness. I possessed eighteen of them and
a great deal of happiness.

When spring came, holes gaped in the frozen surface of the
Neva, disclosing dark waters beneath. The great river burst
its fetters and became a living thing, sweeping blocks of ice
along on its turbulent course.

The transition between seasons is swift. The trees had
barely unfolded their leaves when the ardour of summer was
upon us. Throughout the white nights of the Northland,
when the sun touches the horizon only to rise again, the
shadow of the Peter and Paul Fortress lay mirrored on the
Neva, its slender church spire pointing a glittering finger to
heaven.

In that golden age Russians lived intensely after dark.
They seemed to revive when night fell, and their parties,
always animated and delightful, seldom ended before dawn.
Fashionable society rarely slept at night and did not consider
the nocturnal hours made for that purpose. Sleep for them
was a matter to be liquidated between early morning and

noon, but night was a God-given space of time which they snatched from eternity for relaxation and pleasure. After the war began, this mode of life changed—with men at the front and ladies working in hospitals or sewing for the soldiers. However, parties of young people often repaired to Novaia Derevnia, a gypsy village near St. Petersburg where "tsigane" charmed their leisure with capitivating melodies. This gypsy music is a world apart, and held Russia beneath its spell, exciting the senses and filling the soul with nostalgia. Listeners were deeply moved by these haunting strains, which level rank and abolish race barriers, till all present became as one heart, one people swaying to the magic rhythm. There is a saying among the gypsies: "He who loves the gypsy music will go to hell." Gypsy women were often very handsome. Russian men of wealth and position at times became enamoured of their charms and song and occasionally even married them.

One night I was taken by a party of friends to Novaia Derevnia. It was a white night in July and towards ten o'clock we dined at Felicien's smart restaurant on the Islands. The table was laid in a kiosk overlooking the canal with the Yelagin Palace, residence of the Dowager Empress, Maria Feodorovna, in the background. The scene was bathed in the golden light of the setting sun whose presence at that hour seemed unreal. Towards midnight we went to Novaia Derevnia for an hour's entertainment with the gypsies. We drove in our open victoria behind Kyril, dressed in his summer clothes, a slim chap without his padded winter coat, in a sleeveless black velvet jacket, from which flowed the voluminous sleeves of his pink rubashka (shirt). On his head was a round black cap, ornamented with peacock's feathers.

Entering a small house in the village of Novaia Derevnia, we found eight or nine women clad in full-skirted flowered dresses, with coloured handkerchiefs bound about their

heads, seated on chairs in a row. Some of them were young
and rather pretty, while several older women had been chosen for their deep voices. A man with a guitar stood behind
each girl, accompanying the singers, and occasionally join-
ing the chorus. After champagne and vodka had been placed
on the table, the women began to sing—folk songs and gypsy
songs, Stenka Razin, The Volga Boatman's Song, Two
Guitars, Hey-da-troika, Allah Verdei, and many others,
some wild, some nostalgic, but all expressing the sadness of
the Russian soul. From time to time a woman would rise
from her seat, advance and begin a slow dance, first shaking
her shoulders rhymically, then her whole body until, as the
music grew tempestuous, she quaked entirely from head to
feet.

Some of these expeditions to Novaia Derevnia ended
wildly, but ours was a quiet evening. It was two o'clock and
broad daylight when we left the village and drove to the
Strelka Point on the Islands, the fashionable promenade, to
see the midnight sun touch the horizon and rise again over
the Gulf of Finland. This was the classical way to terminate
such festivities.

Journey to the Caucasus

In June 1916 two loans were made by the National City
Bank of New York to the Imperial Russian Government
which my father negotiated. At this time two of the bank's
vice presidents came to Russia, Samuel McRoberts and
Charles Rich. After the loans went through, the Russian
Government put a private railway carriage at the disposal of
these three American bankers, and arranged for them a
journey to the Caucasus with the amiable Baltic Baron
Maydell acting as guide and host. Besides my father and
mother, Mr. Rich, Mr. McRoberts, Baron Maydell and

myself, our party was composed of Mr. William Patton and Mrs. Patton of Boston, also a former Russian Minister, Mr. Korostovets, and others. There were about fourteen in all.

On a June day we left St. Petersburg in a private railway carriage. Our road led us south by Tula, where arms and samovars were made, then Rostov, among endless fields of sunflowers in bloom, down to the land of Georgia, in the Causasus. Georgia was an independent kingdom for about two thousand years, but under the Emperor Alexander I it became a Russian possession, and the rebellious peoples more or less subjugated.

The magnificent mountain range of the Caucasus, one of the most noble creations of God, stretches from the Black Sea to the Caspian Sea. The Kazbek and the Elbrus are the highest peaks of this mighty chain. The main passes are the Mamison and the Darial, the latter just east of the Kazbek. Through it runs the famous Georgian Military Road, extending from Vladikavkaz to Tiflis, the ancient capital of Georgia. This road was constructed by the Russians from 1811 to 1864 to maintain communication and order among the unruly mountain tribes.

Mythological legends lend glamour to the Caucasus. Here Jason found the Golden Fleece, here on a mountain peak, Prometheus, initiator of the first civilization, was chained by Jupiter for having stolen the fire of heaven to animate the man he had formed from earth.

The Caucasus has always been a source of inspiration to Russian literature. Many writers visited it and described its beauty. The scene of Lermontov's poem ''The Demon'' is laid in the wild mountain passes. Alexander Pushkin, greatest of Russian poets, journeyed to the Caucasus in 1820, remaining for some time in exile for his liberal views which offended the Emperor Alexander I. He wrote there a poem entitled ''The Prisoner of the Caucasus.'' In 1829 Pushkin was again in the Caucasus and related a journey through the gorges where the wild Terek River flows. At that time brigands fell upon travelers, and the poet was escorted by an armed Cossack guard. This was the land of untold grandeur we had come so far to see.

As the train approached Vladikavkaz, the great snow crowned Elbrus rose before our view, dazzling white against the blue sky.

At Vladikavkaz we left the train and drove in automobiles over the Georgian Military Road to Tiflis. This road, hewn out of sheer mountainsides, is a daring feat of engineering, twisting and turning around the brows of thickly wooded spurs. The gigantic scale of the Caucasus mountains over-powered us. We had not eyes enough to contemplate their romantic beauty and majesty. Like pygmies, we beheld snow-capped mountains towering above us. Narrow gorges yawned beneath. Waterfalls rushed tumultuously, plunging into glens and ravines. Dense forests clothed the hills. At one time we perceived the turbulent Terek beating furiously upon the rocks, thousands of feet below, as it took its course through a narrow gorge between great walls of stone. We held our breath before the wild splendour of the Caucasus— so structural, so architectural, it seemed eternal, immortal.

Often no parapet edged the road and the abyss below filled us with apprehension. To add to the discomfort, our automobile was piloted by an Armenian chauffeur who drove like lightning, hurling us around unguarded bends while chasms yawned ominously. Any false movement on his part would have precipitated us instantly into space. In the most dangerous curves he would light a cigarette with his left hand. No command or entreaty of ours could persuade him to lessen his speed.

As we raced along, we came upon a hillsman driving cattle on a narrow road at the edge of a deep precipice. The herdsman called to our driver, warning him to stop, but that individual paid no attention and our car shot forward towards the frightened herd. Like a flash, the hillsman sprang on our running-board, and drawing a "kinzhal" (dagger) from the sheath at his waist, he pressed the blade against the chauffeur's breast. "Stoi!" (Stop!) he ordered, white with rage. "Stoi!" we shouted, "in heaven's name, stop!"

The driver understood and came to a halt. Regaining his self-possession, the mountaineer sheathed his kinzhal and explained to us that recently, at this same place, two horses drawing a carriage had become terrified by a speeding automobile and had plunged into the ravine, dragging with them vehicle and occupants. Determined that the same fate should not overtake his flock, the herdsman would have driven his dagger into the Armenian's heart had the latter not obeyed. Unaccustomed to such primitive methods, we stared at him in amazement and were struck by the beauty of this mountain man, tall and supple, with fine features, an aquiline nose and perfect white teeth. His slender waist was belted into a "cherkeska," the tight-fitting native garment with a full skirt to the knees and cartouches across the breast. Worn with high leather boots and a tall astrakhan cap, it gives the bearer an aspect of great elegance. The Georgian race is handsome in general and the women are often beautiful, but the appearance of this youth, guarding cows in the high passes of the Caucasian mountains, astonished us. With a smart military salute, he departed, guiding his flock across the hills.

The day was blue and gold as the soul-stirring beauty of this romantic land unfolded before our eyes. We penetrated into narrow gorges where wild cascades plunged recklessly down forbidding cliffs. The gorges widened out into pleasant valleys. Mountains soared above us, some powdered with snow. Villages, composed of mud-huts, clung like swallows' nests to the brow of hills. Above all, the Kazbek raised its mighty cone against the sky. Men passed us on the road dressed in the picturesque native cherkeska.

At times we came upon herds of cattle or sheep being driven up for the army of the Grand Duke Nicholas Nicholaevich, Commander in Chief of the Caucasian front, whose headquarters were in the Causasus.

Once we saw a woman seated beneath a palanquin set perilously upon the back of a cow and attended by numerous villagers on foot, evidently a bride journeying to her new husband's dwelling.

We stopped for luncheon in an inn situated at the foot of a mountain where we ate "shashlik," the Caucasian dish made of bits of mutton skewered on a sword, cooked over an open fire and served hot on the blade. Night brought us to the little village of Passa-Naur, where we stopped in a primitive inn.

In the hills nearby dwell the Khevsurs, a curious tribe of unknown origin. We were told that they descend from French Crusaders who passed through these mountains in the twelfth century. This tribe still has in its possession medieval suits of chain armour and helmets which the men wear on special occasions, and no other of the mountain peoples have anything similar. Baron Maydell arranged for us to see some members of this clan, and invited them to the inn after dinner that evening.

Promptly eight or ten of these primitive mountaineers appeared, a strange vision of the Middle Ages, astride small mountain horses. For our benefit they had arrayed themselves in rusty chain armour, with chain helmets on their heads. The men were small of stature, but the close-fitting headdress made it difficult to distinguish their features. Mounted on sturdy mountain horses, gesticulating and flourishing long knives, the so-called descendants of the Crusaders rode their steeds up the steps leading to the wide veranda of the inn, where they executed a mock battle, thrusting knives at each other ferociously and uttering loud, raucous cries. Ghosts of the past, these warriors evoked a vanished world in the silence of the summer night. When they had finished, they dismounted, led their ponies down the steps and, leaving them beneath the trees, returned to perform a knife dance, throwing their long, savage blades upon the floor, leaping over and apparently on them with hoarse shouts. Then, still gesticulating and vociferating, they again mounted their horses and rode off into the night, leaving us with the feeling that centuries had rolled back. Black velvet night enveloped us and the soul of the heavens burned in the stars.

The *Encyclopedia Britannica* (14th edition) writes of this tribe:

> The Khevsurs, a people of the Caucasus, kinfolk to the Georgians. For most part nomadic, they are still in a semi-barbarous state. They are fond of fighting and still wear armour of the medieval type, when the law of the vendetta, which is sacred among them, as among most Caucasian peoples, compels them to seek, or avoid, their enemy. Boys are usually named after some wild animal. Girls receive romantic names, such as Daughter-of-the-Sun, or Sun-of-my-heart. Formerly no Khevsur might die in a house, but was always carried out under the sun or stars. They call themselves Christians, but their religion is a mixture of Christianity, Mohammedanism and heathen rites. They keep the Sabbath of the Christian church, the Friday of the Mohammedans, and the Saturday of the Jews. They worship sacred trees and offer sacrifices to the spirits of the earth and air. Their priests are a combination of medicine-men and divines.

The following day we continued our journey to Tiflis, and descending from the mountains some hours later came upon that sun-baked city in a vast, arid plain, watered by the Kura River.

The bazaars of Tiflis are characteristic. We spent much time there examining beautiful hand-woven rugs, silver filigree, soft silks, rainbow coloured scarves, and raw matrix

turquoises. The city itself offers nothing of particular interest in the way of monuments. A ruined fortress lies on a
hill.

Many other places are to be found in the Caucasus, the
popular Black Sea resort of Sochi, and Gagry, also Baku, the
great oil center, and the spa of Kislovodsk, but my father had
no time for further explorations, and after a short stay in
Tiflis, we retraced our steps over the Georgian Military
Road to Vladikavkaz, where our private car was waiting to
bear us back to St. Petersburg.

Tiflis

All day we strayed in the old bazaars
Of the sun-baked town in the plain,
We bought kinzhals and bright-hued scarves,
And turquoise and filigrane.

We felt the throbbing pulse of the East
In the hush of the old bazaars,
Till the passionate southern night swept
down,
Black velvet, stabbed with stars.

The plaintive tone of a violin
Wailed through the night, then ceased,
But told of love as unchanging
As the charm of the changeless East.

Of love that should be as eternal
And burn with as steadfast a light
As the stars burn over Tiflis,
In the silent summer night.

                                        Lascelle

The Revolution Breaks

In December 1916, St. Petersburg was electrified by the news of Rasputin's murder.

One evening before dinner we were sitting in the green plush salon at the Hotel d'Europe, when the door opened and an English friend entered saying: "Rasputin was assassinated last night and his body thrown into a canal on the Islands. Now we will see many things."

Rasputin, the depraved double-faced "holy man," at whose touch the Emperor's only son, the young Tsarevich Alexei, recovered from his terrible attacks of haemophilia; Rasputin, the debauched Siberian peasant, the evil genius of Russia, was dead. His meteoric career had been cut short by a conspiracy of three men—Prince Felix Yusupov, the Grand Duke Dmitri Pavlovich, and a deputy of the Duma, V. M. Purishkevich, who had plotted against him with the patriotic conviction that by delivering their country from this satanic influence, they were acting for the good of Russia.

On the night of December 15th Rasputin was invited by Prince Felix Yusupov to his palace on the Moika. Yusupov had decided to do away with the evil monk and tried various means of accomplishing this purpose. During the evening cakes were offered to him which had been filled with cyanide, but apparently sugar neutralizes its action and the poisoned pastry had no effect. Later Yusupov shot Rasputin while the latter was attempting to escape through the garden. The body was put in the auto of the Grand Duke Dmitri and deposited in a hole in the ice in a canal on the Islands, where it was found the following day. The tale is told in Prince Yusupov's memoirs.

The Empress was frantic at the loss of one whom she considered the saviour of her son and venerated as a holy man. Mystic and superstitious, she had put her faith in the "starets." (The Tsarevich was a victim of haemophilia, a disease of the blood in the family of the Empress, and transferred only by women to their male offspring. The dread malady took the form of hemorrhages and when an attack came on, the distracted Tsarina summoned Rasputin to the child's bedside and soon the hemorrhage was stayed.) At last he had vanished, the evil power behind the throne whose sinister presence had cast a shadow for so long over Russia. The country breathed again. The news was on every tongue.

In 1871 Gregory Efimovich Rasputin was born in Pokrovskoie, a small village in the province of Tobolsk in Siberia, the son of a poor peasant. The dissolute life of this man caused the people of his village to call him "Rasputin" (the debauched one). He had great religious exaltation and became a monk; he drifted to the Capital where eventually he was brought before the Emperor and Empress under the guise of a holy man and a worker of miracles. He had strong magnetic power and could influence others.

The gift of stopping the flow of blood was not unusual among the peasantry. A Polish friend, Prince Radziwill once told me that he himself had seen it in Poland while on a hunting party. One of the woodsmen had almost amputated his foot with an axe and immediately a certain peasant was summoned who was said to possess this power. The foot was practically severed from the leg and was bleeding profusely. After the arrival of the peasant a miracle seemed to take place, and the blood ceased to flow. "I would never have believed it, had I not seen it with my own eyes," said Prince Radziwill. A mysterious hypnotic power sometimes emanated from these primitive peoples which Rasputin possessed. Upon it was based the influence which this low creature had over the Empress and was one of the myriad threads that wove the doom of Russia.

* * *

The winter of 1917 began pleasantly and the magic charm of life continued. The opera and ballet were a great interest and there were skiing parties in Finland. I had become accustomed to the daylight appearing towards ten o'clock, while night descended about three in the afternoon. I loved to drive in an open sledge in spite of intense cold. In the afternoon, friends came to see us in the green plush salon where a bridge table was always ready, also a gramophone for dancing. At five a huge copper samovar, steaming like a locomotive, was brought in and silver spoons tinkled against tall glasses of weak tea and lemon.

Once I was invited to a soirée in the house of a charming Russian princess O—— to meet some of the young ballerinas of the Marinsky Theatre. My hostess knew that I would be interested in seeing some of these gifted girls who danced so divinely. She herself was an excellent amateur ballerina and occasionally gave performances for the benefit of some charity.

The dancers of the Marinsky Theatre were daughters of respectable bourgeois families and girls of good reputation. They were brought up to consider their work as a vocation and themselves as vestal virgins in the temple of dancing. Often their mothers accompanied them to the ballet school and fetched them when their classes were over. Their technique was perfect and they drifted through the air like leaves in the wind. I found them to be serious minded, entirely absorbed by their art. They had never danced outside of their professional work in the theatre, and did not know the salon dances of the day, the one-step and the tango. Princess O—— suggested that I teach these young ladies the one-step, as an American dance, but the idea aroused a storm of protestation. "The one-step?" they said. "Never! Our mammás would not permit us to dance salon dances." I felt like a black sheep trying to lure them from the path of virtue.

During the winter of 1917 the situation was normal in St. Petersburg, or Petrograd as it had come to be called. Although many Russians prophesied a revolution after the end of the war, no one dreamed how near it was, but the storm was brewing and Imperial Russia was flying headlong to her tragic fate.

The Tsar of Russia, and the Tsarina, Alexandra Fedorovna, lived in the palace at Tsarskoe Selo with their four daughters, the young Grand Duchesses Olga, Tatiana, Anastasia and Maria, and the Crown Prince Alexei, a handsome, winning boy about twelve years of age. In this retreat they had little contact with their subjects. Parents and children were united by the most tender bonds and the simple life they led was more that of a private family than the life of sovereigns. Their misfortune was to have been placed on the throne.

The Emperor was both chivalrous and kind. As first gentleman of the realm he would have been an example to all, but as a ruler he was weak and lacked vision. Nicholas II was quite unprepared for the throne, having neither the upbringing nor the temperament for his autocratic role. To the end, he accepted with mystic resignation everything that befell him, including the final tragedy.

The Empress Alexandra, formerly Princess Alix of Hesse, was half German and half English, her mother having been a daughter of Queen Victoria. She was most unpopular during the war on account of her German origin and was unjustly accused of conniving with the enemy. As a matter of fact she had become Russian with all the exaltation of her mystic nature, and was very loyal to her country by marriage. A tender wife and mother, she was cold and aloof in appearance and lived in a world apart. Even her beauty did not inspire sympathy. Her tragedy was the terrible illness of the Tsarevich which poisoned her life.

In the absence of the Emperor at Army Headquarters during the war, the Empress began to mix in politics. Through her, Rasputin became a power and many of the ignoble creatures he favored were put in office.

The country demanded a constitution but the autocratic Empress was totally opposed to making any concessions and she influenced the Emperor. She wished to hand the absolute power on to the Crown Prince. This was one of the great faults of the regime, together with the lack of agrarian reforms. Nevertheless, the dynasty seemed very secure to the outsider in 1917 and its downfall appeared impossible.

In March, strikes for higher wages began in the Putilov munition factory but no one paid much attention. The people were tired of war and wanted peace. One day a few strikers left the factory quarter of Vyborg in the outskirts of Petrograd and came into the center of the town. The Cossacks who patrolled the city pursued them at first, driving them off, but soon a change came over these troops through contact with the strikers, and they went over to the people. This was a fatal blow to the dynasty as the Cossacks had been one of the principal mainstays of the regime.

The Preobrazhensky regiment revolted, as well as several others that garrisoned Petrograd. There was talk of the Emperor sending troops from the front to suppress the revolt but they never arrived.

One evening before the storm broke, we were invited to Charlier's loge at the ballet. There had been skirmishing that day in the city and the Nevsky Prospect was barred on account of strikers. No one was permitted to cross and in order to reach the Marinsky Theatre, we were obliged to take a very roundabout way, arriving a bit apprehensive and breathless. I forget what ballet was given, but the events of the day had cast a solemn spell over the audience, and the evening was gloomy. Although we could not know it at the

time, of course, we were witnessing the last performance of
the Russian Imperial ballet. Later we all went on to a ball at
Prince and Princess Leon Radziwills', but gloom also pervaded that brilliant soirée and everyone left early. This was
the last gathering of St. Petersburg society. The next day the
revolution broke, changing forever the course of Russian
history.

On the following day, March 8th, my father insisted that
Mammá and I should not go out on the streets. However, I
had some shopping to do in the Gostinny Dvor, the arcade
just across the Nevsky Prospect from the hotel. The street
looked perfectly calm so I decided to risk it and run across,
returning before anyone had time to move. I flew like the
wind and had just regained the Hotel d'Europe side of the
Nevsky when I heard shouts, and a detachment of Cossacks
bore down upon me, riding full speed up the avenue, with a
crowd of strikers flying before it. Quickly I ran into the hotel.
The Cossacks dispersed the crowd; some of the strikers
immediately broke the windows of a bakery shop on the
corner of the Nevsky beneath the Hotel d'Europe, and there
were cries of "bread, bread." After that shots were fired on
various sides. From our windows we could see people brush-
ing along the buildings opposite, crouching on the pavement
when machine gun fire came from the roof of St. Catherine's
Church next door, and from the Old Town Duma across the
Nevsky where the Imperial police had installed machine
guns.

During the ensuing days crowds marched on the Nevsky
waving the black flag of anarchy and the red flag of revolution, singing the French Marseillaise. The mob burned the
Law Courts on the Liteiny, also the police records. They
opened the prisons and released the riff-raff and criminals.
There was constant firing on the Nevsky, and corpses were
to be seen. Shops closed and many of them were boarded up.
Once a bullet crashed through a window of the hotel but no

one was hurt. The Hotel d'Europe was inspected by revolutionary officers and soldiers with bare bayonets, searching for concealed firearms. They knocked at our door and a grim crew entered and looked over the apartment carefully, peering into closets and feeling on top of high pieces of furniture. Finding nothing, they withdrew.

There was little food in the hotel those days. The kitchen was closed. We ate black bread and drank tea. For three days the fighting continued. Automobiles patrolled the streets filled with armed revolutionary soldiers, while others lay on the running boards with rifles cocked, a sinister sight.

We lived in a state of intense excitement. With the exuberance of youth, I was so completely beneath the charm of Russia, that even a revolution seemed a thrilling adventure. The firing was heavy but in spite of all, Charlier, Escaille and a few other dear friends risked going out on the streets and came every day to see how we were getting on. I could never forget this and it attached me to them even more deeply.

One night the situation became so serious that the American Ambassador, Mr. David Francis, invited us to the Embassy for protection with other Americans, but my father decided to remain in the Hotel d'Europe.

Then, suddenly, the revolution came to an end. Without support, forsaken by the army, the great empire of Russia collapsed like a house of cards. Nicholas II was deposed and a Provisional Government was formed under Prince Lvov. The events happened so quickly and were so momentous that people were stunned. It was the end of a world.

There was still much parading on the Nevsky, and the Marseillaise resounded. The hotel servants were called out by mysterious commands to march with the mobs. The shouting and singing made me shiver, and every one felt a great foreboding. Under the influence of invisible committees, our formely meek chambermaid Hilda became militant. One day she entered our apartment about one o'clock,

announcing rudely that she must turn down the beds immediately as "they" had ordered her out for a manifestation
and she would not return that night.

"And I *must* go," she said defiantly.

"Never mind the beds," I answered. "Who makes you
go? Who says you *must* go?"

"Oh, I do not know, 'they' say, 'they' say—ani gavariat."

The ignorant girl had no idea who was the head of this
movement, but the pressure was so strong that she obeyed
without question.

In the weeks that followed there was much talk of one
named Lenin, a Russian political exile in Switzerland, who
as rumors had it had returned to Russia in an armoured train
escorted to the frontier by the Germans. It was even said
that the latter had sent him to make trouble, but once in
Petrograd, little attention was paid to this agitator. A prominent ballerina of the Marinsky Theatre, Madame Kshessinskaia, owned a large house on the Kamenny-Ostrov
which was occupied by revolutionaries. From a balcony,
above the street level, Lenin sometimes harangued the passersby. Driving one day we saw, from a distance, a small
crowd that had gathered around him. Incredibly enough the
Provisional Government did not seem interested in his activities, and no attempt was made by them to prevent him
from saying what he liked. So the Bolshevik Party grew and
gained in popularity.

Soon after the revolution it became evident that it was not
the Provisional Government who ruled, but the Council
(Soviet) of Workers' and Soldiers' Deputies, which had
installed itself in the Duma. Orders were issued from there,
and many officers of the former Imperial Army were brought
to this Council to report, as well as all persons whom they
chose to consider suspect. In the streets the epaulettes and
insignia of former officers were often brutally torn off. General Stackelberg, one of the first victims of the revolution,

was shot on the street and his body thrown below the Neva quays on the ice. Everyone had some tale of horror to tell. Those were turbulent days in the Duma. Socialist meetings were held in the city where anarchy and insubordination were preached. At the front, sanitaires refused to dress the wounds of the soldiers. As for the lower people and the peasantry, they understood nothing of all that had happened. They heard the word "svoboda" (liberty) on every hand and thought it was a new empress. One coachman said: "From now on we will have only eight hours of work a day, from eight in the morning, till eight at night—no more. We want a republic and a tsar."

One thing, however, impressed the peasantry deeply, and that was the removal of the Emperor's name from the church services. The officiating priest had always prayed for the Tsar, the Tsarina and the Imperial family, and suddenly it was swept away, leaving them like sheep without a shepherd, children without a father. "Batiushka, batiushka, little father, do not forsake us," they implored. Alas, only stony silence answered their cry. Nicholas II, Little Father of all the Russias, was a prisoner in his palace at Tsarskoe Selo, and the red flag waved in the land.

Moscow

In the spring of 1917 we rented a villa in Finland, at Terijoki, a summer resort on the Gulf of Finland, opposite Kronstadt, which had been a scene of terror during the revolution. Many St. Petersburg people possessed "dachas" (summer houses) in Finland, and several agreeable neighbours lived nearby. The months went like a dream. We had house guests, and bathed in the Gulf, or drove behind Kyril with his summer clothes and peacock hat.

Many Russian friends came to see us. Panic prevailed as to what terrible fate might overtake them since the disintegration of Russia had begun and the Provisional Government was helpless. What horror for these poor people and how sad for us to witness their agony.

In July the bolsheviks made an attempt to seize power, but the movement failed for lack of leadership. A United States Mission headed by Mr. Elihu Root was in Petrograd at that time. On the day of the coup, excitement prevailed in the capital, and Mr. M. I. Tereshchenko, the handsome Foreign Minister of the Provisional Government, brought charming, grey-haired Mr. Root to my father in Terijoki in order to remove him from the city.

The white nights of this northern clime made a deep impression on me. I never tired watching the midnight sun over the Gulf of Finland, with the warm colours of sunset and sunrise combined. Once I sat all night at my window, reading a thrilling history of Russia in broad daylight.

Upon our return to the Hotel d'Europe in the autumn of 1917, life had become difficult in the capital. Food was scarce and hard to obtain. Instead of offering us flowers as formerly, several of our friends, diplomats, or men in ministries who had facilities, sent us gifts of tea or sugar, which we accepted gratefully. But a young Russian did even better. Upon returning home one evening I found an enormous sack of flour in the entrance hall accompanied by a letter in an unknown handwriting. It was a demand in marriage from an officer whom I knew slightly, but I did not attribute his declaration to my beaux yeux. On the contrary, the astute youth had evidently realized that an American alliance would be useful to him in view of future troubles in revolutionary Russia.

On September 17th, my father went to Moscow to open another branch of the National City Bank of New York. Mammá and I accompanied him.

That day Russia was declared a republic. It happened very quietly and life went on at the usual pace. Towards evening we left Petrograd, driving down the Nevsky Prospect to the Nikolai Vokzal (Nicholas Station). Revolutionary soldiers in blanket coats, armed with bayonets, stood at the door, demanding passports and identification papers before permitting travelers to enter. "Your documents, tovarishchi, your documents," they said. Porters with luggage, citizens and soldiers elbowed each other. In the waiting room candles burned as usual before large gold icons. On the station platforms sat gypsy refugees with ragged children. Hordes of soldiers came and went. They were no longer an army nor obeyed military discipline. It was terrifying to see these men roving about and boarding trains, guided solely by their own will. We shuddered to think what the disintegration of the army meant. The Moscow train was crowded. Panic reigned in Petrograd and everyone was leaving the capital who could do so. We departed on time and eleven hours later reached Moscow where we stopped at the Hotel National.

St. Petersburg was cosmopolitan but Moscow was purely Russian. Abandoned by Peter the Great in his momentous upheaval, Moscow had remained true to old traditions. From the moment the domes of its "forty times forty" churches greeted the eye, the traveler felt that here was the heart of the great Slav nation.

In order to perceive its real mystic sense, Moscow should first be seen from the Sparrow Hills, about four miles distant. There, in 1812, Napoleon viewed his coveted prize lying in the plain below, the spires and domes of her myriad churches gleaming gold, blue and green. Then he swept on, the Grande Armée singing the Marseillaise, and entered the Kremlin walls. Unlike Napoleon, we did not receive this poetical impression until several days after arrival, when we drove there and were enthralled by the old city shimmering like a mirage in the afternoon sunlight.

Where are you lovely Moscow of the hundred domes
Wonder of our land?
There where the solemn city reigned
Nothing but ruins remain.

Take comfort Mother of Russian towns,
See how your invaders shrink,
Hunger and cold cut them down
And at their backs the Russian sword pursues.

Pushkin (translated by Henri Troyat)

We found Moscow crowded with refugees from all parts of
the country. Owners of distant estates had brought their
families here for safety, as marauding soldiers roamed the
countrysides. Izvozchiks (little open carriages barely accommodating two persons) were to be seen in the streets,
also automobiles flying Allied flags carrying English or Belgian officers in khaki tunics, or French officers in blue horizon uniforms. Ambulant vendors sold fruit and sunflower
seeds which the Russian people chewed constantly. The
pavements were strewn with shells. Mutilated soldiers begged alms, and the Cross of St. George, the highest military
order, starred many breasts. Beggars whined, numerous
Chinese were selling shoestrings and white cotton cloth,
even Chinese women with bound feet offered toys on street
corners. These people had arrived in great numbers since the
revolution.

The Petrovka and Kuznetsky Most were fashionable
shopping streets and well-dressed people still purchased im-
ported articles, but long lines formed before shops where
bread, meat, coffee, tea, rubber articles and tobacco were
sold, waiting for hours to be admitted. Black bread was
obtainable only by cards, half a pound per person. White

bread and sugar had practically ceased to exist. Frequently these lines formed in the evening, remaining throughout the night, people talking and chewing dried sunflower seeds. Occasionally women stretched themselves out on the pavement and slept. Some neighbour would always watch the baby and nudge the mother when the moment came to move forward. Russians were kindly souls then and seemed glad to help one another. The Slav nature always understood suffering better than joy.

Army deserters were numerous. There was a grim saying that the troops were divided into two parties, the Octobrists, those deserting in October, and the Novembrists, those deserting in November. These soldiers felt that they must be at home for the division of the lands which the bolsheviks promised, fearing that their families would be cheated, and desiring to be present in order to protect their rights. Alas, these promises were never fulfilled.

The bolsheviks preached peace to the masses, saying that the war was a war of capitalists, encouraged and sustained by them for their own profit. They also promised peace, bread and the partition of the lands as soon as they could seize the government. The ignorant working classes were dazzled by these traps in which they saw the realization of long cherished dreams.

Crowds marched through the streets bearing scarlet banners with inscriptions such as "Peace and World Brotherhood" or "Down with Capitalists." They had no shame in making a separate peace, no thought for their allies. Sick of war, they wanted peace at any price.

The theatres were open. At the (former) Imperial Theatre representations were given and the incomparable Russian ballet still continued at the Bolshoi Theatre. The Imperial Theatre, one of the largest and finest in Europe, was richly decorated with gold and hung with red velvet. The mise en scène was more sumptuous than in the St. Petersburg

Marinsky Theatre, but the dancing in the latter was superior.

On November 3rd we attended a gala performance in the Moscow Opera, organized by Madame Brusilov, wife of the distinguished General, for the benefit of the Knights of St. George. Ladies appeared in evening dress, which was unusual since the war. The national hymns of the Allied Nations were played before the curtain went up. The audience rose and General Brusilov stood beside his wife in a loge. The *Corsair* was a superb ballet and the stage setting extraordinary.

Our drives and walks about Moscow usually ended at the huge Red Place, where rose the fantastic Cathedral of St. Basil the Blessed, founded in 1554 by Ivan the Terrible to commemorate the taking of Kazan from the Mongols. St. Basil's was a bewildering edifice, with numerous bulbous domes painted in bright colours—red, green and gold. This group of cupolas, shaped like pineapples or onions, resembled a growth of exotic fruits, defying description but appealing strongly to the imagination. This church had nothing to do with reality, a vision out of a fairy tale, the enchanted castle in the dark wood, where the brave knight rescued the blond princess from the witch. Dragons surely lurked within. Doves fluttered in the square, pecking at grain offered by loiterers.

The Kremlin had three entrance gates in its great red walls and the most important of these was the Gate of the Saviour, on the Red Place near St. Basil's. A new emperor always entered the Kremlin enclosure by this gate on his way to the Cathedral of the Assumption for the Coronation ceremony. An image of the Christ hung over the arch and no man could pass beneath without removing his headcovering—noble and peasant alike.

I was spellbound by the Kremlin. Fortunately I could not know at that time what sinister fame it would attain in years to come, but for me then it was the image of Holy Russia. I

walked there every afternoon while the northern sun gilded
domes and turrets with mystic beauty. The ancient buildings
had a potent charm. Reverently I contemplated this group of
white palaces, monasteries and churches with golden bulbous domes rising like an apparition from another world
within the red crenelated walls. Religious fervour had animated the men who built these sacred edifices and gave to
their work that magic touch which breathed from the soul of
Holy Russia. Many of the architects were Italians, but drew
inspiration from the ancient churches of the land.

The Kremlin is the heart of Moscow. The name comes
from the Tatar word "kreml," meaning fortress, and the
Russians use the same word. In medieval times the grand
dukes of Muscovy resided within the vast enclosure until
Peter the Great removed the capital to St. Petersburg. After
that the Kremlin remained a museum of the past, of palpitat-
ing memories. Within its walls men have experienced human
greatness and misery. Its stones are dyed with blood. In
olden times palaces overflowed with treasure and the flanks
of the hills were honeycombed with granaries to store provisions in time of siege. In an underground dungeon an ancient
saint, Hermogene, had been confined and pious pilgrimages
were still made to his shrine. In inner chapels, mystic tapers
burned throughout the centuries and paving stones were
worn smooth by the feet of worshipers who kissed the holy
icons.

Besides palaces, monasteries, the Holy Synod and the
medieval chapel "Spass na Boru" (Saviour in the Wood),
the earliest edifice built there, the Kremlin walls enclosed
three cathedrals each of which had a signification in the life of
the sovereigns of Russia.

In the Cathedral of the Annunciation, with its golden
domes, the Imperial marriages were blessed. In the Cathedral of the Assumption, where light filters softly through
slots into the dim, gold-frescoed sanctuary, the coronations

took place. The Cathedral of the Archangel contained the
tombs of the Tsars and princes. Here reposed the line of
rulers from Prince Yaroslav Vladimirovich down to Peter
the Great.

The "terem" or women's apartments, in the old Kremlin
palace, had a medieval aspect. Seclusion of women prevailed at the court of Muscovy and in these rooms where the
tsaritsas formerly resided, low ceilings, walls richly painted
with bright coloured flowers and leaves, combined to create
an atmosphere of conspiracy. In the idleness of seclusion,
dark deeds were plotted. Dim light penetrating through the
yellowish panes of small leaded windows added to the mystery of these painted rooms where all the intrigue of the
Orient lingers. Tradition says that Napoleon lodged in this
palace during his invasion of Moscow in 1812.

Near the women's quarters was an inner chapel where no
ray of light penetrated. Eternal night reigned. Burning tapers
glowed in the darkness, and, as the eye became accustomed,
a silver iconostasis was visible, marvelously wrought and
inset with gem-studded icons. In ancient times, the court
came here to pray in the mystic splendour of this chapel,
while clouds of smoke arose from incense burners swung by
bearded priests in jeweled robes. Gleaming metals and precious stones, set in silence and obscurity.

In the "Golden Chamber," the patriarchs formerly sat in
conclave. Here Boris Godunov held his council. Low-
vaulted, gilded ceilings, frescoed walls, tiny windows forbidding light to enter, niches forming seats for the boyars,
and golden gloom pervading the chamber, made an atmosphere of unsolvable mystery.

Near the terem is the Granovitaia Palata, the great hall
where Ivan the Terrible feasted with the boyars. Here an
English Ambassador was invited and has described the
scene in detail. From an upper window, the palace ladies
looked down, unobserved, as the seclusion of women for-
bade them to appear.

The large palace of Nicholas I, built in the nineteenth century in Renaissance style, was a complete contrast to these medieval buildings. It contained vast reception halls of the orders of St. Andrew, St. George, St. Alexander Nevsky, and St. Vladimir.

I felt so keenly the enchantment of the Kremlin that I wrote the following lines:

The Kremlin

Who shall describe the Kremlin? Let that man come forth
  and try
To grasp the magic of those domes flung out against the sky
Who holds the secrets of the past locked deep within his
  breast,
Who knows the soul of Eastern lands, but also knows the
  West,
Who stains his palette with love and hate, taking for his
  paints
Red from the blood of victims, pure gold from the heart of
  saints.

All things are known to the Kremlin, the might of power, and
  woe
And love of God in holy shrine where mystic candles glow.
From incense-perfumed chapels, where unnumbered feet
  have trod,
Prayers rise to gem-clad icons, and thence to the throne of
  God.

From palaces, churches and convents within the high red
  walls,
Through mysteries of long-dead ages, the voice of Russia
  calls.
Here great rulers were crowned, and wed, here their ancestors lie.

Here is the soul of Russia, The Kremlin can never die.
And the faithful say of these ancient stones where time has
  left its leaven,
"Above Moscow is only the Kremlin, o'er the Kremlin is
  only heaven."

                                                        Lascelle

The Bolshevik Revolution in Moscow

In the autumn of 1917 another revolution was in prepara-
tion. The Bolshevik Party under the leadership of Lenin was
gaining steadily in power, and after a coup d'état in Petrograd in November, which overthrew the Provisional Government, they became Masters of Russia. This revolution
had its repercussion in Moscow and found us in the Hotel
National, where we spent one week under bolshevik fire.
During the days that preceded the storm we lived quietly.
My father was busy with the new branch of the National City
Bank of New York, which opened its doors a few days
before the revolution, only to close them again. Life was
interesting and we met many people. Among them was one
colourful figure, a member of a prominent Moscow merchant
family, whom I mention as a type of that extraordinary class
who were like nothing else in Russia. Some of them were
proverbially vulgar, and others were cultured people of
breeding, but all were fabulously rich and did things in a big
way.

Mr. A —— was a kindly man of ample proportions with a
little beard. He loved horses and had polo ponies and racing
stables. A horse of his once won the Derby, which was the
proudest day of his life. A distinguishing feature about him
was his automobile, painted all over with the stars and
stripes of the American flag—red, white and blue. It was an
astounding sight to see this car flash through the streets of

Moscow, and when it passed, the American Consul literally tore his hair in despair. Just what lay behind this fantastic idea we never knew. Was it sympathy for the United States, or a vague hope of protection should Russia come upon evil days? Who can say. At least it was original, even if highly inappropriate. This Moscow gentleman offered us his loge at the opera, and sent Mammá and me lavish bouquets of flowers. Once I came home to find a box of sweets as big as a suitcase, in pale blue hand-painted satin, containing a supply of bonbons sufficient for a regiment. Another time I found a crystal vase, as tall as I (which means tall), filled with lilacs in full bloom, emitting a heavenly fragrance. It was practically a tree, and I could easily walk beneath it. Everything was done on this extravagant scale.

One night he invited us to dinner in a large house on one of the principal avenues, belonging to his family. This mansion had a fantastic history. Years ago, when his relations wished to build a house, they called an architect and said: "We want you to go abroad, remain a year visiting the countries of Europe and studying their architecture. We will pay your expenses. When you have seen the style which seems to you the most beautiful and most original, you will return and reproduce it for us here." So the architect went to Europe and traveled for a year. Finally he came to Portugal where he saw the Manuelian architecture with shells, cordages and other nautical attributes, symbolic of the great Portuguese era of navigation and discoveries. Enchanted, he returned to Moscow and reproduced a house with these ornamentations carved in stone, and here we dined.

It was an elaborate repast with caviar, vodka, champagne, quail, fresh vegetables and fruits. All the foods Russia had not seen since the revolution were served in abundance. The table groaned. Finally we managed to rise and walked about several huge salons on a digestive expedition, while our friend played the piano. Less than an hour later, the doors of

the dining room were again thrown open and an equally
bountiful supper was served. By this time we could only eat
with our eyes. Such was the measure of the Moscow merchants.

Then the storm broke, shattering old Russia forever. The
following pages are notes I made each day during the week
we were under fire.

Moscow, November 9th, 1917
Hotel National

Tonight, as we sat in our salon, a shot rang out. We rushed
to the windows but all was silent and dark. Soon other shots
followed, shouts and the sound of running feet, then again
the zip of bullets. Several Russian officers who were spending the evening with us went out to investigate, later report-
ing that bolsheviks had attacked the Kremlin, and had been
fired upon by the cadets who held it. (The cadets were young
lads in military training and should not be confused with the
political party of Cadets [K.D.].) They defended their city
heroically.

Moscow, November 10th, 1917
Hotel National

This morning we were awakened by unbroken rifle shots,
while fifteen bullets crashed through our windows. The bolsheviks were firing all over the city, machine guns and field
guns were to be heard. Obliged to abandon our corner suite,
we sought refuge with the American Red Cross Mission
which is stopping in this hotel. Doctor Nathaniel Thayer,
Chief of the American Red Cross Mission, kindly offered us
shelter in their quarters on an inner court, consisting of two
small rooms. (There we remained for a week of daily bombardment, during which time we never undressed and took
turns sleeping an hour or so on the two beds the apartment
offered.)

A French Artillery Mission, under Commandant Mimay, also quartered in this hotel, makes us frequent visits. Other hotel guests drop in. The little rooms are crowded and there is much excited conversation.

The cadets hold the Kremlin which the bolsheviks are trying to capture. The latter's headquarters are in the Skobelev Palace, residence of the former Governor General of Moscow, just behind the Hotel National. The cadets are in the University to our right, also in the City Duma and the Hotel Metropole to our left. The Opera is held by the bolsheviks shooting from upper windows. The Hotel National has become the center of action, a battlefield. Every volley between the two parties passes over our heads. The firing continued all night.

Moscow, November 11th, 1917
Hotel National

Today, Sunday, a big shell dropped on this hotel. The excited guests gathered together in the corridors. It is impossible to leave the building as the bolsheviks shoot at every person appearing on the streets. Wounded are brought in, and the American Red Cross doctors attend them. Mammá and I make bandages. Sisters of Charity and sanitaires, bent on rescuing the wounded, are carried in, also wounded. The bolsheviks aim at anything that moves behind the windows. The streets are empty, save for soldiers lying in wait, crouched low beside the buildings, rifles cocked.

The food problem is acute. Fresh provisions are unobtainable, but the hotel manager performs a minor miracle each day, and provides us with hot soup. Dr. Thayer and his assistant, Dr. Francis Peabody, both very distinguished men from Boston, help us out with a few Red Cross stocks. We make George Washington coffee and eat hardtack with them and Robert Barr, and another officer of the Mission. They are all very kind, cheerful and courageous.

This evening another projectile struck the ridgepole of this building. The shock was terrific. A prolonged sound of falling tiles, smashed chimney pots and shattered glass followed. We are completely cut off from the outside world. The telephone is severed. What strikes me most is that life in other countries can run along as usual, unthreatened by danger. Strangely enough this situation seems almost normal to me now.

Moscow, November 14th, 1917
Hotel National

Today this hotel was deliberately shelled from bolshevik headquarters. After the first few shots, hotel guests came running together, terrified but outwardly calm. Throughout the bombardment, which lasted for several hours, there was not a cry. Herded together on the first floor we waited in silence. Shell upon shell broke and each time it seemed as if the building must crumble, with the din of falling bricks and the clatter of broken window-panes. The air was filled with dust and thick yellow gas from explosives. Our nerves were stretched to breaking.

Towards evening bolsheviks took possession of the hotel. A committee of hotel guests was formed to treat with them. Commandant Mimay, the Chief of the French Artillery Mission, the Italian Consul General, and Dr. Thayer, Chief of the American Red Cross Mission, conferred with the revolutionaries who volunteered to carry a letter to their soviet, to be sent to the Duma. This letter was a protest against the bombardment of an hotel which sheltered non-participating allies and neutral foreigners. The Reds replied: "Are they not Capitalists? Why should we spare them? We do not spare our own Capitalists. We are making a world war."

We dined tonight with the French Artillery officers on tinned beef and trench biscuit from their stocks. We dined by candlelight to the accompaniment of distant firing. The electricity had been turned off. All night the cannons thundered.

Moscow, November 14th, 1917
Hotel National

Today bolsheviks crept upstairs in our hotel and shot from upper windows, thereby drawing upon us the fire of the cadets. It became necessary to seek safety underground. Many people had already spent several days in the cellars, but now word was given and a general rush ensued. We ran to the cellar, past windows where bullets were raining. One young man who wore new boots nervously slid down the whole flight of stairs, which made me laugh. Our nerves were highly keyed but I felt no fear. Excited, I found it a glorious adventure. Mammá told me I was too foolish to understand.

Herded in a subterranean passage, we spent the night—men, women and children—sitting upright on a pile of boards, our heads against the rough stone wall. Sleep was impossible. People talked in whispers and a sick woman moaned. From above came the roar of cannons. At dawn, we went into the boiler room to thaw out.

Moscow, November 15th, 1917
Hotel National

Today the leader of the detachment of Extreme Reds holding the hotel, a doctor of international law, agreed to neutralize the National and fly Allied flags from the roof. Direct bombardment ceased, but heavy firing continued around us all night.

During these terrible days our Moscow friend Mr. A——— contrived to send us an immense basket of various foods, bread, ham and wine. We were deeply touched by his thought of us in danger. How he managed to convey the basket to us we never knew, but it must have been at the risk of the messenger's life.

Moscow, November 16th, 1917
Hotel National

Today a truce was declared. News arrived from Petrograd that the Provisional Government had fallen and that so-called Free Russia had passed into the hands of the victorious bolsheviks.

In Moscow the firing ceased and people began to circulate in the streets. There were still occasional shots. Colonel Mimay was knocked down in a panicky crowd and his arm broken. My father's secretary, Mr. Frederic Grey, was assailed by hooligans on the street and his wallet stolen. The dead were assembled and laid out on the pavement for recognition.

The revolution was over. Hotel guests dispersed and many went to the railway station. Motors and izvozchiks were rare, so they went on foot.

The French officers in the hotel very kindly invited us to the French Artillery headquarters in Petrovsky Park, just outside the city, to remain until we could obtain permission from the new government to return to Petrograd. Dr. Nathaniel Thayer and the American Red Cross Mission were also invited. We all left the hotel together in French military cars.

Moscow, November 17th, 1917

Indelibly stamped on my memory is Moscow yesterday as we made our escape. The dregs of the city stood armed on street corners and evil faces gathered about the hotel doors to watch the guests depart. Red guards with crimson badges tied around their left coat sleeves exercised strict control over passersby. Upon leaving the Hotel National, the French army cars turned into the Tverskaia and we perceived that the top floor of the hotel building had been destroyed during the siege. Empty window frames stared in a sinister manner. Trenches had been dug across the streets and barricades of earth thrown up, behind which the Reds had fired.

The French military cars were stopped by bolsheviks, who demanded our pass. Instantly we were surrounded by Red soldiers, rifles cocked, finger on trigger. They gave us an escort of three soldiers to stand on our running board, bare bayonet in hand. These men wore the usual army blanket coat and grey astrakhan cap. They looked exhausted. Few pedestrians were in the streets and no inhabitants visible in the houses. No one stopped us as our Red escort called out to each sentinel we passed. Moscow was a city of the dead. It seemed as if in another incarnation we had returned and found it deserted and mutilated with all the life hushed in its busy streets and squares.

The French Artillery Mission was quartered in the Petrovsky Park, in the stables of an immensely rich Baku oil merchant, Mr. Mantashev, who had formerly kept his English racing horses in these handsome stone and plaster buildings.

Half an hour later, the car entered the enclosure and the great gates clanged behind us. Above our heads waved the French tricolor as we shook the cordial outstretched hands of our Allies. Never shall I forget the gracious welcome of the French officers, and will always think of them with deepest gratitude. After our little revolutionary experience, it seemed like heaven to be here.

Moscow, November 18th, 1917

For three days we enjoyed the hospitality of these delightful warriors, sitting at their mess-table, sharing their "singe" and "pinard,"* and many other good things, for the mission

* During the war the canned meat served to the French army was called "singe" (monkey) by the soldiers who also named "pinard" the ordinary red wine alloted to the regiments.

was well fed. A change from our recent regime.

The American Red Cross officers went to bolshevik head-quarters in the Skobelev Palace to obtain a pass to return to Petrograd for themselves, for my father, Mammá and me. They described the scene, saying that outside the palace, citizens, soldiers, and armed workmen were assembled with bayonets and field pieces. Once inside, they passed through a crowd of rough soldiers into an inner room where confusion reigned. They were obliged to wait over an hour and during that time a Jew spoke to them in English saying that he was an American and had come over with Trotsky in March. Jews predominated and seemed to be in charge. Finally the sauf-conduits were issued for the Red Cross Mission and for ourselves.

Moscow, November 19th, 1917

Today, sadly we bid farewell to our French hosts, and left the mission in their military cars, crossing the desolate city to the railway station. We went early in order that the cars might return to headquarters before nightfall, and were obliged to wait for several hours in the station as the Petro-grad train only left at midnight. Alarming bands of soldiers surged up and down. We noticed a group of excited Reds gathered around a former Imperial officer in uniform, evidently seeking to find fault with him. For over an hour they questioned him and examined his papers. In the end they let him go, but what a cruel ordeal. The life of a former officer hangs on a thread. If the Reds choose, he is shot or stabbed for any imaginary offense. Among the rough-coated soldiers who invaded the station were many sailors. Their conduct exceeds in lawlessness even that of the troops and their crimes have been atrocious.

*   *   *

Our return to Petrograd was uneventful. We found the city quiet. Food was scarce and in the Hotel d'Europe we received no bread. The Soviet, with Lenin (Ulianov) as President and Trotsky (Braunstein) as Minister of Foreign Affairs, are established at the Smolny Institute—Kerensky has fled.

Journey Across Siberia

At the end of November 1917, shortly after our return from Moscow, we left Petrograd on the Trans-Siberian Express traveling with three officers of the American Red Cross Mission who had been our companions during the Moscow revolution—Dr. Nathaniel Thayer, Dr. George Peabody and Captain Robert Barr. Our destination was the United States.

Dear friends came to bid us farewell at the Hotel d'Europe. It was a sorrowful leave taking, and we all shed tears, well knowing that this wonderful Russia we loved was mortally stricken and could not survive. How and when would we meet again?

For the last time we passed into the Nikolai Voksal (Nicholas Station), where candles still burned before the icons, and hordes of Red soldiers roamed aimlessly. Since the disintegration of the army they were like sheep without a shepherd, coming and going at their own sweet will.

At seven-thirty the Vladivostok Express departed, one of the last organized trains to leave the country. My heart was heavy, and with deepest sadness I watched the lights of Petrograd recede and disappear into the night.

The first day out we traveled through flat lands where piles of firewood lay by the railway tracks, a proof of the lack of transportation. There was fuel in abundance, while in the capital the houses were unheated.

We passed Vologda, Viâtka and Perm, three business cities, then crossed the Ural Mountains. On the fourth day we reached Ekaterinburg, a busy town where mining supplies were sold for the Urals. (Little did I think that this city was to attain infamous celebrity as the spot where the martyred Imperial family was brutally murdered by the bolsheviks, the following year.) The landscape remained flat with frequent izbas. Flocks of Red soldiers roamed about the forlorn railway stations.

We occupied a compartment in a Wagon-Lits carriage, of which there were only two. Our train possessed a dining car where poor meals were served, but we depended mostly on the tinned foods, coffee and trench biscuit which the Red Cross Mission shared with us. When the train stopped we fetched water for tea from the great urns of kipiatok (boiling water) to be found in all Russian stations for the convenience of travelers.

The day carriages were dirty and overcrowded. Wrapped in greatcoats the soldiers of New Russia lay stretched out on the floor of the passageways, their bayonets beside them. We were obliged to step over their bodies in order to reach the dining car. The platforms were also crowded with army deserters who rode as they pleased on the trains.

Not far from Ekaterinburg is Tiumen, the railway junction for Tobolsk, a short distance up the Irtysh River. Here, some months before, the deposed monarch Nicholas II and his family passed on their tragic journey into exile in Jobolsk. After crossing the Urals, the weather became colder and there was heavy snowfall. The train wound slowly through the endless Siberian steppe, stopping frequently. On the track ahead was a freight car laden with deserting troops who had abandoned the front and were returning to their villages in Siberia. These men refused to give us right of way. Therefore the Vladivostok Express crept for days across the snowy plains behind the grey-coated soldiery, whose word had become law in the land. "Liberty or death," they said. On several occasions they requisitioned our locomotive and we waited for hours for another engine to be sent to us in the white wilderness.

Daylight appeared about ten in the morning and night fell by three in the afternoon. We endured long periods of darkness, while blinding snow fell without and fierce winds blew. At times we passed carloads of German and Austrian war prisoners. The journey to Kharbin lasted two weeks, a trip ordinarily made in nine days.

One night the train halted in a lonely station. Suddenly a brick was hurled through our car window, shattering the glass and letting in the freezing night air. At the same time twenty Red soldiers beat on the door of our car with their guns, demanding admittance. Dr. Thayer and my father went out to reason with these men, saying that the carriage was reserved for the American Red Cross, but to no avail. They insisted on boarding the train and traveled in our carriage, remaining, however, in the corridors without invading our compartments. The Trans-Siberian only ran once a fortnight, and they could not wait for the following one, they said, in their eagerness to reach home for the promised partition of the land. Alas, the bolshevik government never held its word. How cruelly they deceived the Russian people who put all their faith in these perfidious promises—lies, all lies.

At Omsk the train halted and we walked on the platform where bread was sold in abundance. There was plenty of food in Siberia but, again, as with the wood, it was a question of transportation, and Petrograd was hungry.

Two days after Irkutsk, we reached the town of Manchuli on the Manchurian border, the extreme limit of the vast Russian Empire which fate had so cruelly destroyed. Intense cold prevailed in this desolate white world, and the wind cut like a knife. A few figures in Chinese costume, with queues, shivered on the platform.

I was torn by emotion upon leaving Russia. In spite of war and revolutions I was completely enthralled and would have turned back gladly had it been possible. The locomotive whistled and drew out of the station, inexorably pursuing its course. I could not believe that this dream was over. The knowledge that something infinitely dear was lost forever made this departure very poignant. Memories of Russia welled within me, not those of dangers run but memories of silent, snowy places, of warm, vibrating friendships, of beauty in ballet and opera, of nostalgic songs, and the sound of bells. Before my vision rose the Kremlin, the incarnation of Holy Russia, with golden churches and gold-clad clergy singing with golden voices the celestial strains of sacred music. The cry of "Gospody pomilui," chanted in the religious services, rang in my ears, "God help us." God help Russia. Tears, burning tears, filled my eyes and fell unheeded on my cheeks.

After leaving the Russian border we continued to Kharbin where we arrived late one night in a snow storm. As the hotel was full, the American Consul and his wife very kindly put us up in their home. We left the station in a sleigh, driving slowly to keep near the American Red Cross officers who were bringing United States mail from St. Petersburg, and several big bags were piled on a Chinese cart. Dr. Thayer, Dr. Peabody and Captain Barr mounted guard, walking beside it through the snow. I recall the grave faces of these fine men that night. Lighted by a lantern on the cart, they seemed the embodiment of duty, a bulwark of our civilization.

Kharbin has always had a bad reputation. It was unsafe to venture forth after dark as thieves fell upon passersby, robbing and sometimes killing them. People rarely went out alone after nightfall, and groups were formed to accompany one another on nocturnal expeditions. Therefore the precaution taken by the Red Cross officers for the United States mail bags was necessary. We heard one shot in the distance, but were not molested on our way to the Consul's house.

We left the Vladivostok Express in Kharbin and from there continued by train to Korea. In Seoul, Mammá fell very ill as a result of our revolutionary experiences in Russia and the poor, insufficient food we had there. When she recovered we took a Japanese ship from Yokohama and, crossing the Pacific, spent a year in our home in Washington, D.C., a large Tudor house at 1825 R—— Street, which Mammá and my father had built a few years previously.

Thus ended my Russian experiences, but two years later they had a sequel in my marriage to a Russian diplomat, Nicolas de Basily, whom I had known in St. Petersburg. During the war he was with the Emperor Nicholas II at Mogilev, the Russian General Headquarters, as chief of the "Diplomatic Chancellery." Fate threw us together again in 1919 when he was Counselor of the Russian Embassy in Paris.

Journeys with Father to Spain and Belgium

Early in 1919 my father went to Paris to resume his duties as vice president of the National City Bank in Europe. We stopped at the Hotel Ritz on the Place Vendôme, and here, a few months later my beautiful, adored mother fell ill and passed on. Her death was a profound grief to me. Mammá's valiant soul made her a lighthouse in the night. All the virtues of the nineteenth century were concentrated in her—high principles, a stern conception of duty, and great moral courage. The word "impossible," she said, did not exist. When she died my father was inconsolable. His world collapsed and later he retired from active life.

During the sorrowful months that followed my mother's death, however, his banking duties called him to Spain where he had been the preceding year with Mr. Frank Vanderlip, president of the National City Bank, and they had been presented to King Alfonso XIII. So in late May I put on my small, round, black cloche hat, and my father and I together set forth on a new adventure.

Madrid, May 20th, 1919

The trip from Paris was long, dusty, warm, and fatiguing. Finally we reached Hendaye, on the French border, where our passports and luggage were examined. We changed trains and ten minutes later submitted to the same formalities at Irun, the Spanish frontier, and thus entered Spain.

Immediately we found ourselves in the beautiful Basque country with well-tilled earth, prosperous fields, and picturesque hills. In the villages the houses were of rough stone

109

or adobe, and their red-brown tile roofs were of the colour of
the soil. No gardens surrounded these adobes, no vines
clung to their austere sides. They are grim, with few windows, suggesting a period when men's dwellings were their
defense. Windowless churches rose above these houses
clustered about them, like a mother hen, in the maternal
manner of village churches. The Basques are a very individual people, honest and industrious, but their nature is
very different from that of the Spaniards. They have a distinct language, which they endeavour to retain and protect.

The sun set, bathing in its luminous glow this peaceful
landscape of fields, orchards in full bloom, and wide
pasture-lands on gentle slopes where sheep were grazing.

Next morning when we awoke, we were crossing the vast
Castilian plain, stretching out to far horizons in its harsh
aridity.

Madrid is a fine modern city with no hint of medieval
Spain, but I seek little touches of local colour, for instance a
boy carrying a flat basket on his head, piled high with
oranges, lemons, and bananas, or a young girl in a pink calico
frock with a red rose behind her ear, seated side-saddle on a
tiny donkey, but these notes are rare. The "guardia civil"
were in green uniforms, with bright yellow belts and straps,
their black oil cloth hats turned up in a revere behind.

Madrid is hot in summer and cold in winter. The wind that
blows from the nearby Sierra de Guadarrama is feared by the
"madrilenos" who declare that it will not extinguish a candle, but can kill a man.

We are stopping at the Hotel Ritz situated on a large
square, and in proximity to the Prado Museum. Each morning I spend an hour in this wonderland of paintings. There is
a saying here: After Madrid, heaven, and in heaven a
loophole to look at Madrid. I should say rather, "to look at
the Prado." I am becoming acquainted with the works of
Goya, the great Spanish painter of the early nineteenth century, whose paintings of the Royal Family, King Charles IV,

and Queen Maria Luisa de Parma, also that of the "Maja desnuda," are so well known. The Velasquez Room is fantastic.

I am often alone as my father is busy with his affairs. We have a Spanish lesson together early every morning in our sitting room, but our progress in that language is not phenominal.

The members of the United States Embassy are most kind to us, especially the charming Magruders, but I go about by myself in spite of the fact that young Spanish girls do not walk unaccompanied on the streets. I decided one morning to take a walk alone. I followed the Alcalà to the Puerta del Sol, the heart of Madrid, thinking that my mourning attire would be a protection. I was the recipient of remarks from the passing male population, which I could not understand, but I grew increasingly uncomfortable when two workmen digging in the street let fall their axes, and whistled at me. I acknowledged myself beaten, and hailing a cab, drove back to the hotel. Of course I know that this reception was not due to my exceptional charms but merely to the fact that females do not walk about alone in Spain.

My father had business with Count Ramonones, Minister of Foreign Affairs, and saw him several times, also his brother the Duke de Tovar. Ince, the latter, sent his young son and daughter to take me for a drive in his automobile to Alcalà de Henares. They both spoke English and were very agreeable. We had a pleasant time together visiting that famous university city with its beautiful old buildings. Then we motored to an estate belonging to the Duke de Tovar where he raises bulls, and saw many fine specimens in the fields. The house was large, built in the old Spanish style with patios and azulejos (glazed tiles), and its beauty charmed me.

My father and I motored with Mrs. Magruder to Toledo and visited that wonderful art city. Unfortunately, I wrote no account of that journey, although the marvelous things we

saw there awed me: the Cathedral with its treasures, the
house of El Greco, the old bridge, the ruins of the Moorish
castle, the honey-coloured stone of the buildings, and the
severe style of Spanish medieval architecture.

We visited the Escorial, in the Sierra de Guadarrama, a
short motor drive from Madrid. This colossal, austere palace
built in the sixteenth century by austere Philp II, King of
Spain, in the hills of Guadarrama, is unique. Everything is of
stone and no verdure softens it. The scale is stupendous, and
like pygmies we crept through the vast apartments, over-
powered by their immensity. This edifice reflects the mental-
ity of the builder, cold, not quite human. It is a vast body in
search of a soul.

Of course, we knew that the dining hour in Spain was
much later than in the rest of Europe, so I decided that nine
o'clock was the appropriate time. I brushed my hair, put on
my black cloche hat, and with my father descended to the
Ritz restaurant. A few people were taking tea in the lounge,
but I supposed that they were belated travelers. We entered
the restaurant and found it empty. Being hungry we seated
ourselves and an army of waiters attended us. The menu was
at least half a yard long, but we ate our way through manfully. About ten o'clock when we were having coffee, the string
orchestra arrived and began tuning their instruments. Towards eleven some diners appeared, and by midnight the
restaurant was full, the orchestra playing, and great animation reigned, but by that time we were exhausted, and hastened to retire.

Madrid, May 29th, 1919

Today is the Catholic fete of the Assumption and we were
invited to assist at the religious ceremony in the chapel of the
Royal Palace, which King Alfonso XIII and Queen Victoria
attended.

About ten o'clock we reached the Palacio de Oriente. Many people were gathered at the entrance gate and in the courtyard, where the king's guard in blue coats with silver galons, white trousers and high black boots stood sentinel. We were escorted by one of the palace gentlemen-in-waiting, and his wife, who guided us through winding corridors and salons to a glass enclosed gallery that encircled the inner courtyard on the first floor of the palace, onto which the chapel opened. The gallery was lined on both sides with spectators, admitted by invitation, to see the king and queen pass on their way to mass. From the courtyard below came the sound of music from the military band.

Upon entering the chapel, the ladies went to the right, the gentlemen to the left, and were separated by two high wooden railings which formed an aisle for the passage of the sovereigns and their suites.

The chapel is not large and the high vaulted ceiling is heavily gilded. At the right of the altar was a dais for the king and queen, with a canopy of fine tapestry, likewise two armchairs covered with tapestry, and two priedieux with cushions. Surrounding the chapel were two or three rows of wooden benches with thick tapestry cushions for the ladies and gentlemen of the suite. The choir was hidden somewhere above and the voices were accompanied by an orchestra of violin and violoncellos, but without an organ.

About a hundred persons were present. Some of the ladies wore lace mantillas over their heads. Candles burned on the high altar. Soon the main doors opened to admit the royal cortège. First came the king's bodyguard, the halberdiers, magnificent-looking men, very tall with fine figures, dressed like those we had seen outside guarding the palace, and carrying shining silver halberds engraved with the name of Alfonso XIII. Then the sovereigns appeared at the head of a long procession of court ladies and gentlemen in gala attire, clergy in purple and white lace vestments, and at the end more followed. It was a sumptuous scene of ancient Spain. The court has rigidly retained its former traditions, and rigourously observes all form and ceremony.

The queen and her ladies wore evening dress, décolleté, no sleeves and long gloves. On their heads, according to Spanish custom on fete days, black lace mantillas were held in place by gigantic combs, many of which were of diamonds set in platinum, marvels of the jewelers' art. Others wore high carved tortoise-shell combs, fine as lacework. Some ladies had diamond diadems in their hair, and on their necks hung ropes of pearls and diamonds. These noble ladies of Spain were very lovely, with their air of high breeding and distinction.

The British-born queen, who had embraced the Catholic faith upon her marriage in 1906, was dressed in a close-fitting frock of gold and wine-coloured lamé, fashionably tight about the feet. The black mantilla draped over a magnificent diamond comb was very becoming to her English blond beauty. Beneath it huge diamond earrings glittered. On her neck hung a long rivière of diamonds. She looked very lovely, but a bit stiff.

Alfonso XIII, on the contrary, carried himself with the greatest ease. He has a regal bearing and is dark and slender with a fiercely turned-up mustachios. He wore a dark blue infantry uniform, highly decorated with medals and orders, and carried a gold helmet from which white cock feathers fell. He has a charming personality, and looks very human and sympathetic. My father, who had an audience with him last year, said that he was very keen and well-informed on all subjects.

The coats of the gentlemen-in-waiting were also of dark blue cloth with heavy hand embroidery in gold. They were tall, handsome men with much allure, as were the officers of the suite, in brilliant uniforms of blue and red, or white and gold with a broad blue cordon over the chest. All carried gold helmets with the cascade of white feathers of the grandees of Spain.

The king and queen took their places on the dais. At the queen's right, at the foot of the dais, sat the Infanta Isabel, the king's aunt, an interesting figure, rather stout with white hair, a white frock, black mantilla and beautiful jewels. Silks, embroideries, jewels, and the heavy gold robes of the officiating priests, all gleamed and shimmered. Clouds of incense filled the Royal Chapel, and the choir raised their voices to the glory of God.

We left the chapel before the service was ended, and stood in the glass gallery through which the cortège passed to regain their apartments—halberdiers, king, queen, courtiers and officers, advancing with measured tread, followed by a military band. The king stood at the head of the historic staircase as the court filed by. The royal anthem was played, and the glittering assembly dispersed.

Madrid, June 1st, 1919

Today at five-thirty we attended a bullfight in the Plaza de Toros. With deepest interest I took my place on the upper gallery, near the exit, in case the famous spectacle proved too much for my nerves to bear.

The passion for bullfighting is profoundly rooted in the Spanish breast. Arenas exist in many of the principal cities, and in the smaller towns the market-place is often used on feast days. At this season in Madrid, the fight is held twice a week, generally late in the afternoon.

The Plaza de Toros is a circular building, a modern amphitheatre. Tier upon tier of seats rise, separated from the arena by a high wooden paling. The top floor is composed of boxes, where ladies usually sit, and has a roof. Here is the royal loge where the king occasionally appears. On certain feast-days the king and queen attend with the entire court, the ladies wearing white lace mantillas, making a brilliant scene.

All masculine Madrid seemed to be swarming in the Plaza de Toros. The huge amphitheatre was filled to the utmost. An air of expectance reigned, even a slight shower did not dampen the spectators' ardour. They merely opened umbrellas over their straw hats. Fortunately the rain ceased before the corrida began, otherwise it would not be possible to continue, the arena being uncovered.

Suddenly the notes of a brass band sounded. The doors of the arena were thrown open and the procession of combatants entered. First the matadors on foot, in close-fitting bright-coloured costumes, red, green, yellow and pale blue, all heavily embroidered with gold or silver. They wore coral pink silk stockings and low black slippers. Their long hair was caught in a chignon on the nape of the neck. Each carried a cape, which plays such a role in the fierce combat between man and beast. Some were bright red, lined with green, some magenta lined with yellow, etc. These brilliant figures were followed by picadors on horseback, armed with long sticks. Then two teams of big black mules galloped in, three abreast. They circled the enclosure while the band played and the multitude applauded with great enthusiasm. Their role was to carry off the carcasses.

Then the great torero, Belmonte, the present favorite, stepped forth in a gold and green suit. Removing his hat, he made a sweeping bow, and the corrida began.

Again the doors of the arena opened, and from a passage where he had been sequestered for several hours in complete darkness, the bull dashed forth. He paused, blinded by the sudden light, then astonished and annoyed he plunged into the ring. It was a pretty play between the animal and the matadors who held out their gay capes to attract him and nimbly stepped aside when the bull came too close. At times the infuriated beast pursued the matador until the latter was obliged to scale the paling in order to escape.

Then the banderilleros arrived with their banderillas, long sticks wrapped in gay-coloured papers terminated by a kind of fishhook which they skillfully planted in the neck of the bull. These banderillas are to goad the beast to fury, thus making him more dangerous and interesting, but our bull was not amused. He stopped short, then turned and trotted off to the entrance. This was evidently not in the program. The audience grew excited and sharp hisses rent the air. He was a "bad bull," they cried. Other banderilleros approached, this time bearing banderillas charged with firecrackers which they implanted in the bull's neck. I could bear no more and turned away.

Then came the third and chief episode, the killing of the bull. Belmonte, the greatest bullfighter of Spain, stepped forth, waving his red cape on his outstretched sword. I could no longer look and thus missed the marvelous play of this great expert, only glancing from time to time, from my half-closed eyes. Belmonte skillfully dispatched the bull.

Then the band played, the mule team galloped in with flying colours to carry off the carcass, while the torero bowed to the enthusiastic spectators, and waved his tricorne hat.

My father had no time for sightseeing, so after a few days in Portugal, we returned to Paris.

Brussels, June 28th, 1919

Today we left Paris for Brussels. Paris was flaming with flags in honour of the signing of the Peace Treaty which takes place at three o'clock this afternoon in the Hall of Mirrors at Versailles, when two obscure Germans will write the names of Müller and Bell on the fateful document which Germany has fought against for so many weeks.

Paris and the Victory lay behind us as our train passed through the region laid waste by the Germans during the recent war. As we approached Noyon we realized what this victory meant to France, why bells were ringing and cannons thundering today. From Noyon to St. Quentin, for over an hour the train ran slowly through scenes of desolation and horror. Towns, villages, and farm-houses lay in ruins, with scarcely a roof which shells had not burst wide open or riddled with holes. The skeletons of former homes lined the streets. Houses gutted and roofless, crumbling masses of debris, silent and deserted. Factories were completely destroyed. Only rusty iron-girders, smokestacks, and twisted sheet-iron roofs remained, tortured and writhing. Many villages had been entirely wiped out, or reduced to rubble, not one stone left upon another to mark where a house had stood. The hamlets were pulverized, the ground covered with mounds of broken bricks, stones, and twisted bits of rusty iron. Every railroad bridge had been destroyed, every church steeple shattered. Trenches and communication-trenches and yawning shell holes scarred the fields. Barbed-wire entanglements lay on all sides, brown with rust. Dugouts abounded. The railway embankments were honeycombed with holes, just big enough for one or two men to take shelter.

Along the tracks German prisoners were repairing the roadbed (which had been completely torn up in places), their faces stolid and expressionless beneath little round caps with a red band. Chinese coolies also assisted in this labour. We noticed plain wooden crosses marking pathetic graves. St. Quentin is badly damaged and her cathedral raises its great frame against the sky bereft of the roof. Only the first row of arches and the towers remain standing. So lies the north of France today, and over these agonized remains, Spring has flung a cloak of scarlet poppies.

We passed German freight cars which are being used by the French, one marked "Breslau," others "Essen" and "Elberfeld." On one were captured camouflaged guns and cannons.

Once over the Belgian frontier, we found rich fields, and pasture-lands where black and white cows grazed, as this part of Belgium has escaped untouched.

Brussels, July 3rd, 1919

We hear many tales of the occupation here. Loyal Belgians grow excited, and their fists involuntarily clench when they recall their sufferings at the hands of the German invaders. The latter took all bronze and copper objects, even in private houses, statues and chandeliers. Doorknobs were removed. The houses were searched by the conquerors and if anything had been hidden, they seized it and fined the owners. Without her husband's knowledge, the wife of a Brussels banker made three cachettes where she put valuable objects, employing two men to tear down the paneling and later close it up again. Soon after the Germans arrived demanding to examine the house. When they had finished they asked the banker if that was all, and in good faith, he answered, "Yes," to which the Germans replied, "Oh no, you have three cachettes. We will show them to you," which they did to the great astonishment of the owner. Then they fined him and removed all the bronzes, objets d'art, etc. However, the housewife told me triumphantly that they did not find a fourth cachette, where she had secreted eight wool mattresses, in the paneling over the fireplace. All wool mattresses were requisitioned. The inhabitants were obliged to give them up and sleep on straw or anything they happened to have at hand. They were obliged also to deliver their mattresses themselves to the Germans, and many pitiful little handcarts passed through the streets, pushed by poor people carrying their only mattress to the enemy.

All the world knows the name of Monsieur Max, the heroic burgomaster of Brussels, who spent four years in a German prison. In the first days of the war, when Belgium was invaded, Monsieur Max went to meet the enemy troops. The German general in command, upon approaching him, offered his hand to the burgomaster, but the latter, ignoring the outstretched palm, said quietly: "General, I only shake hands with my friends."

Upon entering Brussels the invaders quartered men in the beautiful old Town Hall. Upon learning this, Monsieur Max caused a bed for himself to be placed in his own office there, where he slept that night alone. At a late hour German soldiers came to him demanding all the keys of the building.

"I have no keys whatsoever," replied the burgomaster.

"Give us the keys," they insisted, "it is necessary to lock all doors."

"I sleep here alone tonight," said Monsieur Max simply. "My door is not locked. If I, one Belgian, am unafraid, then two hundred Germans need not fear."

Abashed by such courage, the soldiers withdrew.

During our visit in Brussels my father and I had the honour of being received by Mayor Max. We found him in the same office in the Town Hall where he had slept during the German occupation, on the lovely old place with its medieval houses. He is a man about forty years old, of medium height with blond hair, a pointed beard and prominent blue eyes that radiate light and intelligence. He has much personality and it is not difficult to imagine him calm in the presence of the invading German army. My father had a long conversation with Monsieur Max, and, among other things, he told us the preceding stories.

Louvain, July 6th, 1919

Today we motored to Louvain, the ancient university town famed for its beauty and learning, and now, alas, the tragic victim of German aggression. Louvain is about forty minutes from Brussels, and we sped along the excellent road of smooth Belgian blocks beneath tall beech trees that met overhead. On this sunny summer morning, in perfect peace, we came upon the martyred city and saw where the invaders had passed.

On August 25th, 1914, and the ensuing days, enemy troops burned the Church of St. Peter, the University Outer Hall and Library, the Law Courts, the Academy of Fine Arts, and more than two thousand houses, killing over two hundred people, among them women and children.

The senator from Louvain, Baron Orban de Xivry, was to be our guide and we drove to his house. The senator had remained in the town during the entire German occupation, was made prisoner, and conducted himself with the greatest heroism. His residence, a stone house, had escaped the flames that swept over Louvain in 1914, but the entrance portals of wood were scorched and the paint cracked and peeling.

The senator guided us to the Grande Place where stands the fine Town Hall with its six needle-like spires, which for some strange reason had escaped the devastating hand of the vandals, while the Church of St. Peter, just opposite, was set on fire. It is still standing and no damage from the exterior is visible, but the interior has been in part destroyed.

We remained only a few days in Belgium and during this time my father established a branch of the National City Bank in one of the beautiful old houses on the Grande Place opposite the fine Hotel de Ville (Town Hall).

I Marry Nicolas Alexandrovich

Through mutual Russian friends in Paris, Nicolas de Basily and I met again when he was Counselor of the Russian Embassy there. General Butler Ames of Boston and his wife Fifi invited me to visit them in their villa on Lake Como. At that time they also invited Basily. I was pleased to see him again, especially after the tragic fate of Russia which I had loved so well.

The Ameses had a famous villa on Lake Como near Lenno, the beautiful Villa Balbianello, formerly in the possession of the Arconati-Visconti family of Milan, today an historical monument. Founded in the eighteenth century by a Cardinal Durini as a home of rest for convalescent monks of the Franciscan order, Balbianello was an earthly paradise and made upon me an imperishable impression.

Secluded and aloof, on a high wooded promontory extending far into the lake, this Eden possessed a romantic soul-quality, a charm so potent it was like a spell. At the extremity of the point a pale colored villa climbed the hill, surrounded by terraces at different levels. The house was reached by the lake and the moment the rowboat entered the small port enclosed by a high stone wall, ornamented with statues of monks and bishops, the visitor found himself transported into a realm of dreams and beauty far removed from daily existence.

A stairway edged with a carved stone balustrade led from the port to the first terrace where a statue of Saint Francis stands. From there one mounted ever higher, from terrace to terrace bordered with honey-coloured balustrades whose

123

sculpture represented the Arconati-Visconti coat of arms, a
dragon holding a child in its mouth. At the summit a loggia
dominated the lake, encircled by hills and mountains. A
thousand flowers enameled the garden where the fragrance
of jasmin floated. Oleanders, cypresses, and planetrees offered shade and cool. Nothing moved on these enchanted
terraces. Silence. Hours passed and time itself seemed to
pause in contemplation of such beauty and harmony. Below,
the jade green waters of Como shimmered. The spectator
held his breath. Was this reality, or was it a dream?

By moonlight the honey-coloured stones vibrated with
romance. From afar, in the still night, came the sound of little
bells on fishing nets set in the lake, tinkling gently, as in a
dream. Balbianello, what nostalgia your name evokes. Your
image is engraved upon my heart. Never will I forget you.

Nicolas de Basily was also a guest of the Ameses and in
this incomparable setting, surrounded by the affection of our
dear friends, we became engaged and decided to marry in
November, three months later, after obtaining my father's
consent.

On November 25th — the fete of Saint Catherine in
France, patroness of unmarried girls, when all the midinettes
of Paris were reveling joyously in the streets — we went for
our civil marriage to the mayor of the seventh arrondisse-
ment, where the Russian Embassy was situated. The
"maire," with a tricolor sash tied about his ample person,
caused me much amusement and, being nervous on this
momentous occasion, I began to laugh quietly. Nicolas
pushed me with his elbow, his first act of marital authority,
and said severely: "Voulez-vous vous taire?"

The mayor joined us in matrimony. The knot was tied in
my father's presence, with Ernest Peixotto of Paris as my
witness. Nicolas' witness was Vladimir Gorlov, first secretary of the Russian Embassy. Baron Maurice Schilling,
Nicolas' dear friend, was to have been his witness but the

nervous strain of the last moment caused him to forget to tell Schilling the hour of the ceremony. He could not be found, so Gorlov took his place, at the last moment.

I wore a short black velvet frock with a tiny hat of white minoches, and felt utterly bewildered.

November 26th was a cold day. Our marriage was celebrated at noon in the Russian Church of the rue Daru. Clad in white satin, with a Russian kakoshnik in Brussels lace and a white tulle veil, trembling with fear, I went on my father's arm.

Lascelle in wedding dress, with Russian "kakoshnik" on head

The marriage ceremony of the Orthodox Church is very moving, and seems something from another world. During the rites of our union, without organ accompaniment, a choir of angels filled the vaults of the church with their celestial voices. Heaven had descended upon earth. A priest, with a long white beard, good Father Smirnov, clothed in gold brocade, a gold tiara on his head, united us. When he put my hand in that of Nicolas Alexandrovich, I trembled so violently that I feared falling. My husband held my hand in his during the rest of the ceremony, and I was pleased to find him so solidly planted on his feet.

Our witnesses were Baron Maurice Schilling, Baron Léon Rosen, and Admiral Newton McCully of the United States Navy, formerly Naval Attaché at the American Embassy in St. Petersburg. Standing behind us, these dear friends held the crowns above our heads, which is part of the ceremony. Suddenly I became less tense and could smile.

A wedding breakfast followed the church ceremony at the Hotel Ritz, where my father and I had continued to live after my mother's death.

On account of my recent mourning it was a small wedding, but a group of good friends surrounded us—our witnesses, my father, my Aunt Mary Lascelle Struve (Mammá's sister), Baron Bernard de l'Escaille, Belgian diplomat, Ivan Charlier, former Belgian Consul General in Russia, the Russian Ambassador, Basil Maklakov, and his sister Marie Maklakov; dear Monsieur Sazonov (former Russian Minister of Foreign Affairs), a Greek cousin of Nicolas, Alexander de Basily, and his son Dimitri, Albert Kammerer of the French Foreign Office, and Mr. Crosby, a Vice President of the First National City Bank of New York—a happy wedding party.

Our honeymoon was spent on the Côte d'Azur. Upon arrival at the Hotel Carlton in Cannes, I was surprised to find in my husband's luggage an immense brown canvas bag. Later I learned that this mysterious catchall contained seventy-two volumes of both classic and modern authors. My new husband, a great intellectual, had thought it would be agreeable for us to read them together. The Mediterranean was too blue, the mimosas and carnations too fragrant. The brown bag took the road back to Paris unopened. Life presented itself to us in a dazzling aspect. We could not imagine to what extent the coming years would change our destiny. The definite destruction of beloved Russia appeared impossible. Surely order would again be reestablished, and life would hold for us a wonderful future. Full of enthusiasm we returned to Paris. At that moment the ruins of Imperial Russia fell upon our heads.

The Russian Colony In Paris

In the years following our marriage, I lived in Paris with Nicolas Alexandrovich through the downfall of his country and the repercussion it had on the Russian émigrés who had taken refuge there. We were spared, but among those who surrounded us we saw despair, hunger and death. All the glamour of the old Russia I had loved disappeared. Only horror and tragedy remained to tell of the passing of that once great Empire.

My marriage to Nicolas de Basily took place when Russia was dying in agony and the new bolshevik régime, after the treacherous separate peace of Brest-Litovsk, was consolidating itself, although as yet unrecognized by foreign powers. Those were terrible days.

The Russian Embassy in Paris was still active and recognized by the French government. Mr. Basil Maklakov, a prominent lawyer and brilliant orator at the Duma, was sent to Paris by the Provisional Government of Russia as Ambassador. But Maklakov never was given the chance to present his letters of accreditation to the President of the French Republic. Hence Basily, as First Counselor, acted as Chargé d'Affaires, with the title of Minister. But for the staff of the embassy Maklakov was the Chief. Nicolas had deep respect for him.

Maklakov was a bachelor. His faithful sister, Marie, kept his house and watched over him with tender solicitude, at the same time doing the honours of the embassy. Mademoiselle Maklakov was small, dry, with greyish hair tightly drawn back. Passionately Russian, a great heart, glowing with Slav ardour, beat beneath her modest black frock.

We often went to the embassy, in a fine old "hotel particulier," at 79 rue de Grenelle, with a lovely garden and great trees at the back. There we found many prominent Russian émigrés, among them Prince Lvov, President of the first Provisional Government; Paul Miliukov, Minister of Foreign Affairs of the Provisional Government; and Serge Sazonov, Minister of Foreign Affairs under the Emperor Nicholas, a passionate patriot and a wonderfully fine man; Alexander Guchkov, Minister of War of the Provisional Government; and M. de Giers, former Russian Ambassador in Rome; also M. Stakhovich, former member of the Council of Empire. These émigrés were desperately seeking some means of saving their beloved country from the hands of the usurping Soviets. General Denikin (and later General Wrangel) had retreated to southern Russia when St. Petersburg was occupied. They were fighting the Soviets with the remains of the former Imperial Army and were the only hope of these patriots, the so-called White Russian Movement.

The year 1920 brought the complete disintegration of the Russian Empire. My husband's fine moral qualities were well known to me, but at that moment the nobility and force of his character in face of the tragic situation impressed me deeply. His fortitude in adversity was sublime. After having prossessed a large fortune and a high position, everything was swept away from him. Never once did his valiant spirit waver. Without a complaint, a lamentation or a backward look, he quietly went to work. His courage in beginning life anew led him to success, but he was a great patriot and lived only in the hope of serving his country again. Throughout life the pure flame of his ardent soul never ceased to burn for that cause, and his anguish never diminished.

Immediately after our return to Paris, life caught us up. It was already the débacle of Russia. The following year she was to succumb definitely, in spite of the desperate efforts of Admiral Kolchak in Siberia, and General Wrangel in southern Russia. My husband did everything in his power to help them and represented their anti-bolshevik movement in Paris.

Our world had fallen about our ears.

Among the numerous refugees who flocked to Paris, misery reigned. They went to the embassy in hope of receiving some assistance, without realizing that the coffers were empty, as well as the pockets of the Ambassador and Nicolas Alexandrovich.

The most distinguished names of the Russian aristocracy were represented in this influx of émigrés. A number of them had escaped through Constantinople before coming to be stranded in Paris.

Many persons knocked at the door of my husband's apartment, and our entrance hall was never empty. Nicolas Alexandrovich had the reputation of being very generous and also of possessing a large fortune. They could not imagine that Basily had lost everything as they had. The bolsheviks had taken all my husband's lands and estates in southern Russia, his houses in Odessa, and his fortune deposited in the State Bank in St. Petersburg. They took everything. Nothing remained. NOTHING. He had been too patriotic in 1917 when he left Russia to assume his post in the Paris embassy, to carry with him either money or valuables as he could easily have done. Like many of his compatriots, he was convinced by pure patriotism that he should remove nothing from his country, so he came with a few paintings rolled up beneath his arm, precious family souvenirs.

The demands for money of these miserable émigrés were desperate, but they accepted their exile with dignity and resignation. Can one combat the will of heaven? Fatalism perhaps enveloped them and the sadness of the Russian soul, like the vastness of their plains, stretched out ahead, so far, so far.

The majority of these people were pitiful and very worthy of help. Their misery spread gloom over our existence. News would come that someone had committed suicide, another had died, a friend had been shot in Russia. A nightmare and we could give so little assistance, only a drop in the sea.

One episode was absurd. A cheeky little Russian invaded our apartment, coming each day, remaining hours. He wanted Nicolas Alexandrovich to provide a room for him and pay the rent. I could never enter my salon without encountering him. To my husband this seemed normal as he had always had people waiting for him, but this constant presence got on my nerves, and I told Nicolas that I would leave the house if he did not dispose of this bore. So my husband discovered a room, paid the rent, and for six months peace reigned in my household. One day he returned. "Spring has come," he said gaily, "Can you not find me a room in the country?"

Never enough can be said of the suffering of the Russian emigration. Nevertheless with time, the exiles became integrated in the countries where Fate had thrown them and made themselves liked. In general the French people received them well, often assisting them to the best of their ability.

After the Russian revolution in 1917, the French had lost a great deal of money in the "Emprunt Russe," the Russian Loan. Often the small savings of the modest middle class, even the peasant's famous "bas de laine," vanished. In spite of these monetary reverses there was no apparent resentment towards the émigrés. The attitude in France was quite friendly and human. According to her traditions of humanism, France had accepted many other exiles in the course of her history, and the French people understood the suffering of these unfortunate expatriates who had escaped from a lost world.

In Russia, most of these men had positions, a profession, a craft, or else had done nothing, "pomeshchiks" (landowners) living only from their properties. It was difficult to find employment. A few had a little capital and opened restaurants or tea rooms which were very popular with the Parisians, and also foreigners in Paris. The balalaikas had great success, as well as the Russian singers, gypsy and others. At times in this warm Slav atmosphere everyone in the room sang and swayed together in chorus.

When the émigrés had no employment nor means of existence, they became taxi chauffeurs in order to earn their daily bread. Often we called a taxi in the streets of Paris only to find a friend at the wheel and, at times, a prince. One evening, just to laugh, Nicolas gave an order to the unknown driver; "Kleberskaia Ulitsa," (avenue Kléber) he said, and the unknown answered in Russian, "Slushaiu" (very well).

The Russian ladies in exile were admirable. They began to work making dresses, hats and lingerie. Even those who had never before done anything often succeeded in earning their living. Life must go on and they gave proof of heroic courage in providing for their families.

At one time the Grand Duchess Marie Pavlovna of Russia made embroideries for the dressmaking house of Chanel, the great couturière.

Certain great-hearted Russian ladies worked incessantly in an effort to help the needy, arranging balls and benefits for making money to this end, such as our friend Princess Vera Meschersky, Countess Shuvalov, and Mademoiselle Marie Maklakov, sister of the Ambassador, and others.

Princess Meschersky, née von Struve, occupied herself seriously with the émigrés. With subsidies from English friends, she brought help wherever possible. She founded a house of retreat for old Russians without resources in Ste. Geneviève des Bois, a few kilometers from Paris. Often illustrious names were among them. They lived by themselves in a warm atmosphere, fed and protected from the cold. They could bring any furniture or souvenirs to cheer up their rooms, if by chance any bits from the past remained.

The Princess had installed a small chapel in the house whose walls were hung from top to bottom with icons and holy images covered with silver. On Sunday morning an Orthodox priest said mass. Behind the house lay a cemetery, a bit of Russian earth on foreign soil. Here, some years later, we brought our dear friend, Baron Maurice Schilling, Nicolas's dearest friend, whom all our tender affection could not save from an implacable illness. He sleeps there his last sleep, heartbroken at the loss of his beloved country, surrounded by other exiled compatriots who shared his sorrow.

Schilling was a chevalier, a knight on a white horse, who had missed his century. Of a high, noble nature and a fervent patriot, he suffered cruelly from the disaster to his homeland and could not face the destruction of his world.

The Russian Embassy, situated on the left bank of the Seine, in the old aristocratic quarter of the Faubourg St. Germain, was installed in a seignorial mansion between "cour et jardin." During the war, the fine salons of the first floor had been given over for offices where the personnel of the embassy worked. On the ground floor, a large dining room and a large salon opened onto an immense garden, enclosed by walls, with centenary trees beneath whose shade it was pleasant to sit after luncheon and take coffee. The chairs and sofas in the salon were covered with lovely red damask, but already the decline of Russia was visible in the raveled silks where in places the white lining showed through. In this room Mademoiselle Maklakov received her guests and dispensed hospitality.

Profound melancholy pervaded the embassy at that time, just before the definite fall of the Russian Empire. In spite of the turn events were taking, the Ambassador, my husband and the members of the embassy, as well as the numerous émigrés who swarmed there, still hoped against hope that some miracle would happen. They could not believe that their country was about to sink into the abyss.

Dinner at the Russian Embassy

On January 14th, 1920, the Russian New Year, we dined at the embassy. Besides the Ambassador and his sister Marie Alexandrovna, the Comtesse Kreutz, daughter of the Princess Paley, morganatic wife of the Grand Duke Paul, was also present, as well as a few Russian gentlemen, among them Prince Lvov and Monsieur Stakhovich, with his long boyar beard.

It was a sad evening in spite of our attempts at gaiety. The recent defeat of General Denikin, the White Russian leader, depressed us greatly. We sat down to dinner towards ten forty-five and at midnight we were still seated around the great table where heavy silver double-dishes with the Imperial eagles gleamed. Terrible anguish seized these patriots. Russia! What would become of Russia at the edge of the abyss? Would she be saved by a miracle, or would she collapse—Russia, whose fate was being played now in the snows of the beloved faraway homeland?

At two minutes before twelve, the servants set before each guest a pencil, a bit of paper and a lighted candle. According to Russian custom, each person wrote on the paper the wish nearest his heart for the coming year and, folding the paper, held it to the candle flame as the clock struck twelve. If the paper was consumed before the last stroke, the wish would be granted. Fervent prayers for Russia were inscribed on these fragments by the loyal exiles, men of high position, wealth and power, who had lost all in the overwhelming avalanche which had swept away Imperial Russia, and now were homeless and practically penniless in a foreign land.

Midnight struck. The New Year was knocking at the door, but the little papers were not consumed. God had not heard our prayers.

Nicolas Alexandrovich

In my journey through life, the most exceptional qualities I have encountered in a human being are those of my husband, Nicolas de Basily. Nobility of character, intelligence, culture and moral courage, as well as remarkable gifts as a statesman.

Diplomat of Imperial Russia, Chamberlain of the Emperor Nicholas II, he came from a distinguished line of Russian diplomats. He graduated with honours from the famous Lycée Alexandre in St. Petersburg and entered the diplomatic service. Most of his career was spent at the Russian Embassy in Paris. During World War I, 1914–1917, he was in Russia at General Headquarters in Mogilev, the "Stavka," serving as Vice Director of the Diplomatic Chancellery of the Emperor, that is, the Division of the Foreign Office at Headquarters. His chief, Serge Sazonov, Minister of Foreign Affairs, was a great patriot and a dedicated man. My husband was profoundly attached to him, as well as to his superior at the Stavka, General Mikhail Alexeiev, and both of them gave him their confidence and friendship.

During the war years, Basily was Director of the Diplomatic Chancellery of Emperor Nicholas II at General Headquarters, the Stavka, in Mogilev. Thus my husband witnessed the tragic events which tore Russia asunder. He

Nicolas Alexandrovich de Basily

also had the sad duty of writing the Act of Abdication of Emperor Nicholas II. An account of those fatal days forms part of his memoirs.

Early in 1917 he was one of the three representatives of Imperial Russia at the Supreme War Council of the Allies in Paris, and after the abdication of the Emperor he returned to the Russian Embassy there as Counselor of Embassy, with the title of Minister.

In 1938 Basily published a book on Soviet Russia on which he worked three or four years in his study in our home on the rue Alfred Dehodencq near the Bois de Boulogne in Paris.

Originally he planned to write a history of Russia, which he barely outlined, but when he reached the Soviet period, he became interested in comparing post-revolutionary Russia with the Imperial Russia he had served. Much of this book was based on facts and figures he gathered from *Pravda*, and other Soviet publications.

This book, entitled *Russia under Soviet Rule*, appeared in four languages—Russian, French, English and Italian.* The French edition (published by Plon in Paris in 1938) received a prize from the Académie-Francaise, and had great success, as did the other editions.

The fall of the Russian Empire made Basily profoundly unhappy. During long years of exile the flame of patriotism burned in his heart. Only those who have lost their own fatherland can understand his anguish. Until the last breath, his ardent desire was to serve again his martyred country which he so fervently loved.

My husband left some memoirs which, alas, ill health prevented him from completing.** In them he describes the tragic days at the Stavka when General Alexeiev and the other generals sorrowfully concluded that the only solution to the state of revolution raging in the country was the abdication of the Emperor Nicholas II.

Basily was asked to compose the Act of Abdication, which he did in noble terms, setting forth the abdication of the monarch in favour of his son, the Grand Duke Alexei, as the only constitutional solution possible. This message was sent by telegraph to the Emperor then in his train at Pskov, having left Headquarters a few days before.

---

*The titles of these books authored by Nicolas de Basily: *Rossiia pod sovetskoi vlasti*. Parizh, Impr. "Val", 1938. *Russia under Soviet Rule; Twenty Years of Boshevik Experiment*. London, G. Allen, 1938. *La Russie sous les Soviets; vingt ans d'éxperience bolchévique*. Paris, Plon. 1938. *La formazione dello stato sovietico; la Russia sotto il domino sovietico*. Milano. Fratelli Bocca, 1939. *Vent' anni dell' esperimento bolscevico; la Russia sotto il domino sovietico*. Milano, 1940. Fratelli Bocca.

** These memoirs have since been published: Nicolas de Basily. *Memoirs; Diplomat of Imperial Russia; 1903–1917*. Stanford, Ca., Hoover Institution Press. 1973.

My husband describes the terrific tension reigning at the Stavka during the hours of distress awaiting the sovereign's reply. Finally the telegraph announced a message from Pskov, and my husband with several officers of the staff gathered around the telegraphic apparatus, and read on the ribbon issuing from it that the Emperor had changed a few words of Basily's text, abdicating in favour of his brother, the Grand Duke Michael, instead of in favour of his son, the Tsarevich. Otherwise the text remained intact.

Consternation reigned at the Stavka upon receipt of this message, consternation so great as to be almost unbearable. "All is over," they said.

Basily relates that shortly afterwards, he was entrusted by General Alexeiev with a mission to meet the Emperor in his train between Pskov and Mogilev, in order to acquaint him with the steadily increasing rebellion and disorders in Petersburg, and to present to him the list of men composing the new Provisional Government, headed by Prince Lvov.

A private train was placed at his disposal which halted at Orcha, halfway between Pskov and Mogilev, and remained on a side track in expectation of the Imperial trains, of which there were always two. With great agitation my husband waited. He recalled to me the scene before his eyes, the red light of the setting sun on the snowy landscape, lonely and desolate.

At last the Imperial train was sighted, approaching slowly, and stopping at Orcha. Deeply moved to encounter his sovereign under such circumstances, Basily went on board and was immediately received by the Emperor. The complete composure of Nicholas II permitted Basily to regain his own self-control. After an hour's conversation during which Basily informed the Emperor of the most recent events, he was amazed at the way this unfortunate ex-ruler of an immense Empire dominated himself with the greatest dignity. No apparent emotion, only the contraction of the throat muscles betrayed his anguish. Occasionally he said: "Yes, of course."

The Emperor invited Basily to dine at his table and to return with him in his train to Headquarters. Thus my husband was one of the last eyewitnesses of the final days of Nicholas II as Emperor. The small black book in which Basily had inscribed the list of men of the Provisional Government, and which the sovereign had held in his hands, is kept with Basily's papers at the Hoover Institution, Stanford University, in Stanford, California.

During the war when the Emperor was at the Stavka, the Empress often came to see him, accompanied by her four daughters and her suite. These visits caused consternation at Headquarters as for some time Alexandra Feodorovna had been taking part in state affairs, and had greatly influenced the Emperor. My husband gives an account of one of these apparitions at the time when the autonomy of Poland (of which my husband was a firm defender) was a burning question. After the midday meal the party often walked in the gardens which ran down to the Dnieper River. On this occasion, the Empress walked with General Alexeiev, and the conversation turned on this subject. When the dialogue had ended, Alexeiev came to Basily and whispered: "There is nothing to be done. The Empress states that the POWER, as they have received it, must be transmitted without change to their son. When the time comes he will see what should be done." Both the General and Basily were overwhelmed by such intransigence at this late moment.

Later in the day, Basily told the Baroness de Buxhoeveden of this statement, adding: "I fear that our charming young prince will never reign." A slight noise caused my husband to turn. Behind him stood the Tsarevich Alexei. Whether he had heard or not, my husband could not know.

Speaking of the terrible days preceding the declaration of war in 1914, Basily related that he was present in Sazonov's antechamber, when Count Pourtales, German ambassador to Russia, came to present to the Russian Minister of Foreign Affairs the German declaration of war. Upon leaving Sazonov, Count de Pourtales passed through the antechamber where Basily was standing and my husband noted that tears were falling down his cheeks. In making this declaration, the Germans thought that they had nothing to risk, being entirely convinced that Russia was not prepared, and therefore could not go to war. They were right. Russia was not prepared, but they had counted without Russia's sense of honour.

The International Conference at Spa; 1920

In July of 1920, a conference of the Allied Powers was held in Spa, Belgium. Mr. Peter Struve, Minister of Foreign Affairs of the Wrangel Government in South Russia, was delegated by this government on a mission to Spa, in an endeavour to obtain from the Allies represented there the recognition of the Wrangel Government, formed around the remnants of the former Imperial Army, now fighting against the bolsheviks under General Peter Wrangel in an ultimate desperate effort to save Russia. Nicolas de Basily was also delegated on this mission and accompanied Mr. Struve.

I accompanied my husband and with him lived through days of heartache and anguish. I have written down what I saw there, the touchingly friendly reception of the French delegation who consented to recognize the Wrangel Government, and the brutal attitude of Lloyd George, Labour leader and Prime Minister of Britain, who completely ignored the presence of the Russian delegation representing the Wrangel Government, and the appeal they presented to him. Had England possessed a statesman of more foresight at that time, the course of history might have been changed.

Peter Struve and Lascelle at Spa
(Photographed by Nicolas de Basily)

A good friend of Nicolas Alexandrovich, Mr. Albert
Kammerer, of the French Foreign Office, met us at the
station with a huge automobile of the French government.
Having come unexpectedly, Nicolas had not engaged rooms
beforehand. The hotels were full on account of the Conference, and no accommodations were available. We were
forced to search for lodgings. Mr. Kammerer was obliged to
leave us and we found only an ancient fiacre with a broken-
down horse to transport us. Rain was falling in torrents. As
the elegant French automobile disappeared, my husband
cast a glance at the dilapidated cab and abject beast. A smile,
half sad, half mocking, trembled on his lips. "This is what
our poor Russia has come to," he said. "It is not her day for
big autos. At present it is a miserable hack who draws us."

In order to have shelter, we rented a tiny apartment on the first floor of a modest house in the outskirts of Spa, all we could find in the rue de Waux-Hall. On the ground floor was a humble grocery shop. Here Nicolas was joined by Mr. Michelson, a professor of international law of the former University at St. Petersburg. It was Tuesday, July 13, 1920.

Soon after arrival, Nicolas Alexandrovich and Professor Michelson left to pay visits to the various Allied delegations at the Conference. They found M. Philippe Berthelot, Secretary General of the French Foreign Office, also the Polish and Rumanian delegates. M. Alexandre Millerand, Prime Minister of France, was also in Spa, as was Mr. Lloyd George, Prime Minister of Britain, and it was imperative for Nicolas Alexandrovich to see them.

Automobiles sped along the road to "La Fraineuse," a pretty little château hidden in the trees several kilometers from Spa, where the Conference was held. Here M. Millerand (representing France), Lloyd George and Lord Curzon (England), Count Sforza (Italy), and other Allies were discussing the German reparations with the delegates of Germany—Fehrenbach, Simons and the arrogant Stinnes.

The following day, July 14th, Mr. Peter Struve arrived, to Nicolas' great satisfaction. He was a tall man and stooped, with a pointed greyish beard and blue, near-sighted eyes.

Mr. Struve and Nicolas Alexandrovich requested interviews with M. Millerand and Lloyd George for the next day. They found Sir Eyre Crow, a high official of the British Foreign Office. At the Château de Neubois where the French Prime Minister and Marshal Foch were lodged, they saw Marshal Foch, General Lerond, French High Commissary of Silesia, also Messrs. Berthelot, Kammerer, and Vignon of the French Foreign Office.

That night Mr. Struve and Nicolas Alexandrovich talked almost until daybreak in the little salon above the grocery shop. A pall of sickening anxiety hung over them. For hours

Mr. Struve paced to and fro feverishly, his footsteps re-
sounding on the bare floor in the silence of the night.

July 15th was spent composing the text of Mr. Struve's
note to the French and British governments. A young secretary from the Russian Legation in Brussels, Baron
Wrangel, cousin of General Wrangel, arrived and copied it
on the typewriter. The note, written in Russian, was translated into French and English. At ten o'clock that evening,
the note was sent to the Hôtel Britannique for Lloyd George
and Lord Curzon.

"L'épicerie diplomatique"
(Photographed by Nicolas de Basily)

Mr. Struve and Nicolas awaited the answer of the British
with deep apprehension, well knowing that a favorable reply
was doubtful on account of the pro-Soviet tendencies of Mr.
Lloyd George. During this period of suspense, the heavy-
hearted Russians still managed to keep up their sense of
humour. They were amused by the diplomatic grocery shop,
"l'épicerie diplomatique," as they called our quarters, the
last repair of Imperial Russia.

On Friday, July 16th, at eleven o'clock, Mr. Struve and Nicolas Alexandrovich were received by the French Prime Minister, M. Millerand, whom Nicolas knew. I accompanied them in a landau as far as the gates of the Château de Neubois, a pretty gabled villa with geraniums flowering at the windows. After the interview, they returned encouraged and happy. M. Millerand had given them a cordial reception and, in accord with the views they presented, promised the French support and recognition of the Wrangel Government.

The Allied Conference was over. The following day everyone would leave Spa. So far Mr. Lloyd George had paid no attention to Mr. Struve's note, nor to his letter requesting an interview. Nicolas Alexandrovich again attempted to see Lloyd George, but in vain. He could reach only the valet of the Labour leader, not even his secretary. He left his card and the domestic promised to telephone him in case Lloyd George consented to see him.

The evening passed in making notes for the press, especially the French press which was the most sympathetic to the Wrangel cause, and would publish anything Nicolas Alexandrovich wished to give them. At three in the morning, the deeply depressed Russian delegates were still there, Mr. Struve pacing up and down, proffering ideas and observations which Nicolas recorded. With each passing hour, doubts as to the outcome of their mission increased until the anguish was intolerable. They were profoundly humiliated by the attitude of the British, although they had hardly hoped for recognition, knowing their policy.

On Saturday, July 17th, the general departure of the Allied delegates to the Conference took place. M. Millerand and Marshal Foch were to leave on a special train for Paris with the French delegates.

That morning, without one word, without deigning to reply in any manner to Mr. Struve's note and letter, Lloyd George departed from Spa.

Mr. Struve and my husband were in despair.

"C'est le chant du cygne de la Russie" (The Swan Song of Russia), said my husband, back again at the épicerie where we lodged. With mortal anguish he added, "This is the definite end of the Russian Imperial Empire, in a grocery shop." The cause of their beloved country, which these two would have defended with their life's blood, was lost. The last attempt to save it had failed. The fate of Russia was sealed.

Feeling utterly miserable, we sat in a fiacre before the grocery door, making our adieux to the good woman who had sheltered us. It was thundering and raining hard when suddenly someone approached under an umbrella and we recognized M. Albert Kammerer, who had come to tell us that he had obtained places for us to return to Paris in the French official train. The kindly gesture of this loyal friend touched us to tears. In adversity he had not forgotten the fallen ally.

There was much movement on the station platform. A red carpet had been spread before the carriage of the French Prime Minister. Flags were draped and a crowd assembled. Nicolas Alexandrovich and I occupied a compartment in a Wagon-Lit carriage. Delegates and journalists filled the passage ways. Nicolas spoke to several of the latter who promised to help him as much as possible in the press.

We had the third service for the dining car, and it was 4:30 before we lunched. In the meantime we were invited to Madame Berthelot's compartment, where we found Messrs. Berthelot, Laroche, Kammerer and General Le Rond. Gracious Madame Berthelot gave us bonbons and cakes, specialties of Brussels, and we laughed a great deal. These French people were touchingly kind to us. They seemed to be of one accord to prove their sympathy for dying Imperial Russia which, in face of all, was still resisting. My husband was profoundly moved.

General Le Rond came to see us in the dining car. "At last you are lunching," he cried, "but it is very late."

"The hour is of no importance, general," replied my husband with his gentle smile. "We are very pleased to be taken in your train."

General Le Rond put his hand an instant on my husband's shoulder. "I wish you had other reasons to be pleased," he answered significantly.

At St. Quentin the train stopped and Marshal Foch walked on the platform with several of his officers. I saw nearby the fine face of this hero of the war who had an air of greatness and simplicity combined.

At seven o'clock the train entered the Paris station. The last struggle for Imperial Russia was over. Her swan song had been sung.

This tragic ending recalls the famous flight to Varennes when Louis XVI and Queen Marie Antoinette took shelter in a grocery shop, where the king received the decree of the Assembly in Paris to arrest him, an event which in the words of Napoleon "changed the face of the world." One hundred and twenty-nine years later, in 1920, the last efforts to save a vast empire also came to naught in a grocery shop, and again the face of the world was changed.

Journeys in Central Europe

By 1924, Imperial Russia was definitely lost, and no power could save it. The tears, the agony of the Russian exiles were heartrending in face of this catastrophe. In Paris the Russian Embassy had passed into the hands of the bolsheviks, as the communists were then named.

After the holocaust of the Russian revolution in which he had lost his entire fortune, which was considerable, my husband found himself entirely without resources, as were practically all of his compatriots. In order to live, Nicolas Alexandrovich became associated with an important American banking house, Marshall Field, Glore & Co., which he represented for several years in Europe, negotiating loans to European governments, or public works. This occupation took him constantly to different countries where he was again in contact with governments and people he had known formerly as a diplomat.

Thus he traveled to Poland, Germany, Hungary, Czechoslovakia, Yugoslavia, Bulgaria and Italy. I was most proud of him for having been able to succeed in another profession, at a time of life when it is difficult for a man to change his métier and begin again. Nicolas and his Russian childhood friend, Nicolas Raffalovich, worked together. Raffalovich was a brilliant financier and Katherine, his American wife, was lovely.

I always accompanied my husband on his journeys and the following pages are an account of these pilgrimages, a small chronicle of days long past, of some fair countries now lying behind the Iron Curtain. Could we have known then the horrors to follow, wars, and the sad fate of many of the friends mentioned in these tender recollections, we would perhaps not have had the courage to continue on our way. As it was, we were young and life was before us.

January 7th, 1925

We left Paris at night for Cologne and the following morning passed the German frontier at Aix-la-Chapelle (Aachen). The first German I have seen since the war was a fat customs officer who thrust his head in the door of our compartment and asked in thick tones: "Habe' Sie 'was zu deklarieren?" The country was flat and grey, the railway stations well-kept and prosperous. In Cologne we had a wait of two hours for the Berlin train, so we went across the street to a barber shop or "Friseur" for Nicolas Alexandrovich to be shaved. A solid fraülein with honey-coloured braids arranged in "Schnecken" over her ears presided at the counter. I changed 500 francs at the Barclay Bank, receiving 22.50 marks for 100 francs. Money is high here since the gold Rentenmark has been established. Later we visited the famous Gothic Cathedral, just across from the station, a magnificent monument of the age of faith in dark, sad majesty. Nearby is the Hotel Excelsior where the British Army of Occupation have their G.H.Q. Two smart sentinels were presenting arms and marching up and down with a martial air. We saw a few Belgian and French soldiers, but the army of occupation was not in evidence. It was a strange feeling to put our feet again on German soil after the years of war.

At the station, Nicolas ate sausages with a glass of beer, both of them excellent. At noon the Berlin train departed. The sky was leaden, the country drab, with fields and trees. Occasionally pine forests darkened the sad landscape. We entered the Valley of the Ruhr, where many small, newly built workmen's houses attracted our attention, tidy as Noah's Arks. We passed Düsseldorf and Duisburg, center of French occupation, Oberhausen, Gelsenkirchen, Wanne, Essen and Dortmund, with flaming blast furnaces, tall as cathedrals. Great activity reigned. Everywhere cars and piles of coal were visible, also small wagons of coal sliding on wires stretched in the air. Between Hamm, Bielefeld and Herford a veritable hedge of factory chimneys lined the railway tracks. Towards 9:30 p.m. we reached Berlin and went to the Hotel Esplanade near the Tiergarten.

* * *

Berlin, January 9th, 1925

We lunched at the Hotel Bristol, Unter den Linden, an excellent meal with delicious Rhine wine. The restaurant was full towards two or three o'clock, the hour of the German "Mittagessen," a national institution, not to be taken lightly. Later we walked Unter den Linden, in the Friedrichstrasse and Leipzigerstrasse. These streets are animated, but in general the city looks quiet. Afterwards Nicolas went to the Mendelsohn Bank to see Mr. Kempner. We dined at the Pschorr Bräu. At eight o'clock we attended a play by Curt Götz, the German Sacha Guitry, who writes his plays and acts in them himself. Three short pieces were given, and the *Todte Tante* (Dead Aunt) was witty and amusing, being a satire on the proverbial hirsute German professor, his moon-faced wife and numerous offspring. During the entr'actes we walked in the foyer where people stood about drinking beer.

The following days while Nicolas was busy with bankers, I visited the Kaiser Friedrich Museum and viewed the superb collection of paintings (the Netherlands School is especially well represented), the sculptures and the façade of a Syrian palace, the Mschetta or Winter Palace, presented by the Sultan to Emperor Friedrich II.

We also walked by the Cathedral, the Schloss (Castle) and the Lustgarten, a pleasure garden nearby.

At 7:30 we went to the Oper am Königsplatz to see the old Humperdinck opera of our childhood, *Hänsl und Gretl*, always a favourite in Germany. The music is lovely, but witches and gingerbread houses are out of date. The opera was followed by a ballet, the *Puppenfee*, also somewhat antiquated. The "Art Nouveau" style of the theatre appeared very ugly to me. The interior was in bright red wood with bright blue festooned curtains, and strange carved figures representing heaven alone knows what. In the entr'actes we found the entire audience gathered around the buffet, eating sausages and consuming beer.

On Sunday Nicolas and I visited the Kaiser Friedrich Museum and the Royal Castle where Wilhelm II resided, but there is nothing beautiful to be seen in the latter. that evening we saw a play at the Königgrätzer Theatre, called *Der Tokaier* (Tokay Wine) with Emil Jannings, the famous German film star. He played well but his part was somewhat overdone. A pretty blonde actress, Carola Toelle, had the leading feminine role. We are always struck by the difference between the German diction and the French on the stage, the perfect enunciation of the latter being far superior.

Sleeping in a German bed is a great adventure. A sheet is laid over the mattress (the latter usually in three pieces) but there is no upper sheet, nor blanket. A fluffy eiderdown quilt, thick as a feather bed, encased in a white linen envelope, replaced them, but very inadequately, as it is too short to tuck in at the bottom and too narrow to tuck in at the sides. The problem is for the sleeper to establish an equilibrium which maintains the quilt in place, but that is a very high degree of art. He must lie flat on his back and balance the quilt on his stomach, but if his chest is covered, his feet gradually freeze, and if his feet are protected, his chest is exposed. Which is worse? Should he doze off from sheer exhaustion, he awakes, chilled to the bone, to find that the treacherous eiderdown has abandoned him entirely and slipped to the floor. Nicolas Alexandrovich, who is extremely tall, struggled manfully with this situation. One night he could bear it no longer. "There must be some special technique known only to Germans. We must find out what it is," he said and sent for the hotel manager with whom he was very friendly. This agreeable man arrived, clad in striped trousers and a cutaway coat. Nicolas eyed him sternly. "Lie down," he said, "and show me how you sleep in a German bed." We all laughed and the startled manager crawled amiably beneath the high, fluffy quilt to demonstrate German technique. His efforts were fruitless and he could only suggest sleeping with the knees drawn up under the chin. . . . We demanded woolen blankets. Next day they were bought and placed on our beds. As the administration of the Esplanade was extremely nice, these blankets were kept for Nicolas's use on his frequent visits to Berlin. Subsequently, when he arrived in the hotel, the order was immediately given to bring them. "Die Wolldecken des Herrn von Basily," echoed through the entrance hall. Our martyrdom was over.

Berlin, January 12th, 1925

We lunched today at the Kempner's villa in the "West End," a smart suburb beyond Charlottenburg, a pleasant luncheon with Mrs. Kempner, who was formerly Miss Mendelsohn. Mr. von der Meierhauser of the Mendelsohn Bank was also present with his wife.

Later we went to visit an apartment house my father had bought some years ago situated on the Hohenzollernstrasse 11 (later Graf Speestrasse). The manager, Mr. Walter, showed us the house. The rooms are fine and big and the apartments charming. We met Mrs. Walter, their daughter and the "Schwiegermamma," also the family dachshund, and had tea with them. In the evening we attended a Philharmonic concert with the famous Bruno Walter conducting Beethoven's Ninth Symphony with a chorus of voices. A magnificent performance.

*   *   *

Prague, January 13th, 1925

We left Berlin without regret and took the train for Prague. The journey was agreeable and we reached the Czech frontier at Bodenbach where Czech customs officials greeted us with the amiable smiles which seem to be natural to this people. Towards eight o'clock we arrived at the Masaryk Station in Prague and took rooms at the Hotel d'Europe.

We dined in the hotel restaurant and later went out to see the city which neither of us knew. To me it is a delight that my first impression of the old art cities of Europe should be at night, by moonlight if possible, when ghosts of former years haunt the ancient monuments. In the moonlit silence the centuries turn back revealing the soul of the past. Thus we had beheld Venice and Verona, and thus we were to see Prague.

Inquiring our way to the picturesque Old Town Place (Altstädt- erring) from a smiling policeman with white cotton gloves, we were suddenly confronted by a young man who sprang from the earth and offered to guide us. We accepted gladly and, led by this amiable youth, we made a journey into the past. In the old Market Square moonlight bathed the fourteenth century Town Hall, with its admirable antique clock, and the Teynkirche of the same period, cradle of the Hussite religion. The façade of the latter is half covered by old houses with arcades. Here Tycho Brahe, the famous astronomer, lies buried. The pale winter moon lent its magic to this scene, and the historic monuments seemed to vibrate gently as if awakening from a dream. . . . Returning to the hotel by the narrow Celetna Ulice leading to the beautiful Prasna Brama (Powder Tower, part of the old city wall today destroyed), we met a belated citizen who was just inserting his ancient key into the lock of an old house. Our guide politely requested him to show us his key, which he did most courteously, and what a key! We all laughed at this relic of former days, long as a man's hand, which could serve as a weapon of defense in case of need. The young man left us at the Powder Tower after having discoursed at length on the various monuments of the town and on the country in general. He was a lawyer, an intelligent, cultured man, and seemed to find it quite natural to accompany unknown strangers at midnight and do the honours of the city. His courtesy left us with a warm feeling towards Prague.

Prague, January 14th, 1925

Today we visited the Hradchin, the former fortified palace of the ancient kings of Bohemia, which has since been re-modeled. Today its cream-coloured façade has a simplified baroque appearance.

The Hradchin, like the Kremlin of Moscow, is a little world enclosed by walls, set on the summit of a hill high above the Vltava River which flows at its feet. Within the enclosure are palaces, churches and a convent, besides the magnificent Cathedral of St. Vitus. Here dwelt the old rulers of Bohemia, who were crowned in the cathedral. Today the President of the Republic, Mr. Masaryk, resides here, also Mr. Beneš, Minister of Foreign Affairs. These two patriots, as well as General Stefanik, are the forgers of the new Czechoslovak State.

We visited the cathedral founded by the prince-saint Wenceslas in 930, and the adjacent Wenceslas chapel, whose walls are encrusted with Bohemian semi-precious stones, amethysts, lapis, etc. We also viewed the German hall where President Masaryk holds receptions, and the Vladislav hall, now under reparation. Work is being carried on in various parts of the Hradchin as the Austrians had neglected Prague, letting the monuments decay, and treating it as a provincial town.

Nicolas has an engagement to see Mr. Beneš the day after tomorrow.

Prague, January 16th, 1925

This morning I received a visit from Madame Schidlof to whom we had brought a letter from Madame Verdé-Delisle in Paris. I was obliged to take her into the "kavarna" or coffee house as the hotel has no reception room. Madame Schidlof, the wife of a Czech lawyer in Prague, Richard Schidlof, was born Countess Maritza Voinovich of a well-known Dalmatian family. She is a delightful person, speaks at least six languages, is an accomplished pianist and has an extraordinary "charme slav."

The weather is very cold and we are always hungry. The effect of the sharp climate is seen in the numerous food shops, for one is obliged to eat in order to combat the cold. On the street corners, fat women bundled in overcoats sell appetizing hot sausages and the kavarnas are always full.

Nicolas was received by Minister of Foreign Affairs M. Beneš at 12:30.

Office hours in the ministries are from eight to two, then midday dinner. Monsieur Beneš and Nicolas had formerly been closely associated in political work connected with the liberation of the Slavs under Austrian domination, and especially of the Czechs, which aim Russia had pursued since the outbreak of war. Nicolas had worked particularly with the Czech General Stefanik, having collaborated on the formation of the Czech army in Russia. Stefanik had even lived in Nicolas's house in Russian General Headquarters in

Mogilev during the war. After the formation of Czecho-slovakia, he became Minister of War and later was killed in an aviation accident. His death was a great loss for Czecho-slovakia as he was a very intelligent and honest man and an ardent patriot. Nicolas felt his death keenly. Nicolas had worked with Beneš and Stefanik on bringing about the for-mation of a democratic Czech organization which was in keeping with the ideas of the Russian liberals, but not of the Russian reactionaries.

Later we walked to the Karlsmost, a beautiful old bridge built by Charles IV with high, pointed medieval towers. Statues of kings and saints ornament the balustrade on either hand. This bridge, one of the finest sights of Prague, is flung across the Vltava and leads to the Mala Strana (Little Side), the oldest part of the city just below the Hradchin Hill, where ancient houses and beautiful palaces rise.

It was twilight by now and snow was falling, falling gently on houses, palaces, the bridge and the towers of baroque churches. Silently it enveloped the city in its white shroud till a dream world emerged, far from reality. I stood entranced, counting the snowflakes as they fell, until my practical hus-band pulled me by the sleeve and led me to a waiting car.

Prague, Saturday, January 17th, 1925

This morning Madame Schidlof sent her automobile for us to visit the Strakhov Monastery. This cream-coloured baroque building looked pale and frigid in the grey winter daylight of Central Europe. Snowflakes fluttered down to the white earth, making the scene remote, unreal. Snow clothed the baroque architecture in majesty and mystery till I felt I was living in a fairy tale. The library of Strakhov is famous. I could not help thinking of Casanova, who spent his declining years as librarian of the castle in Dux, not far from Prague, and wrote there his scandalous memoirs. I could fancy him at Strakhov. The cold was intense and we gladly returned to the limousine which drove us to the Schidlofs' for luncheon. Later they took us again in their car to see the city.

In Prague we are constantly reminded of former Russia, by women with handerchiefs tied in triangles over their heads, and wagons filled with straw like the Russian country "telega." The general atmosphere of the Strakhov Monastery recalls the Alexander Nevsky Monastery in St. Petersburg. Oil-lamps burning before holy images on houses evoke that loved, lost land. Above all, the hearts of the people are russophile and never forget that they belong to the great Slav family.

Prague, January 18th, 1925

At 11:30 we made an official call on Madame Beneš, who received us in a beautiful big salon in the Hradchin Palace. The view from the windows over the city is superb. Madame Beneš is very blond, and agreeable, with soft Slav manners. Mr. Beneš also appeared to talk with Nicolas.

At 8:30 we met the Schidlofs at Zavrels where we had invited them to dine with us. In the restaurant a number of prominent Austrians were also dining, people of the Austrian nobility—many of them aristocratic in appearance, tall, slender and blond. The ladies were very pretty and elegant.

The agrarian reform made by the new Czech republic has taken away the lands of many Austrian nobles who had possessed vast properties in former Bohemia, repaying them of course, but insufficiently in the opinion of the landowners who, enraged at this procedure, have gone to law. Mr. Schidlof is defending some of them and knows them all, more or less.

Nicolas has taken cold.

Prague, January 19th, 1925

Nicolas remained in bed today with a bad cold. I put off his engagements in various ministries, and called the hotel physician, Dr. Yaroslav Lenz, who arrived, removed his cuffs, put them on the table and examined Nicolas, pronouncing his ailment as grippe.

Prague, January 21st, 1925

Nicolas is somewhat better although still in bed. This afternoon I walked on the Příkope (pronounced Pshi-kopé) and Narodni Třida (the main streets of Prague) to the Masaryk Quay by the Vltava. From there I viewed the Hradchin on the other side of the river, rising marvelously beautiful on its hilltop in the silvery twilight.

A woman in picturesque Bohemian peasant costume passed, wearing a very short full skirt and red woolen stockings, a shawl folded in a point on her head over a white coiffe. Fascinated by this colorful apparition, I followed her for several squares.

We are deeply impressed by the amiability of this people. They are always polite and still keep the charming old Austrian manner of saying "Ich küsse die Hand." Shopkeepers, servants, etc. use this phrase. The hotel chambermaid seizes my hand, kisses it on every occasion and calls me "Frau Gräfin"—I am advancing in the world.

Prague, January 22nd, 1925

Nicolas has recovered. The doctor permitted him to go out in a closed automobile, so he went to the Ministry of Public Works.

In the afternoon I walked to the curious old Jewish cemetery, where gravestones, broken and twisted by age, show between trees and shrubbery (Alt-Neu-Schule synagogue).

Nicolas also went to the Ministry of Commerce to see Mr. Novak, the Minister, returning for luncheon at three o'clock.

The weather is very cold. We admire the "botski" (fur-bordered leather or felt boots) ladies wear on the street to protect their feet from the cold, as in Russia, very cosy and practical.

Prague, January 24th, 1925

Nicolas went again to various ministries. At seven the Schidlofs came to say goodbye, after which we packed our valises to return to Paris and at ten o'clock dined at Zavrels. This restaurant has an excellent violinist who often plays for us during meals. That night, only old Russian folk and gypsy songs flowed from his violin. He played for us alone, putting all his art into the music, that profound, nostalgic Russian music which shakes the soul. As he listened, my husband was deeply moved. Old memories of his former life stirred within him. Suddenly tears stood in his eyes, and I begged him to tell me the cause of his distress. Tears fell on his cheeks. "I was wondering," he said, "if ever I will be able to serve my country again." This is the only time in all the years of exile from his beloved Russia that my husband has had a moment of utter despair, the only time his noble heart has given in to uncontrollable grief. He has always faced the inevitable stoically with no outward mark of the anguish that fills his soul—but tonight the tragedy of his country overwhelmed him and he wept.

*   *   *

Three weeks later we returned to Prague. I saw Madame Schidlof and through her met Madame Rosenkrancova, a Czech singer and teacher who gives lessons to Mme. Schidlof. I also began to study singing with her to fill in the hours when Nicolas is busy.

*   *   *

Prague, February 28th, 1925

A few days ago Madame Bohumila Rosenkrancova gave a soirée to which we were invited, with the Schidlofs. The Mayor of Prague was present, with his wife Madame Karel Baxa, also Madame Hoest, wife of the Danish Minister to Czechoslovakia, and Madame Couget, wife of the French Minister, and Madame Sofianos, wife of the Secretary of the Greek Legation, the Czech Minister to Paris and Madame Osuska, also General Mittelhauser, Chief of the French Military Mission in Czechoslovakia. Among the guests was Madame Germaine Lubin of the Paris Opera Comique, a great singer. Mme. Lubin is making a tour of Central Europe and will perform three times at the Prague Opera (Narodni Divadlo), singing *Louise* and *Faust*. She is a stately, handsome woman, the wife of the French poet Paul Geraldy, author of that delightful book of poetry *Toi et Moi*. Mademoiselle Alvin, a French violoncellist, played at Madame Rosenkrancova's soirée.

A few days later we were invited by the French Minister and Madame Couget to a reception at the French Legation where we saw something of smart Prague society. The Minister of Foreign Affairs and Madame Beneš came late. Madame Lubin was also present, as were the Schidlofs. The Legation is in one of the fine old palaces of the Mala Strana, the Palais Buquoy. The new government has given over several of the palaces to the foreign legations. The beautiful façade and splendid salons of the Palais Buquoy make an appropriate background for the French legation. Mademoiselle Alvin, the violoncellist, played at this charming reception.

The United States Legation is housed in the Schönborn Palace. Mr. Lewis Einstein is the Minister. The Netherlands Legation is in the splendid Nostitz palace (Minister M.

Hoest). The English (Sir George Clark, Minister) is in one Thun Palace and the Italian Legation in another palace. The Yugoslav Legation is installed in the extremely beautiful Palace of the Order of Malta, across the street from the Palais Buquoy.

Prague, March 5th, 1925

Today Madame Pavla Osuska, wife of the Czech Minister to Paris, gave a concert with the Philharmonic Orchestra in the Smetana Hall for the benefit of the Czech Red Cross. Madame Osuska is an artiste with a golden voice who, before her marriage, was a singer at the Opera here, and whom Prague well remembers and gave a great ovation on her appearance. She is a gracious, charming woman and has many friends in Paris where her brilliant husband is much admired. Madame Osuska sang a program of Czech music. *Libusa* is a historical opera by Smetana, and her rendering of the prayer was very fine, as were songs from Dvorak's *Rusalka* and the berceuse from Smetana's *Habicka* (The Kiss), as well as Mašenka's aria from Smetana's *The Bartered Bride*. At the end, the stage was a garden of flowers.

Prague, March 7th, 1925

Today is President Masaryk's seventy-fifth birthday anniversary. Brass bands play in the street and crowds flock about his residence in the Hradchin Palace. This fine old Czech gentleman, a former professor and one of the founders of the new Czech republic, is very popular. We were invited to a reception given on this occasion by Mr. Baxa, Mayor of Prague, in the Community House (Obečni Dum) where we went with the Schidlofs.

In the Obečni Dum is an exposition of paintings by the great Russian painter of the nineteenth century, Ilya Repin, which we also visited. The "Krestnihod" (The Way of the

Cross) is a magnificent painting, bought by a director of the Czech Skoda Metallurgical Works. We also saw sketches of heads for Repin's famous painting, the "Zaparozhe Cossacks," also for the "Chornomortsy" (Black Sea Pirates), which delighted Nicolas. He greatly desired to purchase a sketch of one of the Cossacks but the price was high and he desisted, and it has always been a cause of regret.

The Stavovske Divadlo is a beautiful small theatre built in the eighteenth century by a Count Nostitz. The interior remains intact from that period and the white woodwork with gold trimmings is very lovely, an appropriate setting for old operas. In this theatre Mozart made his first appearance with his opera *Don Juan* which later became so famous. Here we heard the beautiful Russian opera by Tchaikovsky, *Eugen Onegin,* based on Pushkin's poem of the same name, one of the masterpieces of Russian literature. The opera was given in Czech, and Zitek of the Prague Opera sang the bass role of Gremin very well, but the rest was mediocre.

In the Narodni Divadlo (People's Theatre) we attended a performance of Smetana's opera *Taemstvi* (The Secret), a peasant opera with delightful, melodious music. Here we also saw Smetana's best known production, *The Bartered Bride*, on a peasant theme—a charming performance.

Smetana (1824–1884), the greatest of Czech composers, was the first to write compositions using motifs from the old Czech national or folk music, but under the Austrian occupation he was not appreciated at the time. Only later, at the birth of the Czech nation, his characteristic music, imbued with patriotism, had a national appeal and he became popular. His life was one of struggle and disappointment, ending in misery and insanity. Later his talent was recognized and today, exactly one hundred years after his birth, he is venerated as a great musician and patriot. How ironical is fate!

Smetana's great opera *Libusa* (based on the legend of a half mythical Bohemian princess of that name, to whom tradition attributes the founding of Prague and of the Přemysl dynasty) has a historical character and is usually given on national occasions. Libusa became a prophetess who foretold the glory and fame of her city, and as such she has come down through history.

Smetana's other historical opera, *Dalibor*, likewise a half mythological hero of Bohemia, is also very fine. His lighter operas are *The Kiss, The Secret* and *The Bartered Bride*, the latter being the most popular of all his works. His last opera, *The Devil's Wall*, is more modern in feeling and, to me, less interesting.

One of his finest compositions is a symphonic poem called *Ma Vlast* (My Country), in which he describes the Vyšehrad, the cradle of Prague, its glories and downfall, also the Vltava River as it flows through the plains and valleys of fair Bohemia. The last movement depicts the soldiers of Blanik who after the battle of Bela Hora (White Mountain) in 1620 (when the Bohemians were defeated by the Austrians) are supposed to lie asleep beneath the mountain awaiting the moment of Bohemia's need to awaken and rush to her defense. Of course, the legionaries of 1918, the new Czech army, three centuries after the White Mountain defeat, are popularly called the Soldiers of Blanik.

We lunched with Monsieur and Madame Beneš in the Hradchin Palace. Mr. Augustin Novak, Finance Minister, and Mr. Pospišil, head of the State Bank, were also present. The apartments occupied by the Beneš are superb, and we traversed a long enfilade of salons before reaching the dining room. The view over the city is extraordinary.

After luncheon we passed into a smaller salon where Turkish coffee was served. In this room was an ancient baroque Czech stove in cream-coloured faience, a decorative and lovely object.

Mme. Beneš told me what a high regard her husband had for Nicolas and I replied by telling her of Nicolas's admiration for Mr. Beneš.

Prague, March 11th, 1925

We lunched today at Mr. Kramař's, whom Nicolas has known for many years, a charming Czech grand seigneur, and great patriot, whose name is placed beside that of Masaryk, Beneš and General Stefanik in the forming of the new Czech republic in 1918. He now belongs to another, more conservative political party—Narodni (People's). Mr. Kramař is very russophile and loves old Russia. Madame Kramař is Russian. Their fine villa stands on a hill to the left of the Hradchin with a wide view over the city and surrounding country. We lunched in a large dining room in the Russian boyar style with dark, carved wood walls and a most characteristic old green faience stove, which interested me. Mr. Burtzev, the famous Russian publicist and former revolutionary, was also present and the Russian General Voronin, both old friends of Nicolas. We remained for hours after the meal was finished, talking of everything pertaining to Russia, past and present.

In the evening a Slovak woman came to me in the hotel with Slovak peasant shawls for sale, bright-coloured flowers on a white ground. The old ones were lovely and I bought her entire stock for presents. The women no longer wear the traditional dress, which is a pity. The old lady herself, however, was clad in a peasant costume, very full skirts reaching to the knees, tight bodice and high knee-boots—a striking array. On her head was a three-cornered handkerchief worn over a white lace cap. She had soft manners and we understood her speech, as Slovak resembles Russian much more than Czech, which we cannot understand. Upon leaving she seized my hand and kissed it. Poor old lady, last vestige of times that are gone forever.

* * *

We left Prague on March 12th, arriving in Paris twenty-seven hours later.

On March 31st we returned to Prague. Nicolas was detained, and upon reaching the Gare de l'Est in Paris, we almost missed the Prague Express. Fortunately, all the conductors and controleurs of the Wagons-Lits knew him as he traveled so often on the line. "Attendez!" they cried, and held the train a minute for him. "Voici M. de Basily. Il arrive." We raced along the platform and into the train, like a cyclone. We were scarcely seated when Nicolas shouted, "The passports! Where are the passports?" Wrenching open our valises and tossing their contents on the floor, he searched feverishly, like a terrier digging up a bone, and finally brought the missing documents to light. Overcome by emotion we went to bed and slept profoundly until the Czech frontier the following day. Bohemia seemed more amiable than Germany with its splendid forests of firs and birch.

*　　*　　*

Prague, April 2nd, 1925

A sunny spring day. After enjoying the admirable view over the city from Hradchin, Nicolas and I descended the steep Neruda Street, leading from the Hradchin to the Mala Strana Mesto (Little Side Square). This street is lined on both sides with baroque houses of the seventeenth and eighteenth centuries. Nearly all of them retain over the door the individual sign which, in former times, served to distinguish the dwelling as numbers do today. Much fantasy reigns and the signs include holy images, specimens of the animal and vegetable kingdoms, and emblems of the trades. Some are carved in relief on the stone, others are painted and occasionally a statue appears. On one house we saw a deer, on others a swan or a crawfish, a rampant lion holding a chalice in his paws, dated 1726, a carrot, two seated beasts of the Apocalypse, a yellow wheel, a bishop's head, a gold key, a mandonna and child, a statue of an archangel in stone, a painting of a king on horseback holding a white standard, a Medusa's head, a lamb, a madonna, and a baroque shell. The Thun Palace, ornamented with baroque eagles, houses the Italian Legation, opposite the Cernin Palace, now the Rumanian Legation, with negro caryatides and two busts— one "dies," a youth with a sun on his chest, the other "nox," a woman whose head is veiled by a star sprinkled scarf. Still another house bore two red violins crossed on a blue background with yellow stars. On yet another, a brown eagle sits perched on a mountain, and a statue of a saint with an aureole. Two suns ornament the dwelling of the famous Czech poet Jan Neruda, born in 1834, whose name the street bears. Neruda is one of the greatest modern Czech writers—*Stones of the Mala Strana*, and *Holy Friday Chants*, etc.

On the adjacent Smetovni ulice our friends the Schidlofs later lived in another old palace. Nearby is the enormous pile of the Wallenstein Palace, erected by the Duke of Friedland after he retired from the Thirty Years' War. It has a fine garden and is now the Ministry of Commerce (Minister, Ladislav Novak). What a wealth of history and imagination in these Old World streets. Thus the past comes down to us in the eloquent stones of the Mala Strana.

In the afternoon we called on Madame Just (Pani Justova) in her large apartment on the Vaclavski Namesti, with Maria-Theresa furniture and Biedermeier (German Directoire) in light-coloured wood, inlaid. The drawing room was delightful with green ruffled chintz curtains at the windows, masses of flowers and books everywhere—a most characteristic and interesting room.

Prague, April 3rd, 1925

While Nicolas is away on his financial negotiations, I wander about this Old World city. I see numerous book shops, as the Czechs are great readers, also shops with red,

Bohemian garnets, set in old-fashioned gold settings, sombre and uninteresting.

Easter is approaching and often women in peasant costume appear on street corners selling highly decorated Easter eggs on which is written "Veliko Noce" (Czech for Easter, literally "great night"). In every street are several "iadelnias"—delicatessen shops where every variety of hams, galantines, and juice frankfurters all glorify the defunct pig. Salt pickles, beer and bread sprinkled with kümmel accompany these delicacies and towards evening the shops are crowded and look very cheerful. Day and night ample peasant women sit beside their little wagons where steaming hot sausages tempt the passerby.

Today Nicolas called on Mr. Beneš. Later I accompanied him to the State Bank to see Mr. Pospišil and then to the Finance Ministry to Mr. Augustin Novak, the Minister. In the evening we dined with the Schidlofs at the new restaurant Ellner, quite gay with dancing. Some members of the Austrian nobility were also dining there and the Schidlofs introduced us to Count and Countess Dobech and the latter's brother, Count Dietrichstein. Their mother was Russian, born Dolguruky. The Countess had a slight Russian aspect but is very Austrian in sentiment. She wears beautiful pearls. We met a son of the former Austrian Prime Minister Ehrental (who also did his bit in bringing about the war in 1914), whom Nicolas knew. The Czech sugar-king Mendelik was also dining at Ellner's restaurant.

Prague, April 4th, 1925

This evening at seven o'clock, the usual hour, we went to the Narodni Divadlo to see Smetana's *Certove Stena* (The Devil's Wall). The music is fine in parts and quite modern, but I found the opera a bit boring with frequent apparitions of the devil. Wilhelm Zitek, who sang the principal role, is the best singer at the Prague Opera, where there are no remarkable voices at present.

After the opera, the Schidlofs' automobile took us to their house for evening tea in the Russian manner. We found there a samovar and an enormous assortment of sandwiches and cakes, tea and champagne, and hot sausages which Maritza had prepared for Nicolas who loves them. We remained talking with her and Dr. Schidlof until two a.m. Delightful hospitality and very Slav.

Madame Rosenkrancova has invited us to luncheon to meet the famous Italian baritone Matteo Battistini, who is giving a concert here on the 7th and is a great friend of hers.

Prague, April 7th, 1925

We lunched with the Schidlofs, also Madame Just and her brother, Mr. Brumlik, a "beau ténébreux."

In the evening Battistini gave a concert in the Velky Lucerna Sal. This enormous hall seats about five thousand persons and not one place was empty. A tremendous ovation greeted this famous artist who, in spite of his seventy-one years, still enchants his listeners. After the program was over no one left the hall and the entire audience crowded about the platform where he stood. Battistini was obliged to give several encores which were received with wild enthusiasm, among them excerpts from *The Marriage of Figaro* and *Pagliacci*. It was a magnificent demonstration, with the audience on their feet applauding frantically the art of this great singer until they saw they were tiring him. It seems that his success in Vienna recently was also colossal, the critics calling him "the divine Battistini." At seventy-one, his voice has gone off, but his faultless art of emission and perfect diction remain. Battistini is a gentleman as well as a great artist and finesse and taste show in his singing. He looked very distinguished as he stood before us in evening clothes with white waistcoat, tie and gloves.

Nicolas Alexandrovich had known Battistini in St. Petersburg where for years before the war he had sung and was exceedingly popular—always receiving a great ovation. After the concert we went to his dressing room and he was glad to see Nicolas Alexandrovich, as he has very tender memories of Russia.

Prague, April 8th, 1925

Today we lunched with Battistini at the home of Madame Rosenkrancova, a Czech opera singer and a friend of the great Italian baritone. Madame Schidlof and Baron Villani, a Hungarian diplomat, and Hofman, a young Russian singer, were also present.

The maestro has great charm and when he smiles his whole countenance lights up. Black eyes shine in a clean-shaven face with a long, pronounced nose. His heart is so young, his intelligence so keen, it is difficult to believe that he is seventy-one. He wore a black suit and striped black and white tie. He is traveling alone with an old man-servant. His wife, a Spanish noblewoman, died three years ago. He has an estate at Conegliano, near Rome, and divides his time between there and the capital.

In Rome, Battistini lives in a picturesque manner in the Franciscan Monastery of the Forty Saints, the "Santi Quaranti."

"With me it makes forty-one," he said whimsically.

He has splendid apartments in that monastery. In the evening he sometimes invites the monks to visit him, giving them cigarettes and playing the gramophone for them.

"And the ladies, maestro?" we inquired. "May you receive ladies there?"

"Si, si, in an apartment on the ground floor. My wish was to arrange it nicely with pretty hangings, but the Padre said to me: 'What you wish to do is not Franciscan, maestro.' So I refrained."

Every day he rides horseback. "When I do not ride I am ill-natured all day," he said.

After luncheon we gathered round him and Hofman put on a gramophone record of the "Favorita," sung by Battistini. We assisted at the unusual spectacle of a great singer listening to his own voice. The record was so splendid that at the end we involuntarily applauded, which seemed to please him.

As we sat around him, he told us stories of his life in a simple, unpretentious manner.

Once the Governor-General of Warsaw heard Battistini sing the role of Charles-Quint in *Ernani*, and afterwards complimented him on the way he bore his sword, saying he would like to imitate him. Many months later Battistini was requested to intercede with this same Governor for a young Italian boy suspected—without cause—of being implicated in a Nihilist plot, and condemned to thirty years in Siberia. Battistini wrote a letter to the Governor-General in which he said:

"I call to your attention the case of this Italian youth and request you to investigate, as it appears that he is unjustly condemned. Once you did me the honour of saying you would like to imitate the way I handled the sword of Charles-Quint, in *Ernani*. Now, will you not imitate me by saying the words I spoke as Charles-Quint: 'Perdono a tutti?' "

The case was revised. The boy was proved innocent and liberated, thanks to the intercession of Battistini, who had found such a graceful manner in which to make his plea.

Massenet and Battistini were great friends. One day the baritone said to the French composer: "Maestro, why are all your operas for tenors? Why are there so few roles for baritones?"

"Which of my operas would you like to sing?" asked Massenet.

"Werther, maestro."

"I will transcribe it for you and in three months time you shall have it," replied the composer. He did so and everyone knows what an incomparable Werther Battistini was.

The conversation turned on Russia and Nicolas Alexandrovich recalled to Battistini his many fervent admirers in the happy old days there. All his sympathies are for former Russia. He told us that a few years ago when in Norway he had occasion to meet a bolshevik commissar who urged him strongly to come to the U.S.S.R., assuring him of a hearty welcome there. "I cannot go to Russia, you have killed too many of my friends," the singer answered coldly.

In recalling memories of Russia, Battistini spoke of many former friends there, among them the Grand Duke Vladimir and his clever duchess, Marie Pavlovna, born a German princess. He also spoke of the Emperor. "The last time I sang before the Emperor was at Tsarskoe Selo in the Chinese Pavilion just before the war. Taniev, the Russian composer, greatly desired me to sing one of his compositions, which I wrote upon the program to be submitted to His Majesty. When he returned it, Taniev's song was struck out. "I like Taniev, but I do not like his music," remarked the Tsar. (Taniev was the father of the famous lady-in-waiting to the Tsarina, Anna Vyrubova).

"How did you begin your career, maestro?" we asked Battistini.

"I had no idea of becoming a singer," he replied. "I belong to a family of professors and lawyers, and was studying philosophy at the Rome University. At the age of seventeen I was called for military service. Often I sang in the barracks and the men would say: 'You have a good voice, Matteo,' but I paid no attention. Upon returning to Rome I continued to study philosophy but took private singing lessons, purely for my own edification, never thinking of becoming a singer. Several years passed. One day I learned that Mancinelli, director of the Rome Opera, and orchestra leader, was searching for a baritone to sing in *La Favorita*, as two singers had already failed. The soprano, La Galitti, was singing in the title role. As I stood before the theatre one morning, the thought came to me, why should I not apply for the baritone role in *Favorita*? I entered and asked for Mancinelli. He kept me waiting some time, but finally appeared.

" 'What do you wish?' he questioned.

" 'I wish to sing in *La Favorita*,' I replied.

" 'Ah, you are an artist?'

" 'No.'

" 'But you have sung in opera?'

" 'No.'

" 'Then in heaven's name, what do you want here?'

" 'To sing in *La Favorita*.'

" 'When?'

" 'Tonight, if you desire.'

"My calm determination must have made an impression on Mancinelli, for he decided to hear me without delay and called an accompanist. When I had finished these two looked at each other in amazement. Mancinelli said: 'Come with me immediately to La Galitti. If she is willing you shall sing tonight.

"We went to La Galitti. She was one of the last of the great school; un po' rotunda, but she sang divinely. Together we did the grand aria from *La Favorita*. When it was over she cried: 'But this boy is no beginner! I am proud to sing with such an artist!'

"I was engaged at once and Mancinelli promised to pay me three hundred lire for three or four representations. I had no stage clothes. At three o'clock the tailor came to fit my costume. When I went home I said to my mother: 'Tonight I sing in *La Favorita*.' She thought I had gone mad but, nevertheless, came to the theatre."

"I appeared that night. It was a complete success. I was

twenty. I had courage. From that hour my career began.''

"You are an incomparable artist," we said to Battistini, "Art, fame, everything is yours."

"Si," said the great maestro, and for a moment his keen eyes clouded, "Ma sono vecchio, è peccato."

A lively day. Nicolas Alexandrovich went to see Mr. Pospišil at the State Bank, and also saw Mr. Vanuček at the Ministry of Commerce.

We lunched at the Obecni Dum, and later visited the "Old New School," one of the oldest synagogues in Europe, very medieval, with a pointed roof and slits for windows. Women are not permitted to enter the synagogue during religious ceremonies, but are placed in an adjoining room where they can hear, but neither be seen nor heard.

An old Jewish attendant guided us about. He related that three months earlier an unusual wedding ceremony had been performed here, according to ancient Jewish Orthodox rites, which obliged the bride to cut off her hair. She was dressed in street attire with a hat, as no wedding veil may be worn in the synagogue. Before the service the girl retired to the women's room where her lovely long hair was shaved. She then put on a gold cap to wear during the ceremony, afterwards removing it to don a wig, which she must always wear if her husband exacts it. The bride's hair is shaved so that she will not be attractive to other men (nor to her husband either, I imagine). This was a very rare case of the ancient Jewish Orthodox custom being revived today. I had occasionally seen old Jewish women wearing horrible wigs, but never knew why.

Prague, June 1925

We lunched today at Zavchels with the Schidlofs, Maritza charming and stimulating, as usual.

Prince Lichnovsky, former German Ambassador to England, just before the war, was also a guest and we were much interested in meeting him. His conversation is agreeable and witty, and his manners are those of a perfect diplomat of the old school—alas, almost vanished today.

In 1914 he had warned the Berlin government of the danger of provoking England. His attitude displeased Kaiser Wilhelm II, and he was dismissed from the diplomatic service. He had endeavoured to serve his country's interests, but he was misunderstood. Time proved him to be right.

* * *

Belgrade, October 7th, 1926

We left Budapest last night by train for Belgrade. Morning revealed a vast plain with prosperous fields and tidy white houses. This part of Yugoslavia (former Serbia) resembles the great Hungarian puszta. We passed freight cars laden with turnips and other farm produce. Serbia is chiefly an agricultural country, although some mines exist, in general unexplored.

As the train neared the capital, a hill crowned by the ruins of a citadel (Kalemegdán) detached itself from the plain and "Beograd" (White City), Belgrade, lay before us where the Sava rolls its waters into the Danube, the great river of Central Europe.

Upon alighting from the Orient Express in Belgrade, I felt I had reached the ends of the earth, and waves of nostalgia swept over me. It has been said that the border line of East and West lies somewhere between Budapest and Vienna. Already in the fair Magyar capital an undercurrent of the Orient is felt, but in Belgrade, Europe is left far behind. We were in a Slav country which had lain for five centuries beneath the Turkish yoke, only freeing itself definitely in 1878.

Outside the railway station our eyes fell on men in frayed garments, each wearing a close-fitting cap and leather sandals called "opantzi," the national footwear whose name has become synonymous with the Serbian peasant. Various vehicles awaited passengers from our train, principally taxis, but several broad victorias drawn by horses reminded us of Russia. Nearby a group of primitive country carts laden with bricks, cement, and other building materials, drawn by oxen, contrasted vividly with the latest model Citroën which bore us to the Hotel Excelsior.

The drivers of these carts were ragged but placid and comfortable. I observed one of them piloting an empty wagon, of which one wheel remained stationary, as the rim was broken. Three spokes scraped along the ground noisily. The driver reined his horses and leaning down contemplated the disaster. For several minutes he did not move, saying no word to his three companions, who were also mute. Evidently he was thinking: "This wheel is broken. What can I do? Nothing. Then bear it. It is the will of God." With Slav resignation before the inevitable, he slapped the reins on the horses' backs and the cart creaked on.

Belgrade, October 8th, 1926

Our windows overlook the Royal Palace gardens behind whose high walls the king frequently walks. The roof of flat overlapping tiles on the wall itself evokes the Orient.

Architecturally there is little of interest in Belgrade. No Turkish buildings charm the eye as in Sarajevo and Mostar. One small mosque remains to recall the Moslem domination, besides the fortress on the hill and the cruelly pointed pavingstones of some streets (*kaldrina*). The country was too long subjected to strangers for national monuments to arise. The Serbs are essentially a peasant people and have always cultivated the soil, but they are splendid soldiers. The Serb can handle both a plough and a gun. Under the Turkish occupation the national spirit never wavered. The flame was kept burning in secret, for the enemy was always at hand. Belgrade is the capital of a people whose past was spent in fighting rather than in building. This city is an immense village, with the Royal Palace on the main street. The shops are insignificant. Many people are poorly clad, but the wearers of these tattered garments are not always poor, indeed we are told that well-to-do peasants often dress in tatters on principle.

The streets are dirty and badly paved. The pointed Turkish paving-stones are torture to my French slippers. A new Parliament is under construction. Innumerable carts bearing building materials are drawn by great-eyed oxen with upward sweeping horns. The noise they make on the rough pavements is deafening. Piles of superb green and purple grapes, pears, apples, pomegranates and prunes glow in the fruit stalls. Yugoslavia occupies the first place in the world for commerce in prunes. They are employed extensively for making the local liqueur, "slivovitsa." We tried it last evening and found it extremely strong. I saw stars.

In the streets it is easy to believe that we are in the Balkans. We see Montenegrins from whose caps (*kapitza*) the monogram of former King Nicolas has disappeared since their country has become incorporated in Yugoslavia. Albanians, indomitable mountain people, wear the white felt headgear shaped somewhat like a clown's cap, only less high. They are generally armed with a saw, being itinerant woodcutters in large majority. The Serbian peasants with their leather sandals (*opantzi*) and the Bosnians coiffed with a small red fez are picturesque features. Numerous peasant women appear, their heads bound with bright-coloured handkerchiefs. A voluminous skirt is worn over countless petticoats, swinging gaily as the owner walks. Today, in the rain, we saw a peasant girl barefoot on the pavements, carrying her shoes in her hand. Occasionally gypsy women in multicolored rags follow us with extended palms, but in general there are few beggars. An Oriental touch is the fez worn by merchants of "boza," a sweet Turkish drink kept in brass jars and sold on the street. Numerous shops carry

Turkish sweetmeats. We saw a Turk today in a red plush costume with gold embroideries, bearing on his back a tall brass (*boza*) jar in the form of a musical instrument. The national costume has practically disappeared. A few old women still wear the Serbian head dress (a round, close fitting cap encircled by a braid of hair). In former times the feminine costume was very rich.

On the façade of many shops the commodities sold within are painted. As in former Russia, the shopkeeper graphically makes his wares known to the lower classes who cannot read. Golden loaves of bread indicate a baker; an ox or a wooly lamb heralds the butcher shop; soap and cheese, the grocery. A sewing-machine agency bears an elaborate painting of veiled women busily working on these modern Western inventions while mosques and minarets furnish an appropriate background. Thus, for once, East and West meet.

Belgrade, October 9th, 1926

The most picturesque sight in Belgrade is the citadel of Kalemegdán, lying on a high hill at whose base the Sava and Danube meet. Attila and his Huns camped below. Belgrade was the outpost of Christian civilization in Europe, a bastion against whose walls invading hordes of barbarians from Asia beat. In 1389, the Serbs lost their independence at the famous battle of Kosovo, to the Turks. Under Moslem domination, the star and crescent floated from this stronghold. At present it is used by the Serbs as a barracks.

Today we drove to Kalemegdán in a broad victoria drawn by two horses, to visit this historic spot. The road was hedged in on both sides by high stone walls. We passed beneath the gateway of Prince Eugene of Savoy who, in 1717, after a tremendous victory drove off the Turks and occupied Belgrade. On our left rose the round "Neboicha Kula" (Tower without Fear) where the Turks had imprisoned Serbs. Here also Kara Mustapha hanged himself by order of the Sultan after his defeat before Vienna.

In several places we noticed great holes torn in the walls by shells fallen on this citadel during the First World War, of which, of course, Serbia was the original cause.

The carriage wound higher up the hill, through a gateway bearing Turkish ornamentations carved in stone, beneath the picturesque Yakchich Tower, surmounting an inner entrance to the fortress. We stood a long time on the highest terrace in contemplation of the superb view before our eyes, the vast plain where the Danube winds and twists.

Belgrade, October 12th, 1926

Since two days Nicolas Alexandrovich is in bed with grippe attended by a Russian doctor, as Russian émigrés of every class have taken refuge in Belgrade where they are received in a spirit of Slav brotherhood. Many of these refugees are of the intelligentsia and play useful roles here as doctors, professors in the University, etc. This cannot fail to be beneficial to Serbia where the people are peasants and agriculturists principally, and the intelligentsia is lacking. Russian officers also serve in the Serbian army. After holding out heroically against the bolsheviks in the Crimea in 1920, the Russian general Wrangel brought his army to Serbia. It has since been disbanded.

We feel most forlorn and far away. To pass the time I watch the change of the palace guard each morning beneath our windows. Preceded by a military band, a group of soldiers, smart in red trousers, blue tunics and high boots, gun on shoulder, passes along the royal palace garden wall. This breaks somewhat the monotonous rumble of carts in the street.

Mr. Strandman, former minister of Imperial Russia to Serbia, whom Nicolas knew in other days, called upon him. Mr. Strandman still lives in the Russian Legation, looking after the refugees. As yet the Soviet Union has no foothold in this country. Mr. Strandman enjoys a practically unchanged position and is a personal friend of the king.

Peter Durnovo, a dear friend of Nicolas and son of the well-known statesman and former Minister of the Interior in Russia, also visited Nicolas. He has escaped from bolshevik Russia, where he spent two years fighting the communist government and told us extraordinary tales of those days.

Belgrade, October 10th, 1926

Today, Sunday, we motored past the Topschilder race course and park, to the new summer palace now under construction for King Alexander at Dedinie, near Belgrade. This small palace of Byzantine architecture has colonnades and gracefully arched windows. Light tracery of Byzantine motives ornament the capitals of columns, completing a harmonious ensemble. It is built of white Dalmatian stone with a red tile roof. A lovely little Orthodox chapel is connected to the palace by a covered colonnade. The site is unique with a glorious view over woods and hills on one side, while on the other, far below, lies Belgrade and the Danube weaving its silver ribbon through the plain.

The present popular King Alexander is of the Karageorgevich family, a descendant of Kara George (Black George), founder of the dynasty, a cattle dealer of Topola who gained influence through his gigantic size, his Herculean strength, courage and violence. In 1804 Karageorgevich was elected to lead the Serbian uprising and eventually drove out the Turks. He was afterwards made ruler and became a national hero. The Turks, however, took Belgrade again in 1813, remaining until 1867.

After two Karageorgevich rulers, the Obrenovich family came into power, their reign ceasing only in 1903 with the murder of King Alexander (son of King Milan and Queen Nathalia) and his immensely unpopular queen, Draga. At that time Peter Karageorgevich, grandson of old Kara George, was called to the throne.

During the World War in October 1915, when the Austrians were advancing, the Serbs were obliged to retreat, and their aged monarch King Peter led them with the government and a part of the population on foot through the wild Albanian mountains while his son, Alexander, the present king, valiantly fought the enemy at the rear. During this tragic exodus, the people suffered from cold and privation, and many died by the wayside. At the sea coast, Allied vessels met them and brought them to Corfu, where the Serbian government was established. This organized flight of the Serbs is one of the most dramatic episodes of the war.*

Queen Nathalia of Serbia was a cousin of Eva Callimaki-Catargi, mother of Nicolas Alexandrovich (Basily), a Rumanian by birth and daughter of General Roznovano. After the murder of her son, Alexander (Obrenovich), and the subsequent downfall of the Obrenovich dynasty, Queen Nathalia lived in retirement in a convent on the rue d'Assas in Paris. We knew her there and visited her in the convent. Queen Nathalia was a large, queenly-looking woman, with a very sweet character and occupied herself exclusively with works of charity. She was always most kind to us and I liked her very much.

Belgrade, October 16th, 1926

There has been a ministerial crisis here these last days, and King Alexander has returned from Topola. This morning, just as the palace guard swung down the street with the regimental band playing, we saw the king in the royal gardens wearing a khaki uniform, walking beneath the trees

---

* King Alexander (Karageorgevich) was treacherously murdered in 1934 upon his arrival in France on an official state visit, together with Barthou, French Minister of Foreign Affairs. He was an irreparable loss to Serbia. His Queen was Princess Marie, daughter of King Ferdinand and Queen Marie of Rumania.

with the tall, bent figure of Prime Minister Paschich in ear-
nest conversation. The king is good looking, with dark hair
and a prominent nose, a popular monarch with his people.

Tomorrow, Nicolas Alexandrovich's health permitting,
we will leave Belgrade and return to Budapest.

Budapest, October 19th, 1926

After a last conversation which Nicolas Alexandrovich
had with the Serbian Finance Minister in Belgrade, we left
that remote Balkan country and, taking the Orient Express,
returned to Budapest.

As usual upon arriving in that lovely city, we dropped our
valises hastily and ran to dine at the Hotel Hungaria where
Magyari, a gypsy violinist, plays the violin in the restaurant,
tearing the half-wild, half-plaintive notes of Russian and
Hungarian folk and gypsy songs from his strings. He knew
us and came to our table. Playing into our ears, after the
manner of tzigane violinists, he charmed the hours with
those melodies which inflame the heart and leave it floating
midway between ecstasy and despair.

We ate "fogash," a fish from Lake Balaton and a great
Hungarian delicacy, and drank Tokay wine.

Our rooms in the Hotel Ritz on the quay overlooked the
magnificent panorama of the Danube, with the old town of
Buda on the hill opposite. Here rises the former royal palace,
now the residence of the Regent, Admiral Horthy. Further
to the left soars the great Gellert Hill, with the ruins of a
former Turkish citadel. In 1526, after the battle of Mohács,
the Moslem hordes of Suleiman marched on Buda and dev-
astated the city. The Turkish domination lasted for more
than a hundred and fifty years—until 1687.

The view from the Gellert Hill is incomparable, over the
Danube, as the great river flows through Budapest, and
winds its majestic course across the vast plain.

The city is divided in two parts by the Danube: Buda, the picturesque ancient town, dominates the hill, and across the river, in the plain, lies the comparatively modern city of Pest. The government buildings are principally in Buda where the Prime Minister, Count Bethlen, lives. Here also rises the church of Matthias, begun in 1255, where the kings of Hungary were formerly crowned. Pest has an entirely modern character with wide streets and fine buildings, hotels and theatres. A feature of life here is the promenade on the Danube quay, called the "Corso," where all Budapest walks in fair weather. No carriages are permitted and chairs are placed on the pavement where people sit watching the passing throng or sipping drinks at tables before the cafés. In summer there is music. With sunlight on this peaceful scene, one drifts into a state of dolce far niente, not to be found in other capitals.

Budapest is an elegant city and great charm prevails. Social life and night life are very animated. Hungarian ladies are extremely lovely and Hungarian horses are superb.

We lunched with Prime Minister Count Bethlen and his beautiful wife, Margit. They were friends of Nicolas Alexandrovich many years ago when his father was a Russian diplomat en poste in Budapest. Nicolas was then a small boy of seven, with great dark eyes and a sailor suit.

It was a happy reunion of good friends and they recalled with emotion the days when, as children, they had played together at war and wild Indians with Count Alexandre Khuen Hedervary (now Hungarian Minister in Paris), who was also present. An exquisite portrait of the lovely Countess Bethlen by László hangs in the salon.

On another visit to Budapest at the end of the year, without me, Nicolas spent New Year's Eve with the Bethlens. At midnight the door opened and a little Hungarian pig rushed in all tied up with floating ribbons of the national

colours, to inaugurate the New Year and bring good luck.
This, it seems, is a Hungarian custom.

We also lunched with Count and Countess Karoly, other
old friends of Nicolas, and charming, cultivated people.

Budapest, October 23rd, 1926

Last night we attended a new opera by Zoltán Kodály, a
popular living composer. As our automobile stopped before
the Budapest Opera, an attendant hastened to open the
carriage door, an old man with a white beard, clad in a long
tight-waisted coat of dark cloth, and a tocque on his head
adorned with a white aigrette. This characteristic touch delighted me.

The opera was *Hary Janos* (a man's name). The title is
taken from a poem by a famous poet, Arany, who has made
this name a by-word in Hungary, portraying the type of
boastful peasant who seems prevalent here. The opera is a
series of amusing episodes. Janos, drinking with friends,
tells of his exploits as a young Hussard, exaggerating to his
heart's delight. Dressed in a red Hussard uniform, he goes to
the court of Vienna, where he makes a deep impression on
the king and queen. The Archduchess Marie-Louise falls in
love with him, and the double-headed Austrian eagle bows
his head obsequiously when Janos appears. He wars against
Napoleon, whom he takes prisoner, and refuses the hand of
Marie-Louise, offered by the king, to remain true to his
peasant sweetheart. An absurd farce, very Hungarian and
quite delightful.

Budapest, October 26th, 1926

The weather is cold with sunshine. I walked on the
Fisher-Bastion in Buda, overlooking Pest. This is without
doubt the most magnificently situated city in Europe.

We dined tonight with Mr. von Horanski, president of the Agrarian Bank, with whom Nicolas Alexandrovich is negotiating a loan. A delightful evening.

Upon reaching our host's apartment in the Andrassy Ut 46, Nicolas cried out with surprise and emotion that in this same apartment his own father had lived when en poste in Budapest. Poignant memories brought tears to his eyes.

Our host presented me with a beautiful book on Hungary which touched me. In common with all his compatriots, he bemoans the Peace Treaty of 1919 which gave so much Hungarian territory to Rumania and Czechoslovakia. Hungary lives for the day when this treaty will be revised.

* * *

Prague, July 26th, 1927

Motored yesterday to Spindel Mühle in the Riesengebirge (Giant Mountains) to see Mr. Pospišil (State Bank), who is spending a few weeks at this resort (four hours journey). The road led through lovely country of somber forests and golden fields. Occasionally little hunchbacked hills rose gently from the plain. In the distance we saw two ruined towers of the Hruba Scala castle. As we approached the Riesengebirge, the hills grew higher and we ran along the Elbe River, quite near its source, a small stream rippling over stones.

Spindel Mühle is a much frequented resort. We found Monsieur and Madame Pospišil at St. Peter's tea room, and later had dinner with them, returning to Prague at one a.m.

Prague, July 28th, 1927

Lunched at American Legation today with Minister Einstein and his French wife, who were most cordial and agreeable. Colonel James Logan, U.S. Army (former American observer to the Reparation Committee in Paris after the war) was present, also the Austrian Minister to Rome, Mr. Eger and Madame Eger, with several other Austrians, one of them Countess Schwarzenberg, and also Mademoiselle Schönborn. The present American Legation in Prague formerly belonged to the Schönborn family and was recently acquired by the American government. It is one of the fine old palaces of the "Little Side" (Mala Strana), the most beautiful quarter of Prague, with an Old World garden rising in terraces behind, where the Einsteins have planted many flowers, a lovely effect.

*   *   *

From Prague we went by the Orient Express to Bulgaria, remaining a few days in Sofia. I find no account of that journey in my papers, but the principal event was a luncheon at the United States Embassy with Ambassador Charles Wilson, an old friend from St. Petersburg. Colonel James Logan accompanied us.

After luncheon, while taking coffee in the salon, the Ambassador was called to the telephone and soon returned triumphantly announcing the news that Charles Lindbergh had accomplished his lone flight across the Atlantic Ocean from the United States to France, and had landed the *Spirit of St. Louis* in Paris, amid wild acclamations. We were all greatly excited over this amazing feat which seemed almost a miracle at that time.

We motored to a summer resort in the hills, a two hour drive from Sofia, across desolate country with muddy village roads where barefoot girls walked leading flocks of geese, a primitive sight. In the somber forests of that hill station (whose name escapes me) were numerous dachas (villas) where people from Sofia spent the hot season. They looked very desolate. Among them was the dacha of King Boris, but also rather forlorn.

The thing that stands out in my memory of Sofia is streets lined with jacaranda trees in bloom, like a heavenly blue cloud. Of course we heard many tales of life in that faraway country.

* * *

Paris, June 27th, 1925

Tonight the Bal du Grand Prix, the culminating fashionable event of the Paris season, took place at the Grand Opera. All the wealth, rank and beauty of Paris society filled the loges and balconies. This ball is given annually for the benefit of two French charities over which the Princesse Murat presides. A third of the proceeds goes to the Russian refugees in France. Mademoiselle Marie Maklakov, sister of former Ambassador Basil Maklakov, is head of the Russian Committee, composed of various Russian ladies (including myself).

The performance given represented a Night in the Antilles during the first Empire. A yellow and green striped tent covered the stage, flanked by two tall coconut trees. The loges were decorated and many of the occupants wore bright-coloured turbans and fancy dress, giving a brilliant aspect to the Salle de l'Opera. Tableaux vivants and dances were performed on the stage by people of Paris society. The dancers were charmingly dressed, the ladies in long skirts with short Empire boleros and gay native scarves tied around the head beneath flat straw Martinique hats. Madame Nicolas Raffalovich took part in one of the numbers and danced with much grace and art.

Josephine de Beauharnais, reclining in a hammock borne by two blacks, was dressed in a simple white Empire frock with a reddish scarf, but the most elaborate entrée was the Polish singer, Madame Ganna Walska, in the role of Pauline Borghese, clad in a white and gold Empire garment. The red velvet court train, sumptuously embroidered in gold, was carried by four small Negroes in red satin costumes, with tall red hats. The smallest train-bearer was practically eclipsed by a hat several sizes too large which slipped down over his ears. Undismayed he staggered along manfully and received a hearty applause from the audience.

I wore a new white satin robe de style by Lanvin and felt very elegant as I mounted the Grand Stairway.

Paris, June 1925

Another vivid memory comes back to me.

One hot June afternoon we were invited to tea by the Baronne de Brimont, a charming French femme de lettres, in the gardens of a property in Auteuil, belonging to the Duchesse de Clermont-Tonnerre where Madame de Brimont was visiting. That afternoon she had as guest the Hindu poet, Rabindranath Tagore, who was passing through Paris. He arrived with his son and daughter-in-law, all three in Indian costume, the lady in a ravishing sari. The poet himself wore a long brown robe, with a brown velvet cap, the exact colour of his eyes. With his long grey beard he was a majestic figure. Upon the request of Madame de Brimont, he recited for us some of his poems in Bengali which of course we could not understand, but whose musicality enchanted our ears.

I will never forget that afternoon, the heat, the drowsy garden where bees hummed, and roses lay on gray walls, while the rhythm of Rabindranath Tagore's voice flowed like cool water and we watched his handsome, pensive face and brown velvet eyes.

A few days later they all took tea with us and the poet signed for me, in curly Bengali script, a book of his poetry "The Crescent Moon," which he himself had translated into English.

* * *

In 1926 a great tragedy befell us. Alexandre (Sandro, my husband's son by a first marriage) was killed in an automobile accident while driving his car on the road near Angoulême.

The boy had been tubercular from birth, but with unfailing care his father had kept him for many years with an old Russian nurse in Berck Plage on the Normandy seacoast. He was a dear boy, very intelligent, who grew into a tall, handsome youth and at twenty was in perfect health. For his twentieth birthday his father gave him a small, open automobile, painted bright red, such as pleased the young boys then. Delighted with his car, Sandro left Paris, driving alone to St. Jean de Luz where we were to meet him. An accident occurred, we never knew exactly how, but the boy was killed. The grief of Nicolas Alexandrovich was almost unbearable. To lose his country and then to lose his son. What somber tragedy!

Paris, 1938

After several years Nicolas left the banking house of Field, Glore Co. Later he became interested in studying the plans of the Soviets for their proclaimed improvements and steps forward after the Imperial régime. He began to write an account of their activities, basing all statements exclusively on Soviet figures and statistics, which he read in the *Pravda* and other Soviet publications. In his book entitled *Russia under Soviet Rule*, he also writes in defense of Imperial Russia, bringing out the works either achieved or underway at the time of the revolution, and which would have matured just as well under that régime. There were honest men who loved their country and worked for its welfare, but the Soviets condemned all old Russia as rotten and corrupt, and all the emperors as horrifying as Ivan IV.

Nicolas worked about four years on this book, which was published by Plon in Paris in 1938 in French, and received an award of the Académie Française. At the same time it appeared in Russian, English, and Italian. Nicolas was happy to have written these lines honouring his country so cruelly maligned.

We lived in a small hotel particulier in the rue Alfred Dehodencq, a short, private street near the avenue Henri Martin and the Bois de Boulogne. There was a handkerchief-sized garden. Opposite us, on the other side of a vacant space, the Hotel de Rothschild formed a background. No cars passed. Our street was so quiet, so quiet, it seemed to be a bit of country in the great heart of Paris. The neighbour's elderly black dog, "Béber," would often stretch out in the middle of the street for an afternoon nap. In the spring, in another neighbour's garden, an enchanting Japanese plum tree unfolded its pink flowers like a bouquet. The world seemed a beautiful place.

In the evening Nicolas would sometimes read to me passages from classical Russian authors, translating much of it as my Russian was inadequate. We read Pushkin's masterpiece, *Eugen Onegin*, descriptions of Russian countryside and rivers by Gogol, and the poems of Lermontov. I translated into English Lermontov's *The Angel* (which was printed in the *Russian Review*, in June 1942). The thought in this poem is sublime and uplifting and is among the most beautiful poetry ever written.

The Angel

An angel in the midnight sky,
Flew singing to the world on high,
While moon and stars and clouds in throng
All listened to this sacred song.

He sang of sinless souls that rove
At peace in Heavens sacred grove,
Of God Eternal, Great and Strong,
His unfeigned praise rang out in song.

He bore a soul in his embrace
For Life upon this Earth's sad face.
The song, in that young soul enshrined,
Dwelt living, wordless, undefined.

Throughout all life the young soul yearned,
Sublime desires within him burned,
That holy heaven — song at birth
Could not be stilled by songs of earth.

Lermontov (translated by Lascelle)

Italy

All'Italia,
Italia, Italia, o tu cui feo la sorte
Dono infelice de belleza
Onde' hai funeste dote d'infiniti guai.
—Vicenzo Filicaia, patriotic poet of Florence,
1642–1707

Italy, Italy, thou upon whom Fate bestowed
The fatal gift of Beauty
Whence comes thy tragic destiny
Of infinite woes.

(Translated by Lascelle)

Divine Italy. Each year we went from Paris to that enchanted land, at times by car, crossing the French-Italian frontier on the San Luigi bridge, racing breathless and ecstatic along the Mediterranean, glistening beneath the moon and stars.

Or again, we journeyed by train, for trains were still used for travel in those prehistoric days before the automobile eclipsed them.

Always we returned to Balbianello on Lake Como, to those fragrant terraced-gardens above the emerald lake, whose potent charm had brought us together, and still enthralled us.

We knew the great treasure cities of Italy, and the medieval eagle-nests crowning steep, rugged hills. We knew the mountains, the lakes, the seas, the flowers, and the throbbing songs of this many-faced land, the grandeur and the simplicity.

* * *

191

Milan, October 28th, 1925

A new era has dawned for Italy. Fascism, under the dictatorship of Mussolini, has become more than a political movement. The "Duce" has awakened patriotic enthusiasm in his compatriots. He has brought law and order after the communist manifestations following the World War. Fascist police patrols are everywhere, and an air of confidence and hope reigns.

Mussolini is at the height of power, an idol for the Italian people whose enthusiasm is without bounds.

In commemoration of the Fascist March on Rome, led by Mussolini in March 1922, when he took the Eternal City, today Milan is brave with waving flags. Sixty thousand Black Shirts are present. Mussolini, the great dictator, reviewed them this morning from the steps of the Cathedral. The clamour was immense. The vast Piazza del Duomo was so crowded it was impossible for us to approach. On many street corners bands of music played the inspiring Fascist hymn: "Giovinezza, giovinezza, primavera di bellezza." Soldiers and officers were clad in the traditional black shirts with green army breeches and tasseled caps. The ancient Roman salute, which the Fascists have revived, is seen on all sides. This formal raising of the right arm in greeting is dignified and impressive.

In the evening the city was illuminated and a military band played on the steps of the Duomo before a sea of faces. Blue and white searchlights swept the piazza, now and again disclosing the statue of a saint placed high in the lace-work of the famous Cathedral. In the sky the full moon sailed.

Later Nicolas had an interview with Mussolini. He was received in the Duce's office in the Chigi Palace in Rome, a large room with high windows. In the center on a round table the Fascist insignia were displayed. The dictator's desk was in a corner near the window. His greeting was most cordial, and Nicolas was struck by the strength and magnetism of his personality. His face, extremely mobile, showed great animation, especially his eyes, which are full of light. He spoke of the order that must reign in Italy, repeating that foreign capital had every reason to have confidence. Nicolas possessed a photograph of his strong, bold face, signed, but this has also disappeared in the wars and upheavals which have shaken our violent century.

Postscript: Then came the War, defeat, and disaster. Mussolini fell from power and was assassinated on April 28, 1945, on a little road leading from Lake Como into the hills above. With a few faithful adherents he was fleeing on the highroad from Como to the Swiss border, where he hoped to pass into Switzerland. He had spent the night in a house in the hills, and the following morning as he descended to pursue his flight, was apprehended by a group of leftist resistance partisans, lined up against a stone wall, and shot.

A year or so after this murder we were motoring on the road along Lake Como, and mounted the hill to see the site where the tragedy had occurred.

By the roadside we were shown a rough, grey stone wall, sustaining the garden of a modest villa, and told that here the Duce had been killed.

No shot marked the wall. Nothing indicated the great drama of life and death that had taken place. All was still around us, just a quiet country road like a thousand others. After a tumultuous career, in these tranquil hills, the Duce had met his Fate.

"Ca' del Vento," Reggio d'Emilia, October 31st, 1925

Upon leaving Milan we came to Reggio d'Emilia on the weekend visit to Ambassador Panza and his family in their aerie summer home high in the Apennine foothills, "Ca' del Vento" (House of the Wind).

Ambassador Panza was a colleague of Nicholas's father, and my husband was happy to find again these good friends of former times.

Carina, a daughter, met us at Reggio with the automobile. We drove twenty kilometers through picturesque country adorned with cypress trees, up winding roads, higher and ever higher, to the Panza home set on a hilltop with a stupendous view of every side over the Lombard plain, Parma, Piacenza, the Po Valley and the Apennine range as far as Monte Rosa. The ruins of Canossa stand out with their ghosts of Frederic Barbarossa.

The Ca' del Vento soars like an eagle's nest above the earth, with only sun, wind, and clouds for companions. The hill is covered with trees planted forty years ago by the ambassador himself, and the house is a fine massive stone structure.

After fifty years of brilliant diplomatic career, the ambassador retired here, and spends his time looking after the peasants and the lands. In winter the family moves to Rome where he is called by his duties of senator.

We spent happy days with these friends, touched by their exquisite hospitality, surrounded by wide spaces and the living gold of autumn.

Sicily, November 6th, 1925

We left Naples on the night boat to Sicily. The moon has turned the Mediterranean to quicksilver and the sky was powdered with stars. A warm night of "San Martin's summer."

We came on deck early this morning to watch Sicily awaken from sleep. Ahead, across the placid waters, wrapped in the blue mantle of dawn, the island unfolded the cameo purity of its mountainous profile. Then day broke and sunlight flooded the cold silhouette, warming it into life with the passionate radiance of the South. Shimmering like a pearl in opalescent splendour, the vision emerged, transformed, triumphant, at the edge of the limpid sea. Sicily, realm of the gods, lay before us.

After visiting the treasures of Palermo we left for Messina, where we changed trains for Taormina. A young Italian officer sat in our carriage, resplendent with decorations. He courteously drew our attention to several points of interest on the way. He was a native of Taormina and an ardent admirer of the beauties of his land. "E una meraviglia," he exclaimed constantly. We spoke of Sicily, and he mentioned the strong family feeling existing there. Woe to him who offends this sentiment. Strong in friendship, stronger in hate, and he added: "Ogni siciliano ha una piccola Etna nel anima"—"Every Sicilian has a little Etna in his soul"— which in a few words describes the race.

On a plateau, seven hundred feet above the sea, Taormina lies enthroned.

There was something pagan in the classical purity of the panorama morning revealed. No sound. The radiant atmosphere vibrated with peace. Far below, at our feet lay the blue sea. In the distance the unbroken flank of snow-crowned Etna swept down to join it. The majestic outlines and magic colouring dazzled our eyes. In pagan mythology mortals must have felt thus in presence of a goddess. Such beauty was overwhelming.

The only sign of life was a heavily laden donkey toiling up the mountain followed by an old woman. They disappeared beneath the olive trees in the quivering silence.

We climbed to the ruins of the Greek Theatre on a hillside above Taormina and lingered on the sun-warmed stones, thinking of those pagans who had sat there in the morning of time, facing the radiance of the incomparable panorama we were now contemplating.

The most bewildering sensation of the day was the sound of a Sicilian shepherd's flute, played by a beggar seated at the roadside. He piped an air so penetrating, so sweet that our hearts started at the sound. We seemed to have heard it before, an echo from a former existence. All the youth of the world, all the pagan joy of life were in that alluring tune. It awakened the desire to dance carefree, as the nymphs and fauns of the forest danced in the days of the gods. It lured on over hills and dales and away. Surely thus were the pipes of Pan.

In the train returning to Messina we found the same Sicilian officer, and the deputy of Catania. We expressed our profound admiration of Sicily, which pleased them. The deputy burst into such passionate praise of his country and its beauties that we were amazed. Later we learned that he is famous for his eloquence in the House of Deputies.

At Messina the train was put on a ferry for San Giovanni on the Calabrian shore. We left the Sicilian officer waving his hand on the pier. Cordial people, the Sicilians, if one does not cross them, but do not forget that "every Sicilian has a little Etna in his soul."

Rome, January 6th, 1926

Today is the Befana (Epiphany), the day of the Kings' Magi, when little Italian children receive presents, as children in other countries do at Christmas. A popular celebration on the preceding evening in the Piazza Navone enlivens this festival. Toys and sweets are sold at stands erected for the occasion and usually much noise and blowing of trumpets accompanies it. This year, although crowds gathered in the huge piazza, no merry-making cheered them, as the death of the Queen Mother (Margherita di Savoia, widow of King Umberto) has been announced from Bordighera. Flags in the city are at half-mast with knots of crêpe. Shops have closed their shutters, and many bear the sign: "Chiuso per lutto nazionale." Theatres are also closed.

The Queen Mother was born a princess of the House of Savoia. This made her popular; also being the first Queen of United Italy cast a glamour over her, but her goodness, charm, intelligence and nobility of character made her sincerely loved and respected. Blond, small of stature, she had a regal bearing. One hears of her dignity, beauty, and tact, but above all of her fervent patriotism. Her motto in life was that of the Royal House: "Avanti Savoia." She was a patroness and friend of the arts. Her salon was a rendezvous for literary men and musicians. Carducci, the great poet of modern Italy, dedicated a beautiful poem to the "Regina d'Italia," in which the (then) young Queen appears as the very symbol of Italy.

Today in speaking of the Queen Mother, Madame Panza recalled the many evenings spent with her husband at the Queen's villa in Rome, where they often went from nine to eleven when the Queen received a few friends informally, and of the delightful, cultivated atmosphere reigning there. Ambassador P —— had tears in his eyes when speaking of his dead sovereign. Her praises run from mouth to mouth. For those of her generation, Margherita will always be "The Queen."

Rome, January 11th, 1926

The funeral of the Queen Mother took place, the body having arrived this morning from Bordighera. Along the railroad line, quiet crowds assembled to pay their last respects, kneeling, and deeply moved as the funeral train passed slowly by.

In Rome the casket, met at the station by King Victor Emmanuel and the Crown Prince, was placed on a gun-carriage, surmounted by a single huge wreath of Parma violets from the King and Queen Elena. The King and Crown Prince with the Duke of Genoa, Queen Margherita's

brother, followed on foot with Mussolini. Accompanied by a
cortège in which the red robes of the Law Courts, the white
surplices of priests with burning tapers, and the costumes of
the Campidoglio guards added a picturesque note, the bier
advanced through the city to the Pantheon, where the First
Queen of United Italy was laid to rest beside her murdered
husband, King Umberto.

Rome, February 5th, 1926

An American Catholic friend of my husband's whom he
met in Rome had three tickets for a public audience of Pope
Pius XI in the Vatican, and invited us to accompany him. We
accepted. I borrowed a black lace mantilla, necessary for the
occasion, and this morning at twelve-thirty we stood before
the Vatican.

Leaving the fountains on the piazza splashing in bright
sunshine, we entered by the Bronze Door, where Swiss
Guards stood sentinel, their costumes unchanged since
Michelangelo designed them. Ascending the Scala Pia,
crossing the Damascus Court, we continued up innumerable
stone stairways, ever higher, as if the Holy Father dwelt as
near to heaven as mortal man may go. Swiss Guards, armed
with lances, paced up and down the landings, making a
picturesque note with their yellow and blue slashed costumes and blue berets.

Leaving our coats in a loggia, a lackey, sumptuously arrayed in red satin breeches and broché coat with a white lace
jabot, led us through a frescoed hall to another salon hung in
red with a golden throne at one end. Many people were
seated there, the ladies dressed in black with lace scarves
over their heads, obligatory for an audience. Soon a scarlet-
clad lackey requested us to pass into another apartment and
through several salons where the Palatina Guard, in long-
trousered blue uniforms with magenta caps and gold-fringed
epaulettes, and the Pope's gendarmes, very smart in white

trousers, short black coats and patent-leather knee-boots, with high fur bonnets, and the Noble Guard, with gold Mars-like helmets, were on duty, besides the Swiss, halberd in hand, guarding the outer entrance. Dazzled by all this magnificence, we finally reached a large square corner room, really splendid, the walls hung with deep red moiré silk, and the floor a marvel of coloured mosaics.

We waited in silence. Scarlet lackeys passed in and out. A gorgeous cardinal added a note of splendour. Soon a major-domo appeared, motioning those assembled to kneel. Preceded by several purple monsignori, the Holy Father entered. Two officers of the Noble Guard followed. The Palatina Guard presented arms and left, with the Noble Guard.

Pope Pius XI passed before the kneeling crowd, permitting each person to kiss his ring (an oblong sapphire set in massive silver or platinum) worn on the third finger of the right hand.

Attired in a white wool cassock with a shoulder cape and a broad white moiré silk belt, his feet encased in white socks and red velvet slippers embroidered in gold, a small round cap on his head, and a silver chain and crucifix hanging about his neck, he looked impressive, but he was a brisk apparition, small in stature, with grey hair.

His Holiness walked with a rapid step, quickly encircling the room. Our American friend, an ardent Catholic, had brought with him six rosaries to be blessed. They hung on his arm which he raised as the Pope approached, but apparently His Holiness did not see them. In despair, our naive friend extended his arm, murmuring, "Mr. Pope, my rosaries." His entreaty died on the still air. His Holiness passed on, and stood before the fireplace, raising his hand in benediction, and reciting a Latin prayer, then vanished. We rose to our feet. It had all happened so quickly that we wondered if we had not imagined the scene. For a ceremony of a certain religious nature, it was very cold.

Venice, Sunday, September 1st, 1935

7:30 a.m. Domodossola, Italian frontier. Customs officers board the train silently, without the former cry "Dogana italiana, signori." Extremely civil, they did not even glance at our luggage. We were free to pass.

Domodossola, entrance to Italy, my dream. I raised the window curtain of my compartment and saw before me green hills, stucco houses with red tile roofs, and a wild stream, all bathed in luminous sunshine. The beauty of Italy fell upon me like a blow, and tears stood in my eyes.

For almost an hour the train followed Lake Maggiore. The three islands of that vast sheet of water, Isola Bella, Madre and Pescatori, lay etched on the horizon, clothed in early morning mists. Fields, tangled gardens, pastel-coloured houses, churches, campanile, unfolded. The stations are clean and orderly, usually painted a cheerful raspberry hue, covered with vines. Then Milan, and from there flat fields and fruit gardens. The sun grew hot. We passed Brescia, Lago di Garda, Verona, Vicenza, Padua, and at last Venice, where we were invited by our friends from Paris, Nicolas and Katherine Raffalovich, to spend a week in the Palazzo Barbaro on the Grand Canal, which they had rented for the season.

A servant from the palazzo met us at the station, took charge of our luggage, and led us to an elegant gondola hung with red curtains. Antonio, the head gondolier, and his assistant were proud figures in white suits with red sashes, wide-rimmed straw hats whose red ribbons fluttered behind. Antonio, smiling the engaging smile of the Italian people, helped us into the slim, black gondola, and we started on our way.

The Grand Canal was gay with gondolas and small craft in honour of the Regatta which is run each year on this date. *Bissone,* the luxurious gondolas of former times, precede the racing gondolas down the canal in brilliant array. All the population stands on the balconies of houses lining the canal, which are decorated with rich stuffs and tapestries. The air of gaiety and festivity was quite exciting in the golden sunlight.

At the Palazzo Barbaro, a warm welcome awaited us, and we found a large lunch-party drinking coffee in the richly ornamented salon, among them Hélène de Portes, and her husband Henri, from Paris, also Commandant L'Hôpital, former aide-de-camp to Maréchal Foch.

Later, the whole party was invited to the palace of Count Volpi on the Grand Canal, to see the races. We followed to this imposing palazzo, where Count Volpi, former Finance Minister in Italy and former Governor of Tripoli, was giving a reception. The palace is magnificent and in perfect taste, and a copious buffet was served by numerous black domestics in native costume, evidently brought back by our host from Tripoli.

A large dinner-party took place that evening at the Palazzo Barbaro, which brought the guests together. Among those invited was pretty Princess Aspasia, widow of King Alexander of Greece, who, after a short reign, died, having been bitten by a pet monkey.

Venice, Palazzo Barbaro, September 2nd, 1935

I rose early so as not to miss one golden hour in Venice. At eight o'clock I stood alone on the Piazza San Marco. The sun was gilding the bulbous domes of St. Mark's Cathedral, so strangely Oriental at one end of this piazza enclosed on the other sides by classical façades and Corinthian columns.

The famous pigeons walked close to me on neat pink feet, gazing reproachfully at my empty hands. Some reposed on the warm stones, as birds in a nest. A panther-like cat lay ready to spring. Suddenly the whole flock rose as a single bird and flew to the other end of the great piazza, with a whirr of wings like leaves rustling in the wind. I bought grain in paper cornucopias from an early vendor. The pigeons returned, alighting on my arms and hands pecking at the corn, till several tiers of squabbling birds were hanging like bunches of grapes from my outstretched arms.

Then Nicolas Alexandrovich arrived and we breakfasted at Florian's, eating golden fruits, half-peach, half-apricot, nectar of the gods.

Legend relates that the pigeons of Venice are never found dead on the piazza. When some tragic instinct warns them that their hour has come, they leave San Marco and, flying out over the lagoon, meet death at sea. If this is true, what deep dramatic forces move these gentle creatures to quit the scene of their limited existence? Unafraid, when the summons comes, they fulfill their destiny in wide untrammeled spaces, flying to sea for their "rendezvous with death."

After a week at the Palazzo Barbaro, we left for Lake Como, where we were the guests of General Butler Ames, at Balbianello, paradise on earth.

Tuscany, October 16th, 1935

We always come to Italy in quest of Beauty and she never fails us. In October our trip to the medieval hill-towns of Tuscany was what "dreams are made of." Those towns, are practically intact from the Middle Ages where the mystery of past centuries is as yet free of the poison of our twentieth century. Calm and serene, they crown the hilltops, forgetful of a tumultuous past of clashing swords and warfare between these independent communes. In their primitive streets and wide stone-paved piazza, which seems to be an outdoor salon, one expects to see visions with wide-brimmed hats, black capes, and flashing swords.

Never will I forget the poetry of the Tuscany landscape as we drove from Florence through the Chianti hills, to San

Gimignano. On that splendid October day the strangely clear atmosphere shed honey-coloured light. The distant hills grew mysteriously blue, and we understood where Renaissance painters found the glimpses of azure background they depict in their portraits.

The ochre-tinted soil of the Chianti hills made a brilliant background for the vermillion farm-carts overflowing with purple grapes for the wine presses. These scarlet wagons were drawn by two milk-white oxen with upturned horns. Superb as statues, with creamy skins and noble bearing, they passed us unperturbed. Like mythological beasts, detached from this earth, moving majestically, their luminous, sorrowful eyes fixed on a world beyond. Surely Jupiter took the form of one of these to steal away the maiden Europa.

San Gimignano, Volterra, Siena, Pienza, Montepulciano, Perugia, Assisi, and Gubbio in Umbria, Urbino, and Rimini and Ravenna on the sea, each one lovely and historically interesting, but there is no space to describe them here.

Day was waning as we reached Assisi, the perfect harmony of nature gilded by the setting sun. Church bells rang gently, and peace descended upon the waiting earth.

A religious fervour reigns in Assisi. The spirit of Saint Francis pervades it entirely. Time turns back seven hundred years as yesterday. It is most impressive.

Towards noon we entered the lower church of the basilica and wandered about till we reached a stairway leading to the crypt where the saint is buried. Descending to the sanctuary, feebly lighted by red electric bulbs around the coffin which is barely visible, we stood a moment in contemplation. Suddenly the lights went out and we were in complete darkness, alone, alone with Saint Francis. Evidently seven hundred years separated us, but still—it was too much honour for us.

With outstretched hands we groped our way to a wall, and finally stumbling upon the stairway, we fled as if our lives depended upon it.

Fearing that the priests had turned off the electricity and left the church for the midday rest, leaving us locked up in solitary confinement with their great saint, we rushed to the door which was still open. There a priest told us that the fuse had blown out, and the whole church was in darkness.

It was good to feel the fresh air, and the falling rain.

Portofino, August 26th, 1951

On the Mediterranean coast of Italy, below Genoa, lies the small fishing port of Portofino, an ancient village of romantic beauty, built around a tiny bay with a background of high green hills. Tall, slim houses, rose, yellow, red or cream, weary with age, like veterans of past centuries, lean against each other, encircling the horseshoe-shaped bay where brown-sailed fishing boats come from the sea at night to anchor.

Across the Mediterranean from Portofino, above Rapallo on the Ligurian shore, rises a range of hills, among them Montealegre, upon whose slopes a chapel is dedicated to a Miraculous Madonna. Pilgrims mount the long flight of steps leading to this sanctuary, to invoke the Virgin in her shrine hung with ex-votos.

Once a year the Madonna de Montealegre descends from her mountain for a round of visits to the villages of the surrounding countryside. Carried on the shoulders of four men, she is solemnly welcomed by the clergy and the population, and borne through the town to the local church where she remains overnight. Ardent religious feeling pervades these ceremonies.

Tonight the Madonna honoured with her presence the old fishing-port of Portofino.

She was to arrive by sea, coming in a fishing-boat from Zoagli, a village near Rapallo. We dined on the terrace of

Delfino's restaurant on the quay where the procession was to pass.

The village of Portofino was illuminated to receive the Milagrosa. The silhouette of the church, San Giorgio, patron of Portofino, was outlined with electric lights. Myriads of little candles burned on the window sills of the antiquated houses surrounding the bay, like a necklace. In the cobalt blue sky the full moon shed its magic.

On the quay where her boat would land, the clergy in black cassocks assembled, accompanied by acolytes in white robes and old women dressed in black with black lace scarves on their heads, tied beneath the chin. A deep religious feeling prevailed among this group of people awaiting the arrival of their saint, a feeling of anticipation and veneration.

Suddenly, without a sound, out of the deep blue night, silently gliding over the silky sea, the boat of the Madonna approached. Standing erect at the prow, facing forwards, the life-sized statue of the Virgin, framed in flowers and flooded with lights, was an apparition from another world, a phantom, miraculous and mystical. In her long pale blue mantle, she seemed to smile gently. Was this reality, or was it a dream?

Cannons boomed. Fireworks painted the sky, church bells rang. In a long, broadcasted discourse, a priest exhorted the youth to cultivate Christian virtues. Benevolently the Madonna listened to his oration.

The cortège moved forward, the priests at the head, then the acolytes and little children, singing and holding lighted tapers in their hands. Three young men staggered beneath the weight of an immense black and silver cross. Then, borne on the shoulders of four robust youths, the Madonna advanced, accepting with grace the homages offered her. Old women closed the procession, and the people of the village

followed, each one with a taper lighting their faces, grave and
thoughtful, where peace, contentment, and profound religious fervour reigned.

The procession wound around the small port, then entered
the church of San Giorgio where the Madonna was to pass
the night. The chanting ceased, one by one the flames of the
tapers faded. The ceremony was over, but it left an enduring
memory of Christian faith in the silence of a summer night
beside the Mediterranean.

Memories of Paris, 1925–1939

The years between the wars were a wonderful period in Paris. Culture, elegance and intellect prevailed in spite of political rumblings below. Life in "la douce France" alleviated the sorrow of exile for Nicolas and we loved France as a second country. With the humanism the French have always shown, they assimilated the Russian emigration without complaint. Nicolas had some French blood, an ancestor having served in the army of Napoleon and made the campaign of Egypt with him (Colonel Richardot). I have his sword in my possession.

I remember gratefully the attitude of the French diplomats at the time of the fall of the Russian Empire and their friendliness and comprehension in the train after the Spa Conference in 1920 when Russia was irrevocably lost, and we were in despair.

Also, I will never forget the generosity of the French Artillery officers under Colonel Mimay in Moscow when, after having stood together a week under bolshevik fire in the Hotel National during the revolution in 1917, they took us, with the American Red Cross officers, in their automobiles to their headquarters outside the city, in the Petrovski Park where for several days we enjoyed their hospitality, eating their "singe" (canned meat) and drinking their "pinard" (wine) as the soldiers called the army food, but it was very good. During this time my father with the Red Cross officers arranged a "laisser-passer" for us all to return to St. Petersburg, issued by the bolsheviks. Dear France of happy memories.

*　*　*

Between our trips to various countries we took up again
our life in Paris and attended many delightful social events.

In June 1925, we were invited to an elegant soirée given by
the Marquis Boni de Castellane in his beautiful eighteenth
century apartment. Many members of Parisian society were
present. Crystal chandeliers with myriads of lighted candles
added to the eighteenth century atmosphere which prevailed
during that charming evening, but the heat from the candles
was great as the night was very hot. The Russian Quartet
Kedrov, so much en vogue at that time, sang old Russian
songs and others with deep feeling. Boni as usual was a
perfect host.

This same year we lunched with Boni who had combined a
most original repast. Among the guests was the Princesse
Marie Murat (née Rohan) and later Comtesse Charles de
Chambrun, the Duc de Luynes, Madame Cécile Sorel of the
Comédie Française, and Mademoiselle Kiku Yamata, a
young Japanese poetess. "Gilli-Gilli," an Egyptian fakir
who was amusing Paris society at that moment, was also
present. After luncheon we gathered around him in the salon
while the prestidigitator, wearing a long, striped Egyptian
robe and a red fez, performed various remarkable tricks
which left us breathless. However, he would not permit
Mademoiselle Yamata to approach. She sat on the floor
nearby. "Toi, orientale, toi pas blanche," he said to her.
Evidently he feared her Oriental blood would penetrate his
magic. One trick was amazing. Two of the gentlemen present (one was Nicolas) each held the end of a long stick upon
which a ring belonging to a guest had been placed. They held
the stick tightly and never let it go, but suddenly by some
magic the ring was off the stick and returned to its owner.
Nicolas never did know how it had happened.

During the performance Madame Sorel sat like a statue,
erect and immobile. The little finger of her right hand, where
a great pearl glowed, was outstretched and resting upon a

small table, a theatrical pose of the famous Celimène.

Boni had really given a most unusual program to amuse his friends and the party was a great success.

In Paris, our life was varied, my husband having been so long in the Embassy there knew a great part of Paris society—aristocracy, intellectuals, and political circles, as well as the Russian milieux.

Three great houses stand out in my memory and three grandes dames who were deeply interested in politics and often invited my husband, whose brilliant mind and penetrating vision of events of the day and of the future delighted them, and we spent many agreeable hours in their homes.

These ladies were the Comtesse Greffulhe (née Caraman-Chimay), the Comtesse Jean de Castellane, and the Marquise de Ludre.

The salon of the Comtesse Greffulhe in the large "hôtel particulier" of the rue d'Astorg is famous in the annals of that epoch. Many important and interesting people assisted at her receptions, intellectuals and men of science as well as Parisian society, in short, "Le Tout Paris." The grace and beauty of the Comtesse are proverbial. Moving from group to group, she animated conversations and radiated charm. On the cheminée of the grand salon was placed an exquisite bust of the goddess Diana by Houdon. The resemblance to the Comtesse was striking. Always dressed in black, a long scarf of black tulle framed her lovely face. She painted miniatures and I have seen several beautiful examples of her art. A delicate, fine nature and some inner spirit attracted everyone. The grace of a very great lady in every sense of the word. It is said that once a journalist interviewing her, indiscreetly asked her age. "My age?" she replied. "How can I know? It changes every year."

One afternoon we were invited "en petit comité" to be presented to King Leopold II of Belgium and the Queen Mother, Elizabeth, which I describe elsewhere.

Another great lady was the Comtesse Jean de Castellane, née Talleyrand. In her hotel particulier in the rue de Babylone were many family paintings and souvenirs. Among them a portrait of Dorothée de Courlande who married Edmond de Talleyrand-Perigord, nephew of Talleyrand, and acted as hostess in the French Embassy in London when her famous uncle was ambassador. There was also a lovely portrait of the Comtesse herself by Lázló.

The receptions of Madame de Castellane were always most agreeable. Intelligent and keenly interested in politics, she gathered about her intellectuals and mondains, and the conversation was always stimulating.

At times we would visit her alone. Those were delightful hours when she served us tea from a solid gold tea service, while listening to Nicolas' opinions on political events and discussing them with him. I sat silently by and learned a great deal. Occasionally she related some incident in her earlier life in Germany when she was Princesse Fürstenberg. These informal occasions are a happy memory of this gracious lady we were so fond of. There was such an air about the Comtesse that during those visits I always felt as if time had turned back by miracle, I was in an eighteenth century salon, perhaps that of Madame du Deffand.

In 1928 Amelia Earhart crossed the Atlantic, flying her plane alone, a path-finder, and was greeted with great enthusiasm in Paris, after accomplishing this remarkable feat.

The Minister of Aviation at that time was Pierre-Etienne Flandin, an old friend of my husband, who gave a ''vin d'honneur'' in deference to the celebrated American aviatrix to which we were invited. We also attended a reception given in her honour by the Comte Jean de Castellane, president du Conseil de Paris, and Madame de Castellane, in their residence in the rue de Babylone.

When Miss Earhart mounted the stairway leading to the salon on the first floor, her slight, boyish figure and close-cut blond hair were a surprise in that epoch of longish skirts and champignon hats. Amelia Earhart wore no hat, also a surprise, and a precursor of future fashions. She was most attractive, her bearing simple and charming. I said to her: "We are all very proud of you," and she answered modestly, "Oh, don't say that."

Maréchal Lyautey was also present at this reception, his white hair en brosse, a strong personality. One can well imagine the role he played in French Africa.

Another charming hostess we visited was the Marquise de Ludre whose splendid hotel particulier in the Square du Bois de Boulogne was magnificently furnished and filled with treasures of art, among them several busts by Houdon. All was carried out in the French eighteenth century tradition and the result was superb.

The Marquise had great ardour for politics and brought together in her salon the most interesting personalities of the day. It was always an event to lunch there as we sometimes did.

One year, in October, we were invited to spend a weekend at her sumptuous eighteenth century château in Normandy. A vast court preceded the house and behind, on the side of the park, was a great pond where solitary water-birds (poules d'eau) floated in chilly majesty, uttering melancholy cries in the autumnal silence.

Our hostess had put at our disposition two enormous bedrooms and two baths. My apartment was magnificent. The walls of the bathroom were covered with velours de Gênes, and curtains of the same rich tissue hung at the windows. Bathroom fixtures had simply been added to an eighteenth century boudoir. Washing one's hands in these imposing surroundings was a truly royal rite and I always felt like Louis XIV in the bathtub.

Among other weekend guests was Monsieur Maurice Paléologue, French Ambassador to Russia before the revolution and author of *La Russie des Tsars pendant la Grande Guerre,* his memoires of that epoch.

After dinner, in the course of the conversation, the Ambassador related that driving his car en route to Le Perche, he lost his way and finally arrived before a Trappist monastery. Surely the monks could direct him to the château. He knocked at the door and a monk opened. The Ambassador explained that he had mistaken the road as he had not been in that part of the country since the war.

Apparently the Trappist rule of silence had been scrupulously observed during those years. The monk contemplated him in silence, then questioned: "What war?"

Among the outstanding personalities we knew during the brilliant period between the two wars were three Rumanian ladies who occupied prominent places in the life of Paris and were all gifted writers, or orators. One of these ladies was the Princesse Marthe Bibesco whose book *Katia*, the story of the morganatic wife of Emperor Alexandre II of Russia, Princesse Catherine Yurievsky, became famous in the cinema. I had met Princesse Bibesco in the Rumanian Legation at luncheon when Prince Dimitri Ghika was Minister, and she was most kind and gracious to the timid bride I was at that time. She was a friend of Baroness de Buxhoeveden, and I once accompanied the latter on a visit to the Princesse in her apartment on the Ile Saint Louis whose windows overlooked the Seine. After tea she showed us a small room where she wrote, hung all around with white satin which fell in folds like curtains. The room contained only a bed near the window, where the princesse lay and wrote her books and articles while the Seine rolled its waters at her feet.

Helen Vacaresco was a brillant orator and Rumania's delegate to the League of Nations. I once heard her make an improvised speech after a big dinner at the Cercle Interallié which was remarkable. We occasionally went to her when she received in her apartment on the rue Washington where she lived with her mother.

Both of these ladies were distant relations to Nicolas' mother who was Rumanian, Eva Callimaki-Catargi, daughter of the Rumanian Minister of Foreign Affairs and later Minister to Paris and London. Prince Ghika and his lovely wife were also distant relatives as all the families of the Rumanian aristocracy were intermarried and the number was comparatively small.

Another shining light in Paris was the Rumanian Comtesse Anna de Noailles, a poetess and author of *Le Coeur Innombrable*, which was much talked of then. We met her at dinner one night in the house of a Russian friend, Marie Scheikevich, formerly Madame Carolus-Duran, daughter-in-law of the painter Carolus-Duran. The Comtesse de Noailles was a tiny person, brune, with enormous black eyes in a small white face. She liked very much to talk while everyone present listened. That evening she conversed all through dinner and afterwards lay on a chaise-longue in the middle of the salon which had been placed there for her while the other guests gathered around her, listening with great interest to her conversation, a tableau of Madame Récamier.

Marie Scheikevich was an interesting personality, and her salon was a meeting place for writers and intellectuals. Her book of memoirs and her correspondence with Marcel Proust have been published. We often went to her and the conversation was always stimulating. We were very fond of her.

So many other names present themselves to memory as I write, and I recall with emotion the friendship of the Duchesse d'Uzès, the Bentley Motts (the Military attaché at the American Embassy), Pierre de Fouquières, and his beautiful Spanish wife and his brother André de Fouquières, the great mondain, while Pierre was Chef de Protocole, the Comtesse de Portes, Hélène, who made herself famous at the beginning of the war in 1939 and perished in an automobile accident.

A fantastic, versatile Russian lived in Paris at that time. A former diplomat, the Russian revolution left him without a bone in the cupboard as it did everyone else, and he turned

sculptor in order to live. Prince Serge Yurievich had great
talent. He made busts of many prominent men of his day and
his statue of a dancer, "La Natova," was bought by the
French Government and exhibited in the Grand Palais. He
was very "bohème," and his house in Boulogne was frequented by many Russian émigrés, and others. The outer
grill to the property was never locked; anyone could enter
and the house was often empty. Nicolas once asked him why
he did not put a lock on the grill and he answered that he had
never thought of it which made my husband laugh. They
were old friends. He had a beautiful Montenegrin wife, a
relation to the Queen of Italy (wife of Victor Emmanuel III).
In their salon was a large photograph of her cousin, then
Crown Prince Humberto. One night the princess returned
home very late, found the house empty except for a
"clochard," who lived under a nearby bridge and was sleeping peacefully beside the photo of the Crown Prince of Italy.
He aroused himself as she entered and offered to leave, but
he was an old acquaintance and the princess told him to
remain and went upstairs to her room. "Were you not afraid
he would steal something valuable?" we asked her husband.
"Oh, no," he answered "Clochards have a code of honour.
They are very honest."

A Russian seigneur of vast culture, Alexandre Polovtzov,
once master of a great fortune in Russia, had installed with
his beautiful wife an antique shop in Paris, as he also had lost
everything in Russia when the bolsheviks took over. He and
Nicolas Alexandrovich were very good old friends from
Russia, and we saw them frequently. He was most charming
and erudite, and we greatly enjoyed our hours spent with
them. He also wrote books of travel, delightful accounts,
such as the *Land of Timur*, written in French, and a book on
Naples, full of charm, in English, as well as a narration of the
favorites of the Empress Catherine of Russia, all written

with the charm and erudition which characterized him. Unfortunately, his books are out of print today.

Samad Khan, the Persian Minister to Paris, was an old friend of Nicolas' father and my husband had known him for years. He sometimes lunched with us and these were always memorable occasions. He was a most charming man and we always thought of him as a bachelor or widower.

One day, perhaps in 1938, he invited us to his home for luncheon. The Legation was installed in a villa in a quiet quarter of private dwellings. Alone, without Nicolas who was to join me there, I arrived at one o'clock and was introduced into a large, fine reception room where I immediately came face to face with the Orient. A fountain of clear, pure water fell tranquilly down a tiled wall, splashing gently into a small pond below, creating an atmosphere of peace and harmony. At the further end of this salon, on a low platform, an elaborate, high-backed red and gold chair had been placed, evidently in view of a possible visit of the Shah of Iran to Paris.

Madame Philippe Berthelot was the only other guest and together we awaited the host. Suddenly, to my stupefaction, the door opened and a lovely young French woman entered, holding two little girls by the hand. She came to me and said: "I am so glad to know you, Madame Basily. My husband has often spoken about you to me. These are our daughters, Kadeja and Shamsi," presenting the two angelic children. I had the presence of mind not to faint from surprise. Madame Berthelot already knew. Then Samad and Nicolas arrived and nothing more was said. Thus, this dear old Persian friend had been married for some years, but had never mentioned it to us, keeping his wife in the background in true Oriental fashion. With the more free mode of life in Iran, under the Reza Pahlevi régime, he had dared to show her.

After a delightful luncheon, Samad led us to his library and there, seated in a comfortable armchair, with little Shamsi on his knees, he read aloud to us, in Persian, poetry by the greatest Persian poet, Firdousi. We of course understood nothing, but the music of the verses charmed us with harmony and the perfume of the Orient.

Le Clos Saint Nicolas

During those years we possessed a small property in the region of Fontainebleau, near the picturesque town of Moret-sur-Loing, a jewel of past centuries set beside the gentle willow-fringed river Loing (classed as an historical monument). Our property lay between Moret and Montigny, in the village of Ecuelles, at the edge of the Canal-du-Loing, bordered with tall poplar trees. *Chalands* (barges) passed lazily before our door, carrying petrol and other merchandise from one end of France to the other by a network of canals. The life on board these chalands was interesting to observe, the man steering, his wife, a solid bourgeoise, hanging clothes on the line, children eating apples, a black dog barking violently, a canary in a cage between white curtains at the window of the small cabin—a whole world floated by.

Our house, built at the end of the eighteenth century, was very modest, three stories, grey like village houses of that period in France. Behind, a garden was enclosed by high ivy-covered walls. A rustic stone statue of St. Nicolas stood in one corner and the garden was filled with zinnias, making a flame of colour. A large garden surrounded house and enclosed garden and the property was named "Le Clos St. Nicolas."

Here we spent some months in summer in that ideal region of l'Ile-de-France, so evocative of "la douce France," of vanished centuries. My father was with us in this secluded retreat and the days there were quiet, blessed with peace and

Le Clos Saint Nicolas—the garden
(Photographed by Nicolas de Basily)

harmony. Often, late at night, we left Paris in the big white Ballot, with Pierre, the chauffer at the wheel and flew through the forest of Fontainebleau, dark, mysterious and fascinating at midnight to the Clos St. Nicolas, asleep beneath the stars.

Daily we went to the Palais de Fontainebleau to walk in the splendid "jardin anglais," beside the carp pond and we knew every stone of that superb palace built by François I.

An hour by automobile brought us to the Chateau de Lagrange, the chateau of Lafayette, at that time in the hands of Comte Louis de Lasterie, a cousin of Nicolas' friend, Comte Charles de Chambrun, both descendants of the famous French general.

Lagrange was a medieval castle with two immense towers crowned with pointed roofs (en poivrière) and walls at least

Statue of St. Nicolas
(Photographed by Nicolas de Basily)

two meters deep. Lafayette's private study in the tower was intact, and we saw there a personal souvenir of the general, piously kept, a pair of chamois-skin gloves with "General Lafayette" daintily embroidered in pale blue silk on the wrist.

We went there sometimes for tea with Monsieur de Lasterie.

Baroness Sophie de Buxhoeveden

Nicolas Alexandrovich had a childhood friend who often visited us in our home in the rue Alfred Dehodencq in Paris, Baroness Sophie de Buxhoeveden, former lady-in-waiting to the Empress Alexandra Feodorovna of Russia and daughter of a Russian ambassador. The baroness was a person with rare qualities of soul, elevation of character, and loyalty. I admired her greatly and we became very good friends.

In winter she lived in Kensington Palace in London with the Marchioness of Milford-Haven, sister of the Empress Alexandra. The rest of the year she spent on the continent, often visiting friends and at times coming to us. She wrote a book entitled *The Life and Tragedy of the Empress Alexandra*, which is very fine, as well as her pre-revolutionary memories, *Before the Storm,* both written in English, which she possessed perfectly. These books, published in London, are unfortunately out of print today. In the latter volume is a chapter on the "Emperor Nicholas II as I knew him." (My copies of these books are in the Basily Collection in the Hoover Institution in Stanford, California.)

For many years lady-in-waiting to the Empress, she lived in the intimacy of these cruelly maligned sovereigns, whose kindness, generosity and other fine qualities she emphasizes in her books. Her loyalty and devotion to the Imperial family were without limit, and in return they were very fond of her, calling her "Isa" as her friends did, or some other pet name which I cannot now recall.

The health of the Empress was always delicate. Often she lay upon a chaise-longue in the mauve boudoir, surrounded by numerous family photos in the nineteenth century manner, while Isa sat beside her taking down letters the Empress dictated.

The baroness told me many things about the family and their life in Tsarskoe Selo, as we sat around the fire in the evenings, but she was absolutely discreet and did not speak of them generally.

However, one incident she narrated happened at the "Stavka," the Russian General Headquarters at Mogilev on the Dnieper. The Tsar spent the whole war there and occasionally the Tsarina came from Tsarskoe Selo to visit him

with the daughters and her suite. (The Tsarevich was often
with his father at the Stavka during that time.) On one
occasion, after luncheon, they all walked in the gardens to
the edge of the Dnieper. Here the young Tsarevich Alexei, a
charming boy, mischievously seized the parasol the Baroness de Buxhoeveden was carrying and threw it in the river.
The Emperor reprimanded the young prince and he himself
waded into the stream to recuperate the lost property.

Baroness de Buxhoeveden was with the Imperial family
during the agonizing months they were held prisoners in
captivity in the Palace at Tsarskoe Selo. When the bolsheviks came to power, the Imperial family was banished to
Siberia. At that time the baroness was ill with typhoid and
could not accompany them, as did the Comtesse Hendrikova and other members of the suite. The sovereigns
crossed the vast continent in the train, then journeyed by
boat up the Tiumen River, passing the native village of their
evil genius, Rasputin, to them a holy man. Their destination
was Tobolsk. Here they were interned in a house surrounded by a high wooden fence. When the baroness was
well enough to travel, she loyally took the long journey
across Siberia and, after various adventures, joined the family in Tobolsk, but was not permitted to enter their dwelling.
She lodged across the street with the other members of the
suite, and they could only make signs to each other from the
windows.

The simplicity, the kindness, the resignation of the ex-
monarchs were gaining the favour of the population of Tobolsk, as they had that of the guards at Tsarskoe Selo before,
and the bolsheviks decided to remove them to Ekaterinburg
in the Ural Mountains. Baroness de Buxhoeveden, with
Comtess Hendrikova and others of the suite, accompanied
the stricken sovereigns who, upon arrival in Ekaterinburg
were taken from the train and led to the Ipatiev house, to
their tragic, inhuman fate. Isa, on the contrary, was left with

the foreigners of the suite, Mr. Gibbs, the English tutor to the Tsarevich, and Monsieur Gilliard, his French tutor, and others. The name Buxhoeveden is of Danish origin, but the family was entirely Russian. Her name, however, led the ignorant bolsheviks to believe that she too was a foreigner and thus her life was saved and she was able to leave Ekaterinburg with them. The Comtesse Hendrikova was killed in the cellar where the people in power murdered the Imperial family, one of the most horrible crimes in the history of the world.

Another False Anastasia

In 1936 (as I remember) a person calling herself the Grand Duchess Anastasia Nicolaievna, youngest daughter of the murdered Emperor, Nicholas II, addressed a letter to the Baroness de Buxhoeveden, requesting an interview with her in Paris, with the idea that the baroness would recognize her as the daughter of the Imperial sovereigns, so much talked about, and who pretended to have escaped from the inhuman murder of the family by the bolsheviks in a celler in Ekaterinburg in 1918.

The person in question was not the Tschaikovskaia-Anderson who for years had made a world-wide uproar for recognition. No, this was another imposter posing as the Grand Duchess Anastasia. She had lived for some years in the Middle West of the United States, having been taken in and cared for by two very kind American ladies who believed in her implicitly and had brought her to Europe to be recognized and reinstated.

However skeptical, the baroness, who was in Brussels, came to us in Paris so the interview took place in our home at the date given. As the moment drew near for this person to appear, the baroness became greatly agitated. Was it possible? Could such a thing be possible? Her emotion was pitiful.

Breathless, she waited on the third floor of the house, in my father's apartments which she occupied, looking feverishly out of the window for the arrival of the pretended daughter of her Emperor. Nicolas Alexandrovich and I were with her.

At last a taxi stopped before our door. A small foot in a high-heeled slipper descended. The baroness sighed. "That is not my Grand-Duchess," she murmured sadly. It seems that Anastasia had rather large feet and could never have worn small shoes with high heels.

I withdrew, leaving Nicolas with the baroness. A small person, the self-named Anastasia, entered the room with the two American ladies. She threw herself upon the baroness, exclaiming: "Oh, Madame Basily, I remember you from Russia." (I was not married at that time.) The baroness drew herself up with all the chilly hauteur of the Russian court and answered frigidly: "I am not Madame Basily, I am the Baroness de Buxhoeveden." "Oh yes, of course, Sophie, Sophie." The baroness was always called "Isa" by her friends and some affectionate pet name by the Imperial family with whom she lived so many years. She let that pass.

There was nothing in this person in common with Anastasia Nicolaievna. She narrated her escape from Ekaterinburg after the slaughter of the other members of the family. Wounded, she was picked up by a muzhik, put in a cart, covered with straw, and driven away. It was all rather vague. I do not know what else she related as I did not write it down at the time, but Isa kept the record, which she promised to give to me, but we forgot. The pretender, who used the name of Eugénia Smith, recalled several things, saying she remembered them from Russia, things which she could have read in any book on the subject. The interview was long and stormy, with this person and the two American ladies insisting on her identity, but the baroness was inflexible. This was NOT Anastasia Nicolaievna.

They returned the following day. This time the baroness had called in Dr. Kostritsky, dentist to the Imperial family in

Russia, who knew them well and was now living in Paris. He entered, cast one look at the pretender, then said in a low voice to the baroness: "Why did you bother me?"

During this last conversation I was talking with the American ladies in another salon. They were disconsolate at the failure to convince the Baroness Buxhoeveden.

"But she IS the Grand-Duchess Anastasia," they insisted.

"How do you know?" I enquired.

"Why SHE HERSELF told us so," replied these kind, naive ladies.

And so it ended.

The baroness was frequently questioned about the other false Anastasia in Berlin who also claimed to be the daughter of Emperor Nicholas II, whose cries and protestations echoed around the world and made her famous under the name of Tschaikovskaia-Anderson, but was never able to establish her identity.

The baroness replied that after this person had been rescued from drowning in a canal and placed in a hospital, the Grand-Duchess Olga, sister of the Emperor and therefore the aunt of Anastasia, went to Berlin in order to see this pretender and establish if she could possibly be the Emperor's daughter, and her niece. Upon her return to Paris the Grand-Duchess stated: "Decidedly NO," which was conclusive. In her book of memoirs the Grand-Duchess confirmed this statement.

* * *

Days to Remember

Paris, February 2nd, 1935

This Sunday morning Nicolas Alexandrovich and I went to the Bibliothèque Nationale to see an extraordinary exposition of 318 letters written by Napoleon to the Empress Marie-Louise after the abdication when she had left him to return to her father in Vienna, and he remained alone. These letters were recently acquired in London by the French Government from the Montenuevo family, descendents of Marie-Louise and Neiperg. They are of great historical interest, stretching over a period of five years, from his betrothal to the Austrian archduchess, including his invasion of Russia, the abdication, and his exile on Elba. In them he displays a most courageous attitude in face of his tragic fate and vicissitudes. No word of complaint for himself, only solicitude for her and deep regret at having brought her into such a position. From Elba he writes his great desire to have her and "le petit roi" join him, which is pitiful. In these private letters to his Austrian wife, Napoleon shows himself to be really a great man and very human.

These are the letters which Frédéric Masson, the famous historian of Napoleon, so keenly desired to discover and was disconsolate, fearing that Marie-Louise had destroyed them.

                                        Paris, January 1st, 1937

We are at the threshold of a new year and last evening awaited it together, Nicolas and I, sitting quietly at home. 1936 brought communist labour troubles, a Labour government to France and civil war to Spain, while in England, Edward VIII, king and emperor, renounced the throne of Britain for Wallis Simpson.

1936 took away our beloved Scotty, Larry. He went on November 19th, leaving us disconsolate. I walked the streets, weeping.

Christmas was a peaceful day. That evening we gathered a few friends around our table. Two five-branch silver candelabras holding red candles shed warm light upon a mass of poinsettias in the center. Among our guests was Monsieur August de Radvan, a distinguished Polish gentleman, and brilliant pianist, known to all Paris and the honoured guest of many Parisian hostesses.

After dinner and coffee around the fire in the salon, Monsieur de Radvan went to the piano, unrequested, a gracious gesture, and began to play Chopin, which was his specialty. Playing only Chopin, he enchanted the hours by his interpretation of the divine music of his inspired compatriot. With exquisite nuances and delicate sensibility, waltzes and études followed one another brilliantly. At the end the "Polonaise" burst forth with all the fire of patriotism which filled his exalted Polish heart. In this passionate interpretation he laid bare the soul of Poland. We sat in the firelight, listening to this great artist's interpretation of those sublime harmonies, into which he put his whole glowing Polish spirit.

When he finished, M. de Radvan turned towards us his fine face, with black eyes and a crown of silver hair and, by the dying fire, related an exquisite story of Maréchal Foch, who loved Chopin's music. "I was once invited to play Chopin for Maréchal Foch and his Etat-Major. At the end the Maréchal exclaimed to the officers of his suite: 'He who does not know Chopin, does not know Poland, and he who does not know Chopin played by Radvan, does not know Chopin.' A few days later Maréchal Foch came to my apartment, accompanied by several of his officers, to thank me for my playing and to bring me a signed photograph of himself. As we talked together, the Maréchal said: 'I should be happy to hear you play Chopin's "Funeral March" some day; I am sure that rendered by you it would not be the same thing I hear at military funerals.' I should have immediately gone to the piano and played the "Funeral March," but the Maréchal was pressed for time, so I replied: 'A votre disposition, Monsieur le Maréchal. Je le jouerai quand vous le voudrez.'

"The Maréchal left. I never saw him again. Soon after that visit he fell ill and died. The day of his funeral, the cortège followed the wide Esplanade des Invalides to the Invalides, where they buried him, near Napoleon. The windows of my apartment gave onto the Esplanade, and as the cortège passed, I flung them wide open and then and there played

for this great soldier now dead, the "Funeral March" I had
not been able to play for him living."

Paris, January 9th, 1937

Darling Papinka,*
   Last night Nicolas' dear old friend, Charles de Chambrun
and his wife dined here. As you know, Chambrun was the
former Ambassador to Rome. He has just been retired from
the diplomatic service, having reached the age limit. He
spoke of this in his usual brilliant manner, saying: "J'ai
vingt-cinq ans. Mon coeur a vingt-cinq ans. Evidemment
Monsieur Léon Blum a découvert que j'en ai d'avantage, et il
m'a mis à la retraite, mais pour moi, j'ai toujours vingt-cinq
ans."
   It is a pity that Blum did not leave him in Rome, where he
has made many friends, and was on excellent terms with
Mussolini, and might have been useful to France.
   The Comtesse de Chambrun (née Marie de Rohan) is very
intelligent, and always sparkling and amusing. We were
speaking of America and she said: "America is a wonderful
country, but things go so fast there that no one has time to
dream, and if one cannot dream, 'a quoi bon la vie?' "
   Madame de Chambrun writes and paints. One day I was in
her bedroom where she has decorated the walls herself with
flowers, birds and paysages, anything that comes into her
head. Each time she is not feeling well and must stop indoors, she adds something to the wall decoration. Pointing to
a small frog huddled in a corner, she remarked: "Voilà.
Cette grenouille représente mon dernier rhume de cerveau."

Paris, January 30th, 1937

Darling Papinka,
   We have been very busy lately. On January 12th, we
lunched with the Marquise de Ludre. Monsieur Joseph Cail-

---

* "Papinka" is the Russian diminutive for "Papa."

laux was present, which interested Nicolas greatly. We dined one night at the Hungarian Legation. The minister, Comte Khuen Hedervary is a childhood friend of Nicolas'. Their friendship dates from Budapest, when Nicolas' father was en poste there and Nicolas, about five or six years old, wore a blue sailor-suit and they called him "Coco." He and Khuen fought wild Indians together. The Comtesse Khuen, also Hungarian, is charming and does the honours of the Legation delightfully.

Recently the Khuens dined here with Louis Bréguet, the great French airplane constructor, and Madame Bréguet, also old friends of Nicolas. The charming Général Lasson, Chef de la Maison Militaire of the President, and Madame Lasson were also present, with the Montcabriers and the lovely Marquise de St. Chamans, and Ambassador and Madame Frangulis (Greek diplomat). An interesting evening. Ah yes, also the French député, Chappedelaine.

We went to the Comédie Française to hear Racine's *Bérénice* with the outstanding actors Yonnel and Escande. Madame Germaine Rouer in the title role was divinely dressed in a splendid flame-coloured flowing robe by Lanvin. This play has been revived lately with renewed interest since the abdication of King Edward VIII of England last December.

We went to the Sèvres Porcelain Factory one morning on a tour arranged by the delightful Marquis d'Abartiagues, of Basque origin, who often takes groups of friends to some museum or other place of interest.

One afternoon the Comtesse Witte, widow of the former Russian statesman, came to tea with her daughter Vera, Madame Naryshkin. Our Italian friend, Marquis Farinola, and his wife, and the Comtesse de Seconzac were also present. Nicolas had known the Comtesse Witte and her daughter for many years. As a young man in St. Petersburg he was often invited to her home where her illustrious husband was most kind to him. Often he spent long evenings along with the old Finance Minister, who talked to him of many things and took pleasure in the company of this boy of twenty who was preparing for a diplomatic career. These are happy memories for Nicolas and he talked of them to the Countess.

She and her daughter have an apartment in Paris. We called on her recently and saw some beautiful Russian furniture and many photographs of Count Witte.

One day the Countess paid us a visit and remained a long time, recalling old times. Finally she rose, exclaiming: "But it is very late. I must go. In former times in the country in Russia when we went to pay a call on a neighbour, the coachman would inquire upon arrival: 'Shall I unharness the horses?' meaning would the visit be a long one. Surely the horses would be unharnessed here today."

Tonight Welles Bosworth (American architect for Rockefeller for the restoration of Versailles and Fontainebleau) and his charming French wife, dined here with René Grousset, famous Orientalist and savant, curator of the Musée Cernuschi of Oriental art, and author of books of great erudition on these subjects. Mary Churchill Humphrey also dined and we greatly enjoyed these delightful guests.

Paris, February 15th, 1937

Darling Papinka,

We lunched the other day at the Italian Embassy with Ambassador and Madame Cerruti. Monsieur Cerruti is an ambassador of great value. He has a strong, handsome head, like an old Roman coin. The Flandins were the guests of honour at this luncheon and we were happy to see them.

Last week we had tea with the Comtesse Jean de Castellane, who received a few friends. She is always very gracious and stimulating. I have the impression with her of being with a grande dame of the eighteenth century.

On Tuesday we went to the lovely Comtesse Greffulhe to see paintings done by Lady Clark, wife of the retiring British Ambassador to France, Sir George Clark. The paintings

were in the modern style and I greatly preferred two miniatures exposed in a far corner of the salon, admirably executed by the Comtesse herself. One of Sir George Clark was
only half finished, but another miniature of Lucien Romier of
the Figaro was very fine. The most remarkable of all her
work was a miniature of the Comte Greffulhe who died a few
years ago. The Comtesse has great talent for this art.

Nicolas Alexandrovich is dining tonight with friends at the
Cercle de l'Union, one of the oldest and most exclusive
clubs in Paris. It retains its old-world atmosphere. Lackeys
in knee-breeches and silk stockings serve. The library with
solemn leather-bound volumes lining the shelves, and a large
round table, is a fine, dignified room, worthy of former
centuries. Nicolas likes to go there where he finds old friends
and interesting conversation.

Monsieur de Radvan lunched here the other day with us
alone. His conversation is invariably animated and of deep
interest. He quoted Pushkin's famous poem "To the Poet,"
saying that he himself always repeated it before a concert.

In the evening we went to the Comédie Française to see
Le Chandelier by Musset, charmingly done by Madeline
Renaud and Esande, two great artists.

Paris, October 4th, 1938

In early September it became evident that Hitler intended
to annex part of Czechoslovakia to Germany. The Austrian
"Anschluss" had been so successful that he planned to
appropriate the outer fringe of Bohemia, or Sudetenland,
with a German-speaking population of about three million.
On September 15th, the British Prime Minister made an
endeavour to prevent further plundering of neutral territory.
He flew to Berghof, Hitler's retreat near Berchtesgaden in
Bavaria, for a conference with the Nazi leader, but the latter
did not desire a peaceful solution of his differences with
Czechoslovakia. He intended to show the world what New

Germany could do. Mr. Chamberlain again flew to Godesberg on the Rhine, but again the dictator would not come to terms.

On September 13th, my father returned from Morocco where he had spent August in Fedala, near Casablanca. He had contracted malaria, unhappily, and upon arrival, went to the American Hospital under Dr. Fuller's care. This complicated the situation for us in case of war, as he was too ill to be moved.

The French authorities ordered everyone not having a fixed occupation in Paris to leave the city. The whole population was to be evacuated and arrangements were made by them to house the people in surrounding towns and villages. House-owners received a pamphlet from the Prefecture of Police, Department of Passive Defense, as follows: "Ce qu'il faut faire pour vous protéger en cas d'attaque aérienne," "All means of defense will be used to stop enemy planes, nevertheless a few might get through, so do not wait for them to be over you. LEAVE, if nothing keeps you here. At the first serious threat, LEAVE, if you have relations, friends, a house or a cabin in the provinces, LEAVE with your family. You may return as soon as the danger is over. Do not laden yourself, take only clothes and food. Do not wait, LEAVE. To leave in time is to avoid the crowds."

We received one of these booklets which also advised the Paris population to seek underground shelter in case of raids, but there were no adequate shelters, and few gas masks were available. They could be ordered for some future time, but in that hour of need the people were almost defenseless against gases. The city of Paris sent around truckloads of sand, dumping a heap before each house with the order to carry it to the top floors, to be used in case fire broke out caused by incendiary bombs.

A fine spirit reigned in France during those days. The danger from without united the French people. Certain classes of reserves were called out pending the general mobilization, should Hitler declare war. Each man obeyed his duty. The people were calm, courageous, and cooperative. The famous saying became true. "Au-dessus de tout, il y a la France."

War lighting was introduced into Paris. The great luminous globes that make Paris the City of Light by night were replaced by small cups painted black, giving forth a feeble beam, and would not be visible to enemy aircraft. Our little street, usually so cheerful, became lugubrious. The maid's husband had been called to the army, and Helene, poor girl, was weeping. The house servant, Leon, was awaiting the call of general mobilization, and Marie, the cook, was packed ready to leave. My father was still in the hospital, and our dearly beloved home was a sad place.

On September 27th, Hitler threatened to mobilize. We then decided to pack our Russian paintings, which Nicolas had saved from the Russian revolution and send them to Le Havre, where we intended to take my father as soon as he could travel. Covers were put on the furniture, pepper on the carpets, as we intended to close the house. Nicolas desired to offer his services to France, and I too wished to do something.

On the memorable September 28th Hitler threatened to mobilize at two o'clock. My father was then able to travel to Le Havre by car, so we all set off in our automobile with my aunt and the little dog. The paintings were on the roof.

The road was crowded with cars containing families leaving the capital. Men were taking their wives and children to some place of safety before returning themselves to join the army. These cars were pathetic, the heart of the nation seemed to be bare and beating in these families fleeing from the spectre of war, with mattresses, bedding, kitchen utensils, and bird-cages tied on the car or overflowing on the roof.

At six o'clock we reached Le Havre and went to the Hotel Frascati where we had reserved rooms; the house was full of refugees. The following day my dear father was able to embark on a United States ship for New York and our anxiety for him was over.

On September 29th, Chamberlain, Deladier, Mussolini, and Hitler met. Mr. Chamberlain, who it appears dislikes to travel by air, flew like a dove to Munich with an olive branch in his mouth. Peace was saved, but it was a sad peace for the Allies and a bloodless victory for Germany. The tension slackened but everyone wondered when, and where, the Nazi aggressor would strike again.

London, October 1938

On October 18th, five days after our return from Berlin, we left Paris for London and, after a terrific crossing from Calais to Dover, and a night spent in Dover to recuperate, we reached London, the third European capital we had visited since the September crisis.

The city was quite gay. After seven o'clock, the men were in white ties and tails, and the décolleté ladies wore their hair piled high on the heads in curls, after the 1900 fashion now revived, which the British call Edwardian. Piccadilly was astir with high London taxis and crowds entering brightly lit cinemas and theatres. Life seemed easy and attractive, vastly different from recent war aspects of Paris and proletarian Berlin.

Nicolas found here an old Russian friend and colleague, Monsieur Sablin, a former diplomat, who, towards the end of the Imperial régime, was chargé d'affaires in London. His home is still the headquarters for any remains of former Russian enterprises. A fervent patriot, his dwelling was a monument to the Russia he loved and served so ably. All was Russian there and the flagstaff with the former Imperial flag met the eye upon entering, as well as two large brass plaques engraved with the office hours of the former embassy, which Monsieur Sablin had taken with him upon leaving when the bolsheviks seized the embassy in 1917.

The furniture in light Karelian birch, the bibelots, the lovely portrait of the Grand Duchess Marie, daughter of Emperor Nicholas I, the life-sized paintings of various Russian rulers, signed photographs from the Imperial family, and an aquarelle of the Tsarevich Alexei as a small child form a touching shrine of the lost, loved country. The portraits of the martyred sovereigns Nicholas II, last of the Romanovs, and Alexandra Feodorovna add a note of tragedy. Nicolas and I were deeply moved by the atmosphere of old Russia reigning in this home of an exile in a foreign land.

We spent an evening here, a soirée given in honour of the famous school in St. Petersburg, the Lycée Alexandre, which was Nicolas' college as well as Sablins, founded by Emperor Alexandre I and attended by Pushkin. A few members of the Lycée still lived in London. Our host made a charming speech and also mentioned Nicolas' book, *Russia under Soviet Rule,* which had just appeared in English. It was a delightful evening penetrated by Russian charm and Nicolas met many old Russian friends. Baroness de Buxhoeveden was present, also Grand Duke André, son of Grand Duke Cyril.

We lunched one day at the Oliver Harveys (he later became Lord Harvey of Tasburgh), delightful people whom we had met when Mr. Harvey was in the British Embassy in Paris. He is now in the Foreign Office. We also lunched at the Perownes, Mr. Perowne being another diplomat from the Foreign Office. Nicolas had numerous interviews with newspaper men of all kinds concerning his book *Russia under Soviet Rule.* The *Times* gave him a luncheon with several of its staff, who remained until four o'clock talking with him. Nicolas had an interview with Anthony Eden and also Sir Samuel Hoar. They spoke of Russia and the Ukraine. Both were reticent, but asked Nicolas to visit them again when he was in London.

Many Englishmen are not satisfied with Chamberlain's policy since Munich. They do not criticize the peace he made, as neither England nor France were prepared for war, but they find him passive and think that immediate rearmament on a huge scale and conscription are necessary. The newspapers were preparing public opinion for conscription, but Chamberlain believed in the good faith of the Germans. (Now, several months later, we hear that the English are preparing registration which will undoubtedly pave the way for conscription.) One afternoon we had tea with Baroness Budburg, a Russian, and met there Mr. Bruce, former diplomat in St. Petersburg in the British Embassy, who had married the famous Russian ballerina Madame Tamara Karsavina who was also present. We found her very lovely and full of "charme slav." She wore a high fluffy silver-fox hat with a tiny feather and veil and was the portrait of enchanting femininity. Her book, *Theatre Street*, is most interesting.

On Sunday we were invited to luncheon by General Sir Hanbury-Williams whom Nicolas had known during the war at Russian General Headquarters at Mogilev when Nicolas was Vice director of the Diplomatic Chancery there. The general now lives in Windsor in a tower of Windsor Castle called the Henry III Tower. He is a most delightful man, courteous and charming. The Tower was very picturesque and the general is surrounded by family portraits by famous artists, and other fine works of art. One of his ancestors was English ambassador to the Court of Russia in the eighteenth century. A correspondence exists between him and the Empress Catherine II (at that time only Grand Duchess, wife of the heir to the throne). A portrait of the ambassador also hangs in the Tower.

Paris, October 1938

After great suffering, the Grand Duke Cyril Vladimirovich, self-styled "Emperor of Russia," died recently of gangrene of the leg. He was in the American Hospital in Neuilly when my father was ill there. Once we saw his son, the Grand Duke Vladimir, a rather heavily built young man of no particular distinction.

Funeral services for the Grand Duke were held in a Russian church installed in a former garage in the rue Boileau, Auteuil. On account of a shocking dispute concerning the nomination of the Metropolitan, a scission exists in the Russian Orthodox Church (outside of Russia, naturally) and several churches have resulted in Paris, besides the regular Russian church of the rue Daru where the Metropolitan Eulogios officiates.

Nicolas Alexandrovich and I attended a "panaheeda" (service for the dead) for the Grand Duke Cyril at nine o'clock one evening. The garage had been transformed into a chapel. The bier stood before the altar, covered with a former Russian Imperial flag, black eagles on a yellow ground. A similar flag hung from a pole over the coffin. Candles in high flambeaux were disposed around it, and there were many wreaths. The Grand Duchess Helen, his sister, was not present but Nicolas had seen her in the church earlier in the day. His two brothers, Grand Duke André and Grand Duke Boris, were there with their wives, both commoners (the wife of the former is the famous dancer of the Russian Imperial ballet under the old régime, Kshessenskaia). Grand Duke Dmitri was also present, as was the Grand Duke Gabriel.

Funeral services among Russian exiles are usually painful affairs, but on this occasion I saw no evidence of sorrow on the part of the numerous Russians gathered for the ceremony.

After the Russian débacle, the late Grand Duke Cyril, cousin of the Emperor Nicholas II, became head of the house of Romanov and named himself Emperor of Russia, but he had no following. He lived modestly with his family in

St. Briac, Brittany. The death a few years ago of his wife, Grand Duchess Victoria, daughter of the Duke of Edinburgh, affected him greatly. Last year his daughter, Kyra, married Prince Louis-Ferdinand, a grandson of former Emperor Wilhelm of Germany. His son, Vladimir, twenty-one, takes his place as head of the Romanovs.

Paris, December 16, 1938

Each year there is in Paris a public séance of the Académie Francaise where outsiders are invited to hear comments on the books which the Académie had chosen for a prize during the year.

Yesterday, at two o'clock in the afternoon, we attended this séance. As Nicolas' book, *Russia under Soviet Rule*, appeared on the list of prizes awarded, we had received an invitation. The Académie meets in the Institut de France on the quay, and beneath the cupola of the dome.

As we entered the building the Municipal Guard was assembled in the antechamber giving an official character to the occasion. The hall was already filled and we were obliged to sit on stools in the centre. The room is round in shape, and benches are placed in tiers, like an amphitheatre. Four life-sized statues of Fénelon, Bossuet, Sully, and Descartes in cream marble decorated the walls. The benches of the académiciens were still empty. Above a green cloth covered table is a bust of Henri d'Orléans, Duc d'Aumale. We had just found our places when a long, dramatic roll of drums from the Municipal Guard resounded. The door opened and the "Immortels" entered and took their seats. The entire forty were not present but we counted over thirty. Some members were dressed in the classical uniform of the académiciens, green cloth with paler green palms embroidered on their chests. These men occupied the front rows, but the majority were in civilian costume and there were two ecclesiasticals in red robes.

Monsieur André Bellesort, Monsieur Goyau, and Monsieur Henri Bordeaux sat at the green-covered table. Monsieur Goyau, the "secrétaire perpetuel," read his paper, mentioning the most important prizes awarded. It was hot in the dimly lighted room and some of the Immortels dozed peacefully. Nicolas' book received the Prix Thérouanne.

When Monsieur Goyau had finished, Monsieur Bellesort discoursed on the "prix de vertu," which the Académie bestows on persons of humble position whose lives are sacrificed to others. The various examples given showed modest, pathetic existences spent in self-abnegation for some sick or maimed member of the family, years and days passed in an unending round of sordid duties and sacrifices, borne without complaint. It is touching that the worth of such obscure persons should be sought out and recognized by this great literary body. It gives a high, human tone to the Académie Française.

Paris, December 20th, 1938

Darling Papinka,

How happy we were the day you left us in Le Havre to feel that you were getting away from Europe after that terrible crisis in late September when you were in Paris and we thought, as did everyone else in France, that immediate war with Germany was inevitable. Those were hours of anguish and you, in the hospital, were really in no state to endure such strain. But it all turned out well. You reached Le Havre, and how relieved you must have been to feel the vessel moving out to sea, and leave it all behind. Hitler's invasion of Czechoslovakia has made 1938 a momentous year for Europe.

You sailed on September 30th, the day after Chamberlain saved the peace in Munich. Two days later we returned to Paris with all our luggage and two packing-cases of Nicolas' precious Russian paintings, which he had saved from the

bolsheviks twenty years before. We went through Normandy, among apple trees and placid cows feeding in the turnip
fields.

Towards evening we drove into Paris through St. Denis,
and were struck by the dark aspect of the street. War-lighting
still prevailed over all the city. The small black-painted
shades shed just the necessary light, while remaining invisible to aircraft. Nicolas drove the car slowly through the dim
streets which looked as if some catastrophe had befallen
them. Our house in the rue Alfred Dehodencq was barely
discernible in the feeble light. The servants had not yet
returned, as Léon had gone to his native village to await the
call for general mobilization, and the women were still in
their hamlets. There was no light in the house as the electricity had been cut before our departure, the water and gas also
turned off. It was a dismal homecoming, and in the gloom
some awful spell seemed to have been cast about us. We
deposed our luggage and went to an hotel to spend the night.
The following day, gas, electricity and water were reestablished, the servants returned and order reigned.

There was the tremendous relief of a cataclysm averted,
but for how long? People were filled with foreboding, saying
that war was inevitable in six months if Hitler did not
change his tactics.

A week later we left for Berlin. In that city an atmosphere
of tension prevailed. We were the only foreigners visible and
the Germans eyed us in an unfriendly manner. Even in the
smart Hotel Bristol, where all Berlin lunches, no gaiety was
apparent. We saw few ladies and not a single elegant one.
The crowds in the streets looked drab and resigned. The men
wore light-coloured raincoats, almost down to their heels,
and soft green felt hats. The women were dressed in ordinary
coats and all looked as if they were going to market. Even
Unter den Linden no elegance struck our eye and the shops
displayed mediocre merchandise.

We attended a theatre and saw an excellent play, *Ein
grosser Mann Privat* (the private life of a male film star), with

a good actor, Johannes Riedman, who had also written the play. The atmosphere in the theatre was oppressive and the public appeared depressed as they ate sausage and drank beer between acts.

Nicolas saw some of his old acquaintances and discussed the situation with them. None of them wanted war, they said. They had all been through the Great War and knew what war was, but they told Nicolas that the young men were ready for it, and the Nazi Party is principally composed of young people.

I saw airplanes flying over the city and trembled to think that less than a fortnight before, we might have seen these same planes over Paris. Young aviation officers in neat blue suits sent the same shudders through me.

In general the German people had no idea until the Munich Conference that war was possible. They know nothing of what is going on. Many foreign newspapers are forbidden in the country. We asked for the *New York Times,* but it had been banned.

The Nazis are doing a great deal of building in Berlin. Large ministries are being erected in the plain modern style called "Nazi." Several houses have been torn down on your "Graf Spee Strasse," at the corner of the Tiergartenstrasse, to make place for some ministry, War, I believe. Nicholas went to see your house-manager, Wolter. His reception room was divided in two parts by wardrobes, one part forming a salon, the other a bedroom. It was evident that he was sharing his flat with other persons as there were small children playing about. Quite like Soviet Russia. Little Wolter opened wide eyes when Nicolas told him that Germany had almost declared war two weeks ago. He had never heard about it. Everything seemed in order in the house. (This house my father owned in Berlin was later destroyed by bombs.)

I wrote you that Nicolas went to see the head of the Russian Department in the Nazi Party, one named Dürksen, about his book being published in German. He had received offers from various German publishers, but when they see the book they always say that certain changes must be made. (As I remember it was something against the Jews they wanted.) Nicolas had no intention of changing anything, but as this happened several times, he decided to enquire if they had anything against the book. In Dürksen's antechamber he found several Russian priests with long beards and tall boots. When he entered, Dürksen raised his arm and said "Heil Hitler." Nicolas bowed courteously and answered "Guten Tag." The conversation was polite and the Nazi promised to read the book and give Nicolas an answer. That was several months ago, but no answer has appeared. The book certainly was not in accord with Nazi ideas. (It was a question of Nicolas' book: *Russia under Soviet Rule*.)

On the 12th, we went to the Friedrichstrasse Bahnhof to take the Express to Paris. It was heavenly to leave that dismal city of Proletarian gloom, to hear French voices at the frontier, to be again in a free country.

Paris, December 20th, 1938

On December 14th we were invited by the Comtesse Greffulhe in the afternoon at five to have the honour of being presented to the King of Belgium, Leopold III, and the Queen Mother Elisabeth, who were passing through Paris incognito. Nicolas has known for many years the lovely Comtesse and she is always most kind and hospitable to us. She is Belgian by birth, a Princesse Caraman-Chimay, and her sister, Princesse Ghislaine de Caraman-Chimay, is lady-in-waiting to the Dowager Queen, so the Belgian sovereigns go to the house of the Comtesse Greffulhe quite informally. About twenty persons were present that afternoon in the beautiful salon. On the cheminée stands a marvelous cream marble bust of the goddess Diana by Houdon, and an extraordinary resemblance exists between this masterpeice and the Comtesse Greffulhe herself. Among the guests were men of science including a doctor Ramon who became famous a few years ago when he discovered a vaccination serum against diphtheria, and another against tetanus.

The Comtesse asked us not to pay much attention when the Queen entered as she is very shy, so we all continued our conversations and suddenly we perceived among us a quiet little figure dressed in black, with a small round black hat, a fine, sensitive face and a heavenly smile. We were presented, one at a time, and the Queen, very gracious and charming, found a word to say to each one. Nicolas talked with her and she told him that she was interested in learning Russian and wished that she could read the literature. Nicolas replied that there was an excellent English translation of Pushkin's famous poem *Eugen Onegin*, if she would permit him to send it to her. The Queen accepted and the next day Nicolas sent a copy of this masterpiece to her lady-in-waiting for Her Majesty.

A little later King Leopold entered and we were struck by his youthful aspect. He did not look over twenty although he is really about thirty five, I believe. Handsome, with blue eyes and wavy blond hair, and a slender figure. Again we were presented and the King talked for some time to Nicolas about the Ukraine. Both he and the Queen are charming and simple in manner.

Paris, December 27th, 1938

Darling Papinka,

A wave of cold is sweeping over Europe and snow has been falling in Paris for more than a week. We have had a white Christmas. In our quiet little rue Alfred Dehodencq the snow lies almost untouched. The Rothschild palace opposite seems like a Christmas card against the white background. On Christmas Eve we had a tree which Auntie brought (she is spending a week here) and a number of small presents besides your generous checks, and the evening passed very pleasantly in Nicolas' library before the fire. Towards midnight we turned on the radio and listened to French Christmas carols, les chants de Noël. Only your dear presence was needed to make this occasion an entirely happy one. Nicolas gave me a gold Louis-Philippe bracelet, set with diamonds, emeralds, and a line of black enamel, an exquisite gift, and he said to me with that look of deep emotion he sometimes has in his eyes: "Keep this bracelet in memory of tonight. It may be the last we shall spend in our home." Alas, in the present state of Europe it was a prophecy.

We lunched the other day with Charles de Chambrun and his wife in their apartment overlooking the Invalides. Charles and Nicolas are such old and affectionate friends and are always happy to be together. The former Italian ambassador to France was there, Monsieur Cerruti, and Monsieur Leon Bailby, owner and editor of a Paris newspaper, *Le Jour*. A new Italian ambassador to France has just arrived, after an interval of almost a year since M. Cerruti was recalled, as France had not recognized the Empire after the conquest of Ethiopia. The present ambassador, M. Guariglia, had been in Russia as a young attaché years ago at the Italian Embassy in St. Petersburg, and Nicolas had known him there. He dined with us last week with his charming Spanish born wife. Pierre-Etienne Flandin and Madame Flandin were also present. It was not the most propitious moment for them to meet as that same day the Italians had gone back on the Franco-Italian pact which Laval and Flandin had made with Mussolini in 1935. However, they had a friendly talk after dinner. We also had that evening the counselor of the American Embassy and his attractive Hungarian wife. Edwin Wilson is most delightful. Philippe Barrès (nephew of the well-known writer Maurice Barrès) and Madame Barrès, as well as the Marquis d'Abartiagues and dear André de Fouquiéres completed this very agreeble soirée.

Madame Margaritta Sarfatti lunched with us recently. She is Italian and was an intimate friend of the Duce in his young days, even saving his life upon one occasion. She has written the story of his life. However, she can no longer remain in Italy with any ease, as she is Israelite and of late, since Mussolini is following Hitler's lead in the Jewish question, she cannot even keep servants, so she came to France. I have heard through others that the great man would not even see her before her departure. How inhuman is this attack of Hitler upon the Jews!

On Monday, December 19th, a reception was given for the Grand Duke Vladimir, son of Grand Duke Cyril who died recently. The cloak of the pretender to the throne of Russia, which Cyril wore, has fallen upon the shoulders of his son Vladimir. This reception was given so that the Russian monarchists in exile could meet the young Grand Duke and several thousand attended. The Metropolitan Eulogios celebrated the religious ceremony of the Orthodox Church, surrounded by his clergy and the choir, beneath the flag of Imperial Russia, with the two-headed black eagles on a yellow ground. All the monarchist organizations were represented, ex-service men, mutilated soldiers, charitable institutions, officers of the Imperial army, and ladies of the nobility. The Grand Duke Vladimir is twenty-one years old, rather heavily built, and the Russians say he resembles Tsar Alexander III in his youth.

This meeting was held under the auspices of the Union of the Russian Nobility and by the officers of the Guard, in a reactionary spirit which Nicolas does not approve.

A number of Russians think that Nicolas should exert an influence on this young prince, but his entourage would probably be against that, for Nicolas would teach him to be progressive instead of returning to the autocratic principles of the dynasty.

The Grand Duke Dmitri is more open-minded and intelligent and understands that a prince must be of his time.

The Grand Duke Dimitri lunched with Nicolas here yesterday, a man's luncheon with Chambrun and a few others.

Snow is still heaped high in our garden, but it seems that
the thaw is coming. Then we will look for longer days, the
neighbour's Japanese plum tree in flower, and YOU.

Paris, January 1st, 1939

We have not been able to go south, as we had hoped to do,
as Nicolas is writing an article on the Ukraine to appear in
the *Review des Deux Mondes* in February. This is a burning
subject now, with the Nazis proposing to invade the Ukraine
in the spring. The Grand Duke Dmitri wrote an article in a
Paris paper the other day which Nicolas considered excellent and full of good sense. He is certainly the most intelligent of the remaining Romanovs, and it is to be hoped that he
will exercise some influence over the young Grand Duke
Vladimir.

Now that his book *Russia under Soviet Rule* is finished
and published in four languages—Russian, French, English
and Italian—my husband has a little time to himself which he
employs by adding to our collection of Russian paintings
which comprises many of the best painters of the eighteenth
century, such as Levitsky, Borovikovsky, Lampi, Rokotov
and Shchukin. He has a very fine portrait of the Emperor
Paul by Shchukin. This collection is his greatest joy and he
spends hours contemplating them, a sad consolation for his
lost country.

Paris, January 19th, 1939

Last evening we were invited to the Comédie-Française in
the loge of Monsieur Alexandre Millerand (former President
of the Republic). The play was *Cyrano de Bergerac* by
Edmond Rostand, which has finally reached the Comédie
after about forty-one years, as it was first given in 1897. It
was superbly played and beautifully staged. In the audience

we saw Princesse Mestchersky (born Struve) who, since the Russian disaster, has a finishing school for girls in Paris. With her was the daughter of Princesse Hermine, second wife of Kaiser Wilhelm II. Nicolas talked with her and says that she seems very shy. She is only seventeen. She said that she was returning to Doorn for the anniversary of the Kaiser's eightieth birthday at the end of this month.

We are having a momentary lull in European politics, while Hitler and Mussolini think up some new evil. An Italian friend told us the following story. Two friends met on the street in Milan and began talking about Mussolini. One of them said: "What a fine man our Duce is, everything he does is just right, he is really magnificent." Amazed, the other man replied "Listen, are you talking to me, or are you telephoning?" There is little freedom of speech in Italy. As soon as people think they might be overheard, they immediately begin to praise the régime, but there is much feeling against it.

The Russian émigrés are usually very kind to one another, and the old Russian habit of going to a friend's house and remaining, whether he is at home or not, still persists. Recently Nicolas went to the apartment of a Russian acquaintance, and a perfectly strange man opened the door. The host was not at home, but he had lent his rooms to a student to do a bit of work there instead of freezing in some cheerless garret. Another night, in another apartment, Nicolas found every corner occupied by poor exiles, one playing solitaire, another writing a letter. Burtsev, the reformed revolutionary who owns nothing but the boots he stands in, had also sought refuge in the home of this kind-hearted man, who often shares his meals with them, and he himself has just enough to exist on.

Paris, February 1939

On January 30th Hitler spoke before the Reichstag, the first Reichstag of "Great Germany" which has assembled since the Nazis invaded Austria and Sudetenland. Eight hundred and fifty-five deputies were present, including those of the new provinces. We listened to Hitler's speech on the radio which lasted two or three hours. His harangue was moderate and he launched no new thunderbolts. Europe breathes again, momentarily.

On January 24th the former German Kaiser Wilhelm II celebrated his eightieth birthday at Doorn in Holland with all the pomp and splendour of his former court. Dressed with all the insignia of his past power, he received a delegation of the old army, headed by the ninety-year-old Field Marshal von Mackensen in a splendid uniform and plastered with decorations. A grand dinner followed where wine glasses were struck together, heels clicked and swords clanked in Teutonic style.

This is the season of receptions now and we have a handful every afternoon—Kammerer, Berthelot, Patenotre, Curial, Vacaresco, Phipps, Souza-Dantos—all salons where Nicolas meets diplomats and political men with whom it interests him to talk.

Last Friday we attended a big ball given at the American Embassy by Ambassador Bullitt. The Duke and Duchess of Windsor were present and the cynosure of all eyes. The Duchess looked very well in a white frock with gold trimmings and was most amiable in manner. Everyone watched her, but the ladies kept their distance for fear of being presented and thus having to make, or not make, a curtsey to the Duke's wife, as he requested, but she had not received the title of Royal Highness in England. This makes the Duke unhappy as he wishes her to have it and all the honours which accompany it. The Duke himself looks quite young, but his face is pleated, which detracts from the youthful appearance.

The Princesse Martha Bibesco was present also, wearing a black lace Eugénie frock and her superb parure of emeralds. It is said that this parure was given by Napoleon Bonaparte to the Polish Comtesse Marie Walewska, perhaps only a legend.

Paris, February 1939

Recently Nicolas went to Brussels to see his aunt, Princesse Euphrosine Urusov, his father's sister. He found her quite well. She is almost eighty, small, slender and active. She lives in a very pleasant house of which she has one floor, four rooms, in the good residential section of the city where she has resided a long time, a refugee from Russia where she owned vast estates. Two nieces live with her so she is not alone. They all exist on what Nicolas gives his aunt. The flat is furnished with anything from good arm-chairs to a canvas deck-chair, but there is a canary in a cage, a few potted hyacinths, and the rooms are warm and cosy. On Sunday afternoon the doorbell kept ringing constantly and many Russian and Belgian friends arrived. Aunt Zozo gave them tea and held a regular "salon" where all the topics of the day were discussed. It was a great satisfaction to Nicolas to see that his aunt could live decently on what he was able to give her. She could live much better alone of course, but she prefers the two nieces to be with her, which we of course understand. They were most happy to meet again and Nicolas spent two days with her. How greatly her present mode of life differs from the days when she lived on her estates in the Ukraine, before the Russian tragedy, when they often sat down forty persons at table.

War Is Declared

Then came the end of that fair life. The hour of 1939 had struck. Nazi hordes invaded France and this society was dispersed, never to be the same again.

In the spring, after the so-called peace of Munich in September 1938, Hitler was again rattling his saber and Europe trembled with apprehension.

Towards the end of June, at the close of the Paris season, the Comtesse Greffulhe had a garden party. Tables were set beneath the trees and friend greeted friend more warmly than usual.

"This is perhaps the last reunion before war comes," they said nostalgically. The Comtesse was there, as gracious as ever, but we never saw her again. Hitler loosed his thunderbolts and in September war was declared.

The summer of 1939 we spent at Cauterets in the Pyrenées with my father. Leaving Paris, we went there by car in a roundabout way through Dordogne, the southern province which has conserved the gentle beauty and enchantment of "la douce France" of former centuries. The woods, the fields, the streams, and the numerous stately châteaux with steep pointed roofs of this ancient land repose so tranquilly, so sweetly in the landscape that it seems a dream. One would not be surprised to behold a knight in shining armour ride down the highway, lance in hand, a tableau of the France we loved.

We passed the château of Fénelon, asleep in the fields like the Sleeping Beauty of the fable. The entrance gates were locked. We rang and rang, but no creature moved. Silence,

249

awaiting the kiss of the prince. In later years how often the disillusioned bishop must have thought of these scenes of his youth, and of his mother's "tour aux confitures."

One evening we stood at sunset on the crenelated battlements of the then half-ruined Chateau de Beynac like lord and lady surveying their vast estates. Across the fields the gentle Dordogne River flowed quietly and the peace of God reigned over the land.

Upon leaving Cauterets we motored to Cannes and there, on September 3rd, learned that France had declared war on Germany. Consternation reigned at the Carlton where we stopped.

Dismayed by this appalling news we hurried to find a place in the Paris train for my father and fortunately obtained the last one, but we had the car and a trunk which the railway refused to take. Nicolas discovered a small trailer to place the trunk in and we started off in our car with the trailer rattling behind through Aix-en-Provence where soldiers were already bivouacing and straw was spread on the square of the Grande Fontaine in that enchanting city of fountains.

Nicolas was excited and anxious to reach Paris to offer his service for any task. Upon arrival he wrote letters to the Quai d'Orsay and to his French ambassador friends to enquire what he could do, translating, Red Cross work, anything. There appeared to be nothing. Everyone was stunned. Deeply deceived, he decided to go to the United States and endeavour to raise a little money for the French Red Cross.

Great anxiety reigned in Paris. Citizens carried gas masks as they went about their business, in case of German air raids and poison gas.

In our little hôtel particulier in the rue Alfred Dehodencq near the Bois de Boulogne, feverishly we packed furniture and our precious collection of Russian eighteenth century paintings. These were to be stored so as not to leave the house habitable in case of Nazi occupation of Paris. Every few moments I ran to the window to scan the sky for the Luftwaffe, but no air-raid signals were heard, and no Nazi planes appeared. This surprised the population as they had feared that Hitler's first move would be an attempt to take Paris. Why did he not do so? Paris was literally without defense and it would have been a simple affair. Happily the Führer had other plans and beautiful Paris was saved from destruction.

We sent the women back to their villages, weeping. The young valet-de-chambre was called to the army. We were alone but found a man and a boy to assist us besides the professional movers.

During the four or five days we spent packing and scanning the sky for Luftwaffe planes over Paris, at evening we drove to Fontainebleau to spend the night, in case of German air-raids. We took two rooms in a modest hotel on the great place d'Armes, opposite the Château, where the windows were painted a dismal dark blue, and dined in a small café nearby again with dark blue windows. Several young soldiers were seated there, each one alone at his table, writing a letter, sipping coffee, or merely gazing into space. We were filled with pity at the sight of these sad youths, and Nicolas, with his warm compassionate heart, called them to our table, ordered coffee for all, and talked to them of their homes and occupations. The gloom lifted a bit as the conversation warmed their hearts, but they were mortally sad. There was no enthusiasm as in the First World War, nevertheless they were doing their duty.

These men were waiting to be sent to different "secteurs" at the front, and wanted a dog, a mascotte, to take with them. Nicolas spent a whole day searching throughout the countryside to find one. At evening he returned with a splendid wolf-hound who delighted the boys. "Merci Monsieur, merci Madame'' they cried as they went off in a truck to their barracks, ''We will bring him back to you the day of Victory.'' Alas poor youths, alas Victory.

The moment had come to leave our beloved home. With sadness we closed the door. My husband turned the key in the lock and we went out into the night. That was the end of our happy life. Fate was against us and we never returned.

*　　*　　*

We left Paris on the Rome Express because my husband had business in Rome. Soon we sailed from Genoa on the Italian liner *Rex*, arriving in New York about November 9th.

It was autumn 1939. At that time President Franklin Roosevelt was still under the spell of the recent renewal of diplomatic relations with the Soviet Union. An uneasy atmosphere of pro-Soviet sentiments permeated the State Department and leftist intellectuals in the country.

I believe that Nicolas had a letter of introduction from the American Red Cross. In Washington he went to the State Department ready to accept any modest work. He was received by an official of the Department whose name, unfortunately, I do not recall.

''You are Russian?'' inquired that individual who must have been of a subordinate category, as I cannot imagine a high official so ignorant and unfeeling.

''Yes, I am Russian,'' answered my husband, who was well known in diplomatic circles and had excellent relations with American envoys in several European capitals. His former high position in the Imperial Russian Ministry of Foreign Affairs, including service as Director of the diplomatic chancellery at Russian Army Headquarters during the war, and finally his last post as Russian chargé d'affaires in Paris made him welcome in foreign offices.

"Then why do you not go back to your own country?" asked the State Department person.

"Sir", replied Basily, "you are certainly aware that there has been a change of régime in Russia. It is no longer my country."

Thus the interview ended, but it clearly reflected the pro-Soviet tendencies of Roosevelt's administration.

It was then that, sad and disheartened, we moved to South America, where my husband spent the rest of his life.

Conclusion

In 1941 my beloved father died and we left the United States where we had gone after leaving France in order to be near him.

In 1942 we flew to South America in a tiny two-motor plane that fluttered like a butterfly along the Pacific coast of the South American continent, flying between the colossal Cordillera de los Andes and the ocean, at such low altitude that we could see people working in the fields, or walking on the roads with their donkeys. It was the childhood of aviation. From Chile our toy plane fluttered across the Andes,

Granja San Nicolas near Punta del Este (Uruguay)
(Photographed by Nicolas de Basily)

255

Lascelle in Granja San Nicolas
(Photographed by Nicolas de Basily)

through the Uspallata Pass, beneath the gigantic peak of the
Aconcague to Argentina, a perilous adventure. After two
years in that, then, lovely country, we crossed the Rio de La
Plata and dwelt for many years in Uruguay, beneath the
Southern Cross. My husband's fragile health required a mild
climate, as he suffered from emphysema, and found it in this
little country where we formed many endearing friendships.

Near Punta del Este, the famous bathing resort, we bought
a country place, with eight hectares of vineyards, orange and
lemon groves, and vegetable gardens which I named the
"Granja San Nicolas," (*granja* meaning farm). We built a

house in the old Spanish Colonial style, pale pink walls, a red tile roof, and grilled windows with stone mouldings above them. The garden was redolent with the fragrance of gardenias and red roses. Rows of tall cypress trees sheltered the fruit plantations from cold winds. Here long hours of silence passed, broken only by the flight of birds and the wind in the vineyards. Four bullocks ploughed the earth between the rows of grape vines, dreamy-eyed, and careful not to injure the vines. The voice of the peon leading them rose gently in the drowsy heat of summer, calling them by name to encourage them, "Quiero-ver-te. No-mi-toques, Voluntario, Delicado."

Thus we lived in the solitude of a Uruguayan farm where Fate had thrown us. The South American birds were wonderful. Many varieties of hummingbirds darted like arrows through the gardens, seeking the corollas of fuschias.

Nicolas de Basily in living room of the Granja

Many friends came to us there. The Uruguayans were most cordial and foreign diplomats en poste in Montevideo also came on Sunday afternoons when the tea table was always set, and we were awaiting them with pleasure. It was only a two-hour drive by car from Montevideo.

The Grand Duchess Marie Pavlovna of Russia resided in exile in Buenos Aires, and sometimes came to visit us at the Granja. We spent delightful hours with this gifted princess. Her books of memoirs are fascinating and she drew and painted extremely well. I possess among my treasures a beautiful gouache she made for me of the Maldonado country cemetery, with a high ochre wall, a blue-domed chapel, and dark cypress trees. I often accompanied her on sketching tours. We sat on tiny camp stools before the Maldonado cemetery. While she painted I read aloud to her from a Spanish book by Azorín. I was just beginning to learn Spanish, as was she. This absurd situation amused us beyond words and we laughed merrily. She had a wonderful sense of humour.

Often Nicolas and I talked with her of Russia (she was a cousin of the Emperor Nicholas II). She was heartsick over the fate of her loved country. One night, in our salon, she sat beneath the splendid portrait of her ancestor, the Emperor Paul I, by Shchukin, and wept over the destiny of Russia and her own sad fate. She was quite alone in the world, sorrowful, but outwardly courageous. I admired her great spirit and was fond of her. However, she varied often in temperament, at times simple and charming and again very "grandduchess."

My husband's health was failing in spite of our desperate efforts and medical consultations in Uruguay and the United States. I felt the need of inner strength and help.

In a small structure within the granja, Nicolas Alexandrovich and I made a tiny sanctuary, painted pale pink within and without, with a high narrow dark wood table where two tall silver church candlesticks were placed. Two ancient

Spanish wood carvings of polychrome angels knelt there in prayer, and above hung a cross of South American beaten silver. I often went there for prayer to alleviate my distress.

I remember tenderly our last Christmas Eve at the Granja San Nicolas when the farm people and house servants (all Spanish) gathered there with us for a moment's prayer on this holy night. The voice of Josefa, one of the young Spanish

Sanctuary at Granja San Nicolas
(Photographed by Nicolas de Basily)

housemaids, rose in song, and the harmonies of old Spanish Christmas chants broke the silence beneath the Southern Cross. The candles on the altar flickered and the sanctuary came alive. My husband smiled his gentle smile (1960).

Alas, my fervent supplications were in vain. The following year we left Uruguay and the Granja. Soon after I lost him, but through my tears I see the image of that humble retreat we had made together, while hope still burned within us.

Red Roses

How can I leave you, my roses?
Red roses dear to my heart,
In this distant, silent garden,
Where jeweled humming-birds dart.

Clad in deep crimson velvet,
Your grace is beyond compare,
Your fragrance a thing from heaven
As it floats in the garden there.

You lift your lovely faces
Imploring my face above.
"Do not forsake us," you whisper,
"We live sustained by your love."

Life tears me from you, red roses,
The hour has come to part,
But my spirit will haunt this garden,
Red roses, dear to my heart.

Lascelle

Granja San Nicolas
March 21st, 1961

Written at the moment of departure from the Granja.

*   *   *

In the anguish and solitude which follow the loss of a loved one, the heart's blood flows out drop by drop, like the wound of the king of the Holy Grail. In this silence which his voice will never again break, thought turns back to former times when youth was radiant, and happiness seemed, "So near, so possible" (Pushkin).

In 1919 when I married Nicolas de Basily in Paris, the fate of Imperial Russia weighed heavily upon him. Throughout all life the flame of patriotism burned in his heart, and his ardent desire was to serve again the country he so passionately loved. Alas, he died after long years of exile, without a gleam of hope that some day this dream might be realized, and his fatherland restored.

I have lost him. The rainbow is fallen, the book is closed, but these pages evoke days spent with Nicolas Alexandrovich in what is today a lost world, memories of a vanished past, so remote, it now seems to be a dream.

> Be still my heart
> Be still my sorrow
> Only tonight
> Again tomorrow
> Unending pain
> Will fill my breast.
> Be still my heart
> Now let me rest
> Until tomorrow.
>
> Lascelle

Nicolas de Basily died on March 20th, 1963.

* * *

Thus my story ends and I am alone.

In 1967 I created a foundation in memory of my husband at the Hoover Institution at Stanford University in Stanford, California, founded by Herbert Hoover, former President of the United States. In this great documentation and research center are united Basily's papers from the First World War, 1914–1917, which Emperor Nicholas II, as Commander in Chief of the Armies, spent at Russian Headquarters at Mogilev (the "Stavka"), and Basily was Director of the Emperor's Division of the Russian Foreign Office at Headquarters. Here he worked beside the Emperor during those years. The Minister of Foreign Affairs, Serge Sazonov, was his chief and General Alexeiev was general of the army. Basily had the sad duty of writing the Act of Abdication of Emperor Nicholas II. He has narrated all this in his memoirs. They are the thrilling account of an eyewitness of the final days of Nicholas II as Emperor, the last of the Romanovs.

I have given his papers to the Hoover Institution, also Basily's library of some 7,000 volumes, many old Russian editions, rare today, which form the "Nicolas de Basily Collection," to which we add, from time to time, new books on Russia to bring it up to date.

I also presented our collection of Russian eighteenth century paintings, so dear to my husband's heart, among them the portraits of the sovereigns of the Romanov dynasty of that epoch. All these paintings are by the most famous Russian artists of that time—Levitsky, Borovikovsky, Rokotov, Shchukin, and others, as well as several examples of other European painters—Reynolds, Hopner, Joseph Vernet, Guardi, etc. These paintings my husband and I collected over the years. They were our most treasured possessions. Today they hang in the Nicolas de Basily Room at the Hoover Institution in Stanford, California.

In the eighteenth century, when California was still a Spanish possession, a chain of missions was flung by Spanish

Franciscan monks along the "Camino Real," the Royal Highway, leading from north to south, a day's journey apart. A monk, riding a donkey, could leave one mission in the morning and reach the next by nightfall. The country was wild and these missions were like oases in the desert. Some ruins of the old hostelries remain, others have been restored. One of these is the Carmel Mission, which I visited a few years ago, enjoying the picturesque Spanish Colonial architecture, but the feature which impressed me profoundly was the little library where the head monk, Junipero Serra*, a Spaniard, conducted his affairs. It was a very small room, wood-paneled, with a few books on one wall. A high-backed Spanish chair, a bare oak table, and a tall copper candlestick with a half-burned candle were the only furnishings. Yet in this tiny sanctuary, severe and monastic, the Spanish monk had lighted the fire of learning. His candle was dim, but it was burning, showing the way to enlightenment in a still uncultured country.

Today, when great universities widely disseminate knowledge and the face of California has changed, I think of the little taper glowing in that quiet, consecrated room.

As Junipero Serra did, over two hundred years ago, I too have lit my modest candle, and formed here a small sanctuary of Russian paintings and literature of former centuries, little known outside of their native land, Imperial Russia.

---

* Miguel José Serra was born in the village of Petra, Mallorca, Balearic Islands, Spain, in 1913. In 1730 he took the Franciscan Orders under the name of Fra Junipero Serra. Arriving in California in 1769, he began to build the chain of Franciscan missions along the Camino Real leading from south to north. He established nine of California's original twenty-one missions, and converted many of the Indian inhabitants to Christianity. Fra Junipero Serra died in California in 1784.

Appendix

KOREA, LAND OF MORNING CALM

A BOOK OF MEMORIES

BY

LASCELLE DE BASILY

PARIS, NOVEMBER 1933

Preface

In the northwestern part of Korea, not far from the Yalu River, the boundary between Korea and Manchuria, is the Province of Unsan, a wild mountainous region of romantic aspect with high hills, broad valleys, deep gorges, and turbulent streams.

"Over the hills, hills again, hills without number" is a Korean saying most true of their country.

Gold exists in some of these northern hills. In the latter part of the nineteenth century an American gold mining company obtained from the Emperor of Korea a concession of fifty square miles in Unsan Province, about thirty miles from the Manchurian border, as the crow flies. Here they operated under the name of Oriental Consolidated Mining Company. There were a hundred white men who served as superintendents and mill-men, also several hundred Chinese and Japanese, principally cart-drivers and carpenters. A few thousand Koreans actually worked the mines.

In the beginning of the twentieth century this concession was like a little kingdom over which my father, although a banker by profession, ruled for some years as general manager of the mining company. He and my mother remained there during the summer months. In winter they traveled to Japan, China, or Europe where I was in school. My summer vacations were spent with them in Korea.

In a grove of sacred pine-trees was my parents home, built like a temple with upward-sweeping grey tile roofs, set in the midst of a wide valley hemmed in by hills, two miles from the nearest mine.

267

Whites and natives alike loved and revered my father for his kindness, good humor, and sense of justice. He understood the Korean language and liked the people. Frequently they came to him to arbitrate their dissensions, accepting his judgment as final. It was a real tribunal.

In the following pages I set down what I saw and heard at that time in Korea, Land of Morning Calm.

Outline of Korean History

The map of Asia reveals Korea, a small mountainous peninsula directly south of Manchuria, separated from China by the Yellow Sea. To the east lies Japan. Geographically sandwiched between the two great powers of the Far East, Korea has always been a bone of contention between these countries which cast greedy eyes upon her and growl at each other over her head.

The early history of Korea is obscure and legendary. The first date considered authentic is 22 B.C. when the Shang dynasty fell in China, and Kija, a Chinaman, invaded Korea with five thousand followers. He began there a peaceful reign and made laws for civilizing the half-wild people. He was wise, just, and good. His capital was Pyengyang in the north. His grave is still shown in that city, guarded by grotesque beasts carved in stone. Ruins of the fortified wall he built are also visible.

The name of Kija stands out in the mists of legends of that time and it is supposed that he was really a historical character. His dynasty lasted a thousand years although no known written records exist.

During more than two thousand years, Korea was alternately independent or vassal to Japan or China, principally the latter. She was repeatedly invaded by the

Chinese and the Manchus, by the Mongols, and by nomadic tribes.

In his very complete and excellent book *The Passing of Korea*, Mr. H. B. Hulbert says:

"With the opening of our era there were three powers in Korea, Silla in the southeast, Pakche in the southwest and Koguryu in the north. The kingdom of Silla was by far the most highly civilized of the three kingdoms. Eventually almost the whole of the present territory of Korea was in her hands. Three centuries later luxury sapped her power."

In 1592, Hideyoshi, the great shogun of Japan, invaded Korea, as part of a plan to conquer China. At that time the remarkable Korean Admiral Yi-Sun-Sin put a Japanese fleet to flight. Mr. Hulbert calls this commander the "Korean Nelson," and says:

"Yi-Sun-Sin, assuming charge of the Korean fleet in the South, had invented a curious iron clad in the shape of a tortoise. The back was covered with iron plates and was impervious to the fire of the enemy. With his ship he met and engaged a Japanese fleet, bringing sixty thousand reinforcements to Hideyoshi's army. With his swift tortoise-boat he rammed the smaller Japanese craft right and left, and soon threw the whole fleet into confusion. He incinerated the struggling mass by launching fire-arrows and a terrible conflagration broke out which destroyed almost the entire fleet. A few boats escaped and carried the news of the disaster back to Japan.

"This may be called the turning point in the war for although the Japanese forces went as far as Pyengyang, and the king had to seek asylum on the northern frontier, yet the spirit of the invasion was broken."

Frequent invasions and raids together with foreign pirates in Korean waters caused this country to adopt a policy of absolute national seclusion, which was enforced with great vigor for several centuries, Korea thus becoming known to the outside world as the Hermit Kingdom.

In 1876, by the Treaty of Kanghwa, Japan recognized the independence of Korea. The Hermit Kingdom was then opened to the world. Treaties with several Occidental powers soon followed.

Towards 1784 Christianity was introduced into Korea, principally by French missionaries. The natives were hostile and persecuted them mercilessly, probably through fear of foreign domination.

In 1894 Japan declared war on China for the purpose of settling the international status of Korea, the constant intrusion of China in Korean affairs making the little country appear under Chinese suzerainty. Japan was victorious in the conflict. In October 1895 the Korean queen, Min, a bitter enemy of the Japanese, was brutally murdered by them one night in the Seoul palace.

In 1904 Japan went to war with Russia, Korea again being the case. A Japanese army invaded the coveted Korean territory which they had ever regarded with jealous eyes as a foothold on the continent.

The following year, Japan, victorious, forced a protectorate upon Korea, which struggled vainly to rebel. In 1907 the emperor was compelled to abdicate in favor of his son. In 1909, Prince Ito, one of the great forgers of modern Japan, then vice-regent of Korea, fell beneath the knife of a Korean fanatic acting in a frenzy of patriotism. It was all to no purpose. Korea was without ammunition, defense, or support. In 1910, Japan calmly annexed Korea to the despair of the weaker nation. No one protested. Korea did not interest the world. So the Japanese walked in, as the Germans did a few years later in Belgium when the whole world rose up in defense of this gallant little kingdom.

The Koreans were sorrow-stricken at the loss of their freedom. A Korean army officer, General Prince Min Yong Whan, committed suicide, preferring death to foreign domination (November 1905).

The People

Korea is called "Cho-sen" in the native language, meaning "Land of Morning Calm". To one who knows the country this seems logical. The mornings are often serene and calm, while in the afternoon strong winds blow, making the trees bend and the white garments of the inhabitants flutter madly.

In spite of repeated foreign dominations, Korea has kept her individuality and language. The latter is quite distinct from Japanese or Chinese.

A Korean mourner wearing wide mourning hat
(Photographed by Helen Struve Meserve)

The people are kind and gentle but without initiative, and very poor. Nevertheless they are hospitable, and generosity is one of their salient and most sympathetic traits. The country-folk, who have nothing to spare, offer their pipe to smoke, or pull a turnip or carrot from their small garden-plot and press it upon you.

One of the first things that strikes the traveler in Korea is that both men and women are dressed in white. This custom originated many years ago when the country was thrown into mourning by three succeeding deaths in the ruling family. The prescribed period of mourning for each member was three years. Thus the population mourned for nine consecutive years. At the end of that time the impoverished nation accepted white, the color of mourning, for the national dress. Alas, it is usually far from immaculate and the robes of the masses have nothing in common with cleanliness except on their New Year's Day when all are arrayed in new, or at least clean, garments.

The Journey

At that time Korea was difficult of access. To reach it we took an antiquated Japanese steamer in Nagasaki. After crossing the famous Tsushima Straits from Japan, we sailed one evening at sunset along the coast of Korea, the Hermit Kingdom. Hills rose abruptly from the water's edge, concealing his forbidden land from the gaze of indiscreet outsiders. Twilight painted the sea with amethyst shadows. Myriad islands rose out of the haze. Night fell and our ship cut through silver waters beneath the moon.

We stopped to coal at Fusan, a small fishing-port. During this time we went ashore, and climbing a pine-covered hill found, beneath the trees, a Japanese inn where we lunched.

A diminutive Japanese girl brought us food, but the September sun was hot, the climb long, our throats parched. We needed liquid refreshment as well. Our gestures were obvious enough, heads thrown back, a significant thumb pointing down our throats; this seemed quite clear to us but not to the serving maid. She looked perplexed. Suddenly we spied an advertisement for champagne hanging on the wall. If it was impossible to get water, we would take champagne. Solemnly we pointed a finger at the sign. Then she understood and laughing, brought and set before us a huge bottle of warm champagne.

The following morning we reached Chemulpo, a seaport about twenty-five miles from the capital, Seoul. There is nothing of historical interest in this town which sprang into being after Korea was opened to the world and the customs installed there in 1883. At that time the village counted only a few fishing-huts. It has since grown into a straggling town of native and Japanese houses with a few European buildings.

We left the ship on a tender which brought us alongside a primitive jetty where a crowd of white-clad native porters shouted and struggled for possession of our luggage. On their backs were strapped a kind of wooden frame, called "jighis" on which they carried their loads.

How poor this town seemed to us with its low dwellings lining the boggy streets, how utterly forlorn in the falling rain. Chemulpo is built on a hillside and stone steps often replace the road. Halfway up we paused and, looking back over the bay, saw there the Korean Navy, consisting of one ancient man-of-war.

We stopped in the house of the agent of the mining company, an American with a Japanese wife.

Next day we continued our journey north to Unsan Province. From Chemulpo we took a Japanese steamer overnight to Chinnampo where we boarded a small launch, property of the mining company, remaining at open sea for twelve hours, tossed by high waves. This brought us to Anshu, a town on a hill at the mouth of a large river bearing the same name. Once a flourishing settlement, Anshu was practically destroyed during the Chinese–Japanese war of 1894–1895. Now inside the ruined walls desolation reigns.

The night was spent in a native house belonging to the company and early the next morning we set out for Unsan, traveling in sedan-chairs, each carried by eight coolies. The rainy season had just come to an end (September). The rivers were swollen and the coolies waded through, holding us in our chairs high above the turbulent waters. There were no bridges as they had either been taken down before the rains began, or else been swept away by the torrent. Korea has a rainy season like India and during the summer torrents of warm water deluge the land. Korean bridges are therefore fragile constructions, built of logs, straw, dirt and loose stones. During this rainy period the natives ford the streams, often a dangerous proceeding on account of high waters.

We traveled all day. The sweating coolies groaned beneath our weight, four at a time carrying each chair. A relay of four ran alongside encouraging them with grunts and shouts, ready to take their places when the first relay was exhausted. Once the coolies of a stout member of the party rebelled and ran away across the fields, but were pursued relentlessly by several white men and brought back, puffing and sighing.

At times our road led past houses where barking dogs heralded our advent, bringing white-robed inmates to the door. Korean dogs are wolfish beasts with pale blue eyes. They appear vicious but are in reality cowardly. One word or the gesture of picking up a stone puts them to flight.

The villages were picturesque with thatch-roofed mud houses overgrown with trailing pumpkin vines. Strings of red peppers and gourds hung beneath the eaves to dry. At a distance a Korean village is difficult to distinguish from the earth. Occasionally we saw clean compounds but usually they were very dirty. Black razor-back pigs, nosing in rubbish heaps, regarded us suspiciously.

White-clad women passed, balancing on their heads large earthenware jars of water. Their carriage was superb, erect and supple. Frequently they stopped and in sweet voices asked our destination, Korean etiquette on the road.

Once we noted with amusement several men fording a deep stream who had removed all their clothing, which they held in their hands high above their heads, still wearing their black horsehair hats.

In the outskirts of a village a pony lay flat on his back in the road, his four feet tied together and attached to a pole, while a blacksmith hammered his shoes on with odd three-cornered nails. This is the correct native manner of shoeing an animal.

Another day on the road spent in similar fashion brought us to our journey's end, my parents' home, Sonamo, Puk-Chin, Unsan Province, Korea.

Sonamo-Among-the-Hills

My parents' home was several miles from any mine or camp in a wide valley surrounded by high hills. The house was placed on an eminence at whose base two rivers flowed, met, and continued together across the fields. A grove of sacred pine trees crowned this knoll where formerly the natives had offered prayers to their gods.

My mother had great talent for painting and architecture, which she had studied for years in Europe. After having been but a short time in Korea she herself drew the plans for a house of native design which she built with only the help of a local Korean contractor, Pak. With the talent and imagination which characterized her, she seemed instinctively to feel how each detail should be carried out. The result was a

house of picturesque beauty which the country people came
from miles around to see, saying it looked like a temple and
was the best example of Korean architecture in that part of
the country.*

No false note jarred the harmony of the admirable proportions. The walls were of stone and grey stucco. The
framework was painted dull red. The characteristic part of
the building was the heavy roof of curved grey tiles sweeping
upwards at the corners after the manner of temples. Small
animals, red, green, and indigo, rode astride the roof-pole.
The native contractor, Pak, insisted on adding these grotesque beasts to keep away the evil spirits, a Korean belief.
Beneath the eaves tiny brass bells tinkled gently with any
vagrant breeze. Their tongues were made in the form of fish,
which native superstition declares to represent the element
of water, thus preserving the building from fire.

Pak, the contractor, made a wonderful sign with Korean
characters in gold on a white ground, testifying that "a good
and kind gentleman named Meserve lives in this house." He
hung this sign on his own initiative over my father's study
door. On the front veranda he placed a similar sign in Korean
verse which translated means: "Listen to the murmur of the
water from this veranda."

The house lay like a temple, serene and remote beneath
the pine trees of the sacred grove. My parents called their
home "Sonamo," the Korean name for pines.

The interior of the house was finished in European style,
several of the rooms being oak-paneled. The ceilings were
formed by great oak beams and rafters, which are the main
beauty of a Korean interior.

During the construction of the house my mother went
each day to inspect the work. In Korean fashion, the
framework was first made in horizontal position and then put

---

*For a photograph of the house see page 23.

in place, upright. The local carpenters, accustomed to constructing only one-story huts, had never built stairs. With bits of wood my mother made a miniature model staircase which they copied.

The extensive grounds were surrounded by a high stone wall. A gate-house, also built in native style with a sweeping tile roof, guarded the entrance. The latticed doors were stretched over with rice-paper.

On either side of the entrance gate stood a "devil-post." Such posts are frequently seem in Korea, placed near the village or valley, and are supposed by the natives to have the

Devil-post at entrance to Sonamo and gate-keeper "Fizzle"
(Photographed by Helen Struve Meserve)

power of driving away evil spirits. Our posts were trunks of trees about five feet high roughly carved to resemble demons, and painted red. Their grotesque countenances grinned savagely and their outstretched arms brandished sticks. These primitive specimens of Korean art had been placed there by a poor native whom my mother had sent to the American Concession Hospital where he was cured of consumption. To prove his gratitude this Korean begged leave of my mother to place these devil-posts at her door. One was named the "Biggest Man in the North" (of Korea). The other was the "Biggest Man in the World." Under their guardianship no harm could come to his benefactress, another proof of Korean generosity.

The grounds were laid out in gardens. Japanese stone lanterns, stepping-stones, and a stone-lined pond made a picturesque setting for the house beneath the pine trees. Nasturtiums, petunias, zinnias, marigolds, and asters, each in their season, added a brilliant note of colour—hardy flowers, the only ones resisting the hot heavy downpours of the rainy season in June and July. In September frosts nipped them. Making a garden was a difficult task in a country where the elements combine to defy mankind.

The native gate-keeper at Sonamo, a reduced "yang-ban" (or nobleman) watched over the property during the day. Energy was not his forte. He usually reclined on the floor in the gatehouse, smoking innumerable pipes. From time to time he applied a cautious eye to a hole poked with his finger in the rice-paper door to see if any trespassers were about. Indignant at his laziness my mother discharged him every Saturday night. On Monday morning, after a restful Sabbath, he would appear imploring Mammá on bended knee to take him back, which she always did. He had become a habit. She called him "Fizzle," as he was such a perfect failure.

"What does Fizzle mean in the American language?" he once inquired.

"Oh, Fizzle is a number-one American name," my mother answered.

"Many, many thanks," he retorted, bowing low and shaking his clasped hands together as if congratulating himself.

Fourteen servants were necessary to keep up this establishment. The cook was Chinese. He adored my mother with the faithfulness of a good dog. When she was ill, he slept at night, of his own free will, on the floor before her door, to be near in case she needed anything. During her absence he gambled and drank like a fish, and no one could manage him, but he led an exemplary life when she was there. His cuisine was delicious. The first house-boy, gardener, and two mafoos (grooms) were also Chinese. Mammá's maid, Marie, was French. A doll-like Japanese amah (maid) named Cheo, trotted about the house on straw sandals, decorative but inefficient. The second house-boy, gate-keeper, his assistant, a water-coolie, and also the interpreter were all Koreans. Two native night watchmen guarded the house during our sleeping hours. The Koreans are a peaceful people but at times Chinese bandits came down from Manchuria. My father always slept with his gun beside him.

The vast valley lay before the house cut by a single highroad leading south which my mother in this distant wilderness called "The Road to the World." Behind the house a path trailed northward by mountain fastnesses to Manchuria. Hills hemmed in this wide valley, chameleon hills, changing with every passing season, flushed in spring by wild pink azaleas, clothed in emerald green by summer rains, brown in autumn, in winter, white. Silence reigned, immense, overpowering, broken only by the song of the river, by tinkling bells beneath the eaves, by crickets in summer, by crows in autumn. Solitude. Meditation.

Here we lived with books, hundreds of books, as companions. The piano was a great resource in leisure moments.

In the afternoon the horses were brought around by the Chinese mafoos and we started off for a long ride. This was

Japanese table in living room at Sonamo
(Photographed by Helen Struve Meserve)

the most agreeable part of the day. My parents had Austra-
lian horses while I trotted along on a China pony, Pat. We
rode by hills and valleys, past grey villages where the
friendly natives always greeted us. At times they would pull
turnips or corn from their tiny plots to offer. Korea is a poor

country. The natives are pathetically poor, but their generosity never fails. It is an admirable trait of their character. They are certainly the most likeable nation of the Far East and their sweet nature makes up for some of their faults, such as lack of initiative.

One evening on one of these rides we came upon an old woman washing cabbage in a stream. Nearby stood a low mud dwelling with pumpkin vines covering the ragged thatch roof. Magpies hopped about the compound for they are almost a domestic bird here. A naked brown baby sat in the doorway devouring an ear of corn. The old woman smiled as we approached and offered us her pipe to smoke. All Korean women smoke long slender pipes. "How many children have you?" she asked my mother. This is always the first question of Korean females. The old lady finished her washing and went to the house. Asleep on the floor of the poor room lay several men with their hats on, their heads supported by blocks of wood which in Korea serve as pillows.

Our friend reappeared and pressed into our hands an ear of corn, all she could give. She expected nothing in return and would have been surprised had we offered her money. A sweet sense of hospitality and generosity alone had guided her.

The Governor of the Province

Several times a year the governor of Unsan Province made a trip from his walled capital of Yeng-Ben to the American Concession. These visits were not purely disinterested as he always tried to "squeeze" my father, in Oriental fashion, but he obtained no satisfaction. All Korean officials squeeze. The country is governed on a system of squeeze. The governors squeeze the magistrates, the village headmen squeeze the people and are in turn squeezed by the magistrates. Therefore the Koreans live from hand to mouth, planting just enough rice or millet to last them the year, well knowing that any surplus would be taken from them. If a Korean is well-off his friends and relations come to his house and remain until the last grain of rice is eaten, the last oriental piece of money spent. When they leave he often accompanies them to enjoy the hospitality of some other mutual friend or relation. To refuse hospitality is unknown. Even in public inns the night's lodging is free (that is the right to lie on the floor with other travelers in a common room). Food alone is paid for.

The governor's sedan-chair and bearers

The Governor traveled in a closed chair hung with black cloth, preceded by yamen (palace) runners who cleared the way, proclaiming in a loud voice that the Governor of the province was approaching. Numerous gentlemen-in-waiting attended him and occasionally he was accompanied by his dancing-girls. He was a keen old man, a picturesque figure in flowing white robes and black horse-hair hat, fan in hand.

When our house was finished the Governor came to call. He sat in the drawing-room on an European chair, drinking tea with my parents and admiring everything politely. Behind his chair stood an interpreter, hands tucked into flowing sleeves.

"Pray tell His Excellency," said the Governor designating my father, "that this house is like heaven, but I never dreamed I would go to heaven and get a cup of tea besides."

On another occasion the Governor lunched with us. As usual an interpreter stood behind him, and also one behind my father. The Governor sat uneasily on the extreme edge of his chair. When olives were passed to him he ate them with relish, and then, lifting the tablecloth and bending his head, he spit the stones upon the floor.

My father had ordered California canned fruit served at the end of a perfect meal composed by Mammá's expert hand, as the Koreans had a high opinion of these fruits and thought no foreign meal complete without them.

Our native house-servants were excited at having this high official at table. Yi, the head house-boy, on offering to me a full dish of canned peaches let the bowl slip. The ripe California fruits in their glistening juice slid down the front of my pink silk frock to the floor. After a stiff meal it was good to have a provocation to laugh. I laughed and my parents laughed. We laughed immoderately and the governor watched us with round wondering eyes. Then he turned to his interpreter. "Tell His Excellency and his family how deeply I appreciate their courtesy to me by making light of this catastrophe."

This was an Oriental conception of courtesy, for no man

My father (left) with governor of Unsan Province

must ever pain another over any mishap, or even over disaster such as death. Etiquette prescribes that one must laugh and say that it is nothing. Our occidental lack of manners had been construed into exquisite courtesy by this Far Eastern potentate.

Market Day

Near our house was a tiny hamlet called Puk-Chin where every five days market was held and people from the surrounding country poured in to buy provisions. Some came on foot, others astride tiny donkeys, their feet dangling to the ground. The small, sturdy, vicious Korean horse figured prominently in these processions, saddled with a pack, and a native astride without stirrups. There was something biblical in the sight of these white-robed men with black horsehair hats straddling their miniature mounts. Bulls are also used as beasts of burden. Occasionally a closed palanquin, perched at a perilous angle on a bull's back and lurching with each movement of the beast, sheltered a Korean lady who must never be seen in public.

Market was held on the main street of the village, merchandise being exposed on straw mats spread upon the ground. The merchants crouched beside. Millet and rice were the principal articles sold, the peasants buying just enough to suffice five days till the next market. Silks were displayed, wooden combs and long slender pipes. In winter sheepskins and cotton-wool served to pad the wadded winter clothing. An admiring group was always to be found besides the mat where black horsehair hats for men were exposed.

The village street was crowded with men and boys talking, laughing, or quarreling. Towards sundown they mounted their steeds, returning through the mountains to valleys whence they came. When the sun had set and the last white figures had passed along the road, Puk-Chin settled down to the evening meal. The air was sweet with odours of smoke curling up from wood fires where the evening rice or millet simmered. Inquiring stars filled the heavens and the solitude was intense.

The Korean Woman

The social status of the Korean woman is greatly inferior to that of the man.

When a Korean man marries he brings his wife to his parents' house. If he has brothers they also marry and bring their wives home. The young couples live with the parents. The mother-in-law is often harsh and tyrannical with her sons' wives, who are subordinate to her and must obey whatever she dictates. Her word is law. Often the life of the young wife is one of drudgery and hardship. Therefore every Korean woman looks forward to the time when she herself will become a mother-in-law and can in turn exercise her authority.

The Korean wife is a household slave. She prepares food for her husband and serves his meals but may not sit down to eat with him.

The Korean woman has no name. In childhood she receives one such as "Beauty" or "Life-Long Blessing," but loses it upon marriage and becomes known as the wife, and later the mother, of So-and-So. Sometimes she is taught the "Unman," or native script, but generally cannot write even her own name. When this is necessary she traces on paper the outline of her hand with outstretched fingers.

From the age of eight years girls are kept in seclusion and must never appear in public. Even the poorest man in a mean dwelling has an inner room for his daughter. It is a disgrace for a young girl to be seen by a man. She remains hidden most of her life, even after marriage, which usually occurs in her sixteenth year.

The woman of the higher classes rarely leaves her husband's house from the day she goes there a bride. This naturally does not apply to the coolie class whose women work in the fields and do all manner of hard labour.

The Korean woman has no social life, being always occupied with household affairs. Besides cooking, the principal duties of the young girl and woman are sewing and ironing. These tasks occupy her constantly as the white clothing needs frequent cleansing. In winter padded garments are worn which must be ripped apart before washing and afterwards sewed together. Ironing in Korea has nothing to do with a hot iron as in our countries. The garment is laid upon the floor, and the woman, kneeling, beats it with two slender wooden sticks. This treatment eventually flattens out the material and restores the original gloss, but the process is long. The sticks are manipulated as a drummer beats his drum, falling alternately with rapid rhythmical regularity. This monotonous sound is heard at all hours of the day and night in Korean villages. Washing is done by the older women at the river or village well.

Swing day in Korea
(Photographed by Helen Struve Meserve)

In spring, in the fifth moon which usually falls in June, a day called "Swing Day" is set apart when the young girl is permitted to leave her seclusion. On that day all men are supposed to remain indoors. The young girl puts on her gayest raiment and goes with her playmates and the older women to the hillsides where for this occasion swings are hung from the branches of the pine trees. Here she spends her annual holiday playing and swinging with her young girl friends. On that day the hillside behind Puk-Chin village seemed a garden with little maids in bright-hued garments, rose-red jackets, and cornflower-blue skirts, dresses white as the opium poppy and yellow as lilies, intermingling like flowers. Green frocks fluttered like leaves tossed by wind. The poor little recluses in their long-roped swings flew far out over the ravine, skirts blowing, black eyes sparkling, then back again and up till they seemed lost in the branches above. They frolicked throughout the long warm day, the cuckoos calling from the trees. Midnight found them still swinging in the light of the crescent moon.

The Korean woman (even of the peasant class) has a soft voice and sweet manners. Her costume is quite distinct from either Chinese or Japanese dress. A full skirt of transparent material is tied under her arms and worn over baggy trousers. A short jacket covers the shoulders, not quite reaching to the top of the skirt, thus leaving the breast exposed. Her black hair is parted and done in a coil in the neck, fastened with silver pins. Peasant women wear their hair in a braid wound about the head.

The Korean woman has many children. She carries her baby strapped to her back. The little ones are often pretty. A Korean mother is proud if her child has a big stomach. This means that she can afford to feed him well. These people are so poor that life to them is one long struggle for food. If her means permit, the mother often stuffs her offspring with rice or millet to obtain rotundity of figure.

Marriage in Korea is a great event for men as well as for women. Only a married man is really of consequence. An expression for marriage in the Korean language, is "to take the hat" or "to take the topknot." Only after marriage may the Korean man wear the topknot and hat to which he had no right before. This rule is very strictly observed. Before marriage the man wears his hair in a braid down his back, no matter what his age. In general the Korean marries young and there are few bachelors. It is said that, in the rare cases of a girl remaining single by preference, at her death she is buried beneath the high-road that the constant passing to and fro may keep her soul from finding rest.

Marriages are arranged between the parents of the man and those of the young girl by an intermediary, or "go-between." The man seldom sees his bride until after the wedding ceremony which is most simple, bride and groom bowing low to each other several times in presence of witnesses. The new wife, muffled in draperies and laden with jewelry, is conducted to her husband's home in a closed chair or on a pony, according to his means.

Polygamy is occasionally practiced in Korea but less than formerly, the people being too poor generally to support more than one wife.

Korean Dwellings

This Land of Morning Calm has a strange beauty, half wild, half calm. High hills stand sentinel, jealously guarding peaceful valleys where thatch-roofed mud-huts seem more like a growth of huge mushrooms than a village.

From afar a Korean town is difficult to distinguish as the low mud-houses blend completely with the greys and browns of nature.

A Korean dwelling is constructed in a peculiar manner.

The framework, made of the trunks of trees, is put together in a horizontal position and erected afterwards. A network of rice-straw rope is strung between the timbers, and the interstices filled with mud-balls. This forms the wall, which then receives a thick inner and outer coating of mud. These humble dwellings, never more than one-story, are well adapted to the wind-swept valleys. When the autumn wind whistles between the hills, the Korean in his low hut scarcely heeds it. The houses are often built with two compounds, or courts—the outer for the men, the inner for the women. The windows, which serve also as doors, are wooden frames stretched over with rice-paper. These fragile panels are very convenient for curious natives desiring to observe others, while remaining themselves unseen. They merely poke a hole in the paper with their finger and apply one eye to the aperture. The roof of the ordinary Korean dwelling is always of straw. Rounded grey tiles are used for the houses of the well-to-do.

An individual feature of Korean houses is the primitive heating system. In the air-space between ground and floor, flues conduct the heat of a fire (generally built outside the house) under the mud floors, thus warming them, a comfortable economical arrangement, as the natives sleep on the floor, their heads resting on a block of wood, and have no bed-clothes. The hotter the floor, the deeper the slumber of the native, but the unhappy European unused to this system, gasps for breath and wonders if the house is on fire. This system of flues is called in Korean "kang."

The main, and often only, beauty of a Korean house is the vaulted ceiling, made with fine oak beams and rafters. The rooms are small and unfurnished, save for an occasional chest in which the family wardrobe is kept. These chests, sometimes made of fine wood with iron or brass trimmings, are very ornamental, and are much sought after by foreigners. Low round tables used for serving meals are removed when the repast is finished. Rice or millet, forming the principal food in this country, are piled in brass or porcelain bowls. Dried fish and a highly-seasoned relish made of cabbage, called "kimchi," is served with it.

A pretty custom is that of hanging bells under the eaves of houses. With the faintest breeze a gentle tinkle is heard.

The Korean enters his hut and seats himself on the floor without removing his hat. In Europe this would be impolite but in Korea it is the contrary. The Korean, however, leaves his straw sandals before the door.

The moutain villages of northern Korea are most attractive in autumn after the leaves are dead, and before the first snow covers the brown hills. Then golden pumpkins and gourds lay ripe among their withered vines on the roof. Strings of scarlet peppers and yellow corn are hung to dry beneath the eaves. The atmosphere is crisp and radiant.

When day has vanished behind the hills, and night steals down on the valley, the Korean remains in his mud hut through whose paper windows the light of a bean-oil lamp flickers. He rises with the sun and retires at nightfall. The belated traveler finds the hill villages lighted only by the stars.

Beliefs and Superstitions

Buddhism still exists in Korea to a small degree but the religion of the country is ancestor worship, based on filial piety, one of the greatest Oriental virtues. This cult consists of offerings of food and incense before the tablets and on the graves of ancestors. Fortune never favours a man who forgets his forebears. This same ceremony is performed before the tablets of the spirits of the Sky, Earth, Mountains, and Rivers, and various other protecting spirits. The Koreans believe that every hill, river, and tree is inhabited by a good or evil spirit. The very air is peopled with spirits and the natives have many ways of propitiating them.

Beneath the gnarled pines on the hillsides are tile-roofed shrines called "devil-houses," where the spirit of the mountain dwells. Nearby bits of white paper and gaily coloured rags are tied around the trunks of trees and attached to bushes, which the natives place there as a propitiatory invocation to the spirits.

Sickness is also an evil spirit and must be treated with respect. Smallpox, very prevalent in Korea, is addressed in the highest terms. While "His Excellency," as he is called, is a guest in the house, nothing is done that might anger him.

The "mudang," or woman witch-doctor, stands on the lowest rung of the Korean social ladder. The people resort to her to dispel the alarming spirits surrounding them. She sits by the sick, the noise of her drums and cymbals frightening away the spirit of disease. At all hours of the day and night the sound of her gongs may be heard in every village.

In spring, for about a week, the "Mudang Festival" is held. The witch-doctors, an empty bottle in one hand and a cork in the other, run through the valleys and on the hillsides endeavouring to catch evil spirits and thrust them into the bottles they hold. Once captured the spirit cannot escape to again torment its former victim. The mudang is paid for this service rendered to some person possessed by a devil. Often she runs for days before the elusive spirit is secured. The longer she runs, the higher the reward.

When Koreans first saw white people dancing they thought it was a form of devil-chasing.

The devil-posts occasionally seen by the roadside are also supposed to frighten away evil spirits. These posts have roughly carved hideous faces. Once we passed a secluded valley whose entrance was guarded by two war-like figures brandishing sticks, their eyes and mouths painted black. What demon could withstand these grim apparitions?

Koreans have necromancers to help them choose a propitious site for a grave. This choice is an important matter, usually considered while the person is alive. Should an unlucky spot be chosen for a father's grave, ill-luck will surely pursue his descendants. Korean graves are generally found on the hillsides, rarely in the valleys. If circumstances permit, an entire hill is bought in order that the grave may be in a lonely place, completely isolated. The graves of the poor are merely grass-grown mounds but those of kings and nobles are surrounded with slabs and posts of stone. Grotesque stone beasts stand guard in the solitude.

Mourners in Korea wear a special costume, a grass-cloth robe bound around the waist by a piece of rope. A large scalloped hat of split bamboo covers head and shoulders. Three years is the allotted time for mourning father, mother, or husband. During that period men in government positions go out of office. Even though guilty of crime they may not be approached.

Early one autumn morning a mournful dirge broke on the air. Rushing to the windows we beheld a funeral procession slowly advancing along the road near Sonamo. The bier, borne on the shoulders of eighteen coolies, was draped in scarlet cloth. Bright-coloured papers floated from it while a gaudy dragon, coiled on top, glared with large green eyes. Four boys preceded the bier bearing the red and buff banners upon which the virtues of the dead are inscribed. Then came a small table where food is placed for sacrifice. The men of the family followed (no women are allowed) and a company of friends closed in behind. They crossed the river on the stepping stones and continued their way between fields of yellow millet, the notes of the sad monotonous chant echoing from down the sunlit valley.

The following panegyric chant, written by a Korean on the death of a white man on the American Concession, has a certain eloquence.

"Alas, as for this world, it is only a place for strangers to tarry in a brief time. It has been so from of old. Years and months pass like the flowing of a stream. It is like the early dew on the grass, moved by the morning wind, or like a grain of millet on the waves of a broad ocean. Therefore the hour of death is not the same for all. It is not possible to tell when the moment will come to put off the body and enter Nirvana like Buddha. This man was one of the best of men. His presence was as delightful as the days in spring. His intellect clear as the moon.

"We had hoped he would not grow old in a thousand years. His friends mourn for him and even the grass and trees are sad. It is impossible to record our grief. We weep and know not what to say.

"Alas, how sorrowful. We shall see his face no more. We write these words of everlasting farewell, our tears flowing in sorrow.

"Pak Kio Sam prostrates himself and presents this funeral dirge to the dead."

Summer Rains

The climate of Korea is very healthy, cold in winter and hot in summer, but between June and August there is a most trying rainy season. For about six weeks heavy, devastating streams of water pour from heaven upon the earth. Moist heat reigns. Mists veil the hills. Gnarled pine trees stand motionless in the warm air. Brown villages lie desolate, without life. Black pigs and naked babies play about, crouching beneath the eaves when the rain falls heavily. The doors of the houses are thrown open. Women seated on the floor within sew or prepare the meal of rice or millet in the dingy kitchen. Men smoke eternal pipes or, stretched out on the floor, sleep the long dark hours away. Earth holds her breath, waiting. Then the rain descends in torrents, impetuously, angrily, falling on the roof like ramrods, cutting deep gashes in the roads and swelling the streams till they boom along with a noise like the faraway beating of drums.

Occasionally the crushing rain ceases, only to descend again with doubled energy. Peals of thunder announce an approaching storm. Lightning flashes behind the hills. It requires courage to live through the summer rains.

The houses are picturesque at this season smothered beneath pumpkin and gourd vines whose glowing yellow globes lay ripening on the thatch roofs, while millet and Indian corn grow to man's height.

Winter in Korea is very cold and the North lies for months beneath a blanket of snow.

Autumn and spring, the best seasons, are truly delightful. In spring myriad fruit-trees in blossom spread their flower-laden branches throughout the land. Violets and lilies-of-the-valley abound. Wild pink azaleas flame on the hillsides. Blue swallows and wild pigeons nest in our roof.

In autumn the weather is crisp, invigorating, and sunny. Ears of yellow Indian corn hang beneath the eaves of thatch-roofed huts and baskets of bright red peppers are spread upon the roofs to dry. The noise of insect life is stilled and save for the murmur of the stream the nights are very silent.

The Walled Town of Yeng-Ben

The time-old walled town of Yeng-Ben in northern Korea is the seat of the governor of Unsan Province. My father, having business with this official, set off one November morning for Yeng-Ben accompanied by Mammá and me. We traveled partly in sedan-chairs carried by eight coolies, partly on horseback. As usual on such expeditions, Kim, our interpreter, a Korean house-boy, a Chinese cook, and a Japanese amah trotted behind, mounted on native ponies. Two mine superintendents journeyed with my father, each with his house-boy. We formed quite a cavalcade together with a cart for luggage, bedding and provisions.

Northern Korea is a succession of hills, valleys, and narrow passes. Turbulent streams tumble over rocky beds. We passed through this wild beauty, valley upon valley revealing glimpses of straw-roofed huts cosily tucked away with smoke curling up from the "kangs."

Natives passed us mounted on ponies already burdened with heavy packs. This is the prevalent mode of transportation, but the sturdy quadrupeds do not seem to mind. Bulls are also used for transporting merchandise.

Eleventh century walls near Yeng Ben
(Photographed by Helen Struve Meserve)

The distance from the American Concession to Yeng-Ben is not great; nevertheless the journey took two days as the roads in this primitive land are in a sad state, furrowed with ruts and strewn with rocks. We forded streams, as native bridges loosely built of logs, straw and stone are destined principally for pedestrians.

On the evening of the second day we reached the entrance of a canyon through which Yeng-Ben is approached. On either side rose hills wooded with gnarled pine trees. Yeng-Ben Mountain looked down upon us.

A turn in the road brought us upon the wall of Yeng-Ben. This great wall does not immediately encircle the town but runs for miles along the crests of hills surrounding the valley. The town, scarcely more than a big village, lies in the hollow.

In former times Yeng-Ben must have been an important center to warrant such extensive fortifications. It was difficult for us to learn then anything definite about the history connected with this wall as Koreans are very vague and inaccurate. Kim, the interpreter, told us of great stone battles having taken place from the ramparts. These missiles become deadly weapons in the hands of the natives.

In his excellent book, *The Passing of Korea*, Hulbert tells us that in the eleventh century, a wall (similar to the Great Wall of China) was built in the northern part of Korea (probably in 1033):

"In the far North one can still find remnants of a mighty wall that was built clear across the peninsula from the Yellow Sea to the Japan Sea to keep out the wild barbarians who made sudden and sanguinary raids on the peaceful citizens of Koguryu. Remains of this wall can still be seen today in the vicinity of Yong-Byun (Yeng-Ben). It was twenty-five feet high and two hundred miles long."

Undoubtedly this was the wall we were then contemplating, built eight or nine centuries ago. The massive wall is neglected, like all else in this country, and broken in places.

Main street in Yeng Ben
(Photographed by Helen Struve Meserve)

It is impressive, now following the outline of a near hill and disappearing in the dense growth of trees, then visible on a distant ridge silhouetted against the sky. The entrance gate is built on a foundation of Roman arches, the enormous slabs of granite neatly fitted together.

Passing through an inner gate surmounted by curving roofs of grey tiles, we came in sight of Yeng-Ben in the valley below. There is nothing of interest in this big village of mud huts. The governor's palace alone is worth mentioning. We walked in the streets, which were exceptionally animated as it was market day. White-coated merchants sat on their heels besides goods spread on mats on the ground.

A government house had been placed at my father's disposal, built around a court, one-storied with a tile roof. Our rooms were about seven feet by nine, with low ceilings.

There was no furniture. We entered by small paper doors and sat upon the floor beneath which a roaring fire had been made in the "kang." Fresh straw mats had been laid for us. We had brought along camp beds with us.

We dined in our apartments that evening. The cook prepared the meal over a brazier, and the house-boys served us on individual tables not a foot high. Candles in tall brass holders placed on the floor cast a dim light.

A cook is always an essential member of our party on such trips as the food found by the wayside is not to be contemplated.

After dinner as we still sat upon the warm floor the door opened and Yi, our head house-boy, appeared followed by a strange woman clad in scarlet garments from head to foot, including a small red hat. Her face was painted red and white and large silver pins were thrust into a knot of hair low on her neck. Without a word, she entered, and crouching upon her heels in native fashion, silently contemplated us with round unwinking eyes.

"This is a harlot," said Yi cheerfully in his Christian-mission-taught English. "She wanted to see the foreign lady."

"Take her away, Yi," ordered my father sternly. The scarlet figure faded reluctantly into the night.

Upon arriving, my father had sent word to the Governor who requested us to call on him later. At eight o'clock we stood before the palace, one-storied as are all buildings in Korea. The feeble light of a lantern guided us across a dark court, past the spacious summer apartments to the low winter quarters. Stepping over a high door-sill we found ourselves in a small plain room lighted by a single candle in a tall brass candlestick. The governor sat cross-legged upon the floor, dressed in a long white silk coat and a horsehair hat, his men-in-waiting and dancing-girls grouped about him. He rose, extending a limp left hand. Chairs having been provided for us, he reseated himself on the floor and offered each member of our party a large black cigar, expressing his surprise when Mammá refused. Kim, our native interpreter, stood before us, his hands tucked into his flowing sleeves.

The Governor was much interested in my father's gold watch, holding it so long we feared the owner would never recover his property. The Governor finally relinquished it to examine Mammá's rings. The diamonds dazzled him. He spoke to the interpreter: "Tell His Excellency next time he goes to America I would greatly appreciate his bringing me a few precious jewels."

He then asked my father's age. He already knew it as they were old acquaintances, but he was merely being polite.

"Thirty-eight," answered my father.

"Impossible," exclaimed the Governor. "I am sixty and you look much older than I."

This was exquisite courtesy in a country where age is venerated and not abhorred as with us.

When conversation lagged we requested some music. The singing-girls, clad in long, full, multicoloured skirts bound under the arms, seated themselves in a corner. Their glossy black hair was smoothly parted and done in a large coil at the nape of the neck, fastened with heavy silver pins. Six musicians with gongs and fiddles took place in an outer room. The girls then sang a droning song punctuated at intervals by a beat of the drum. The harmony of Korean music is excellent but to Occidental ears all melody is lacking. One note is held until the singer apparently tires of it and drops on to another, thus making a drawling, nasal sound. The performance was monotonous, and when the song finished we took our leave and went out into the star-lit night.

Next morning my father had an interview with the Governor. Mammá and I, attended by a great part of the population, explored Yeng-Ben, threading our way along narrow streets among numerous pigs and children that always impede progress in a Korean town. Once we heard loud chanting voices issuing from a house nearby and, looking in, found a school-room where twenty small boys seated on the floor were swaying back and forth droning their lessons aloud beneath the sharp eye of a master. As we opened the door the noise ceased and twenty pairs of black eyes regarded us curiously.

A speciality of Yeng-Ben is the silver work. This metal is treated much in the same manner as cloisonné. The designs are formed by a strip of iron the width of a hair, and the silver beaten into it. The result is very harmonious.

We visited a silversmith and saw a few boxes made in this manner, but the people are too poor to have a stock, working to order only. We saw an interesting ornament against the evil eye (which the natives fear greatly). Two tiger claws were held by soft gold roughly worked to resemble the face of a tiger. The Koreans often wear such ornaments but the claws are held by bright-coloured enamels instead of gold. The tiger, formerly so plentiful in Korea, is venerated by the natives. His image is embroidered on the coats of high officials.

We climbed to an open pleasure-house on the mountain. No sound arose from the brown town below and we forgot its existence looking across the valley to the hills beyond, crowned by the great wall.

That afternoon we attended the trial of native thieves having stolen gold and amalgam from the American mines.

We found the governor in the same room as on the preceding evening. His stolid countenance bore an official frown and a pair of horn-rimmed spectacles. All the available space was occupied by men-in-waiting and dancing-girls. The doors of the apartments were open. Outside, prostrate upon the ground, were the shivering prisoners, who dared not raise their eyes to the governor's face. His remarks were greeted with cries of approval from the attendants. He asked my father if he would like to have the men killed for their offense. The question was of course perfunctory. My father replied that death was not necessary. The governor then pronounced the sentence: a year's work on the roads. The worst culprit, however, was first stripped, then laid face down on a board, that chill November day, while the attendants gave him thirty lashes, provoking groans and cries.

After the trial a dance was given in my father's honour in one of the summer buildings. Four of the girls were dressed in full bright-coloured gowns with pieces of striped cloth shaped like long narrow bags falling over the hands. Musicians with drums and fiddles sat on the floor. At first the dance was only a swaying of the body and a lifting of the hands with their gay coverings, but gradually it drifted into quicker movements.

Next morning we left Yeng-Ben, turning our faces to the North. The great mountain silently watched us depart till a range of hills hid it from our view.

Hyang-San Monastery

"Buddhism, once powerful in Korea, fell into disfavor and eventually became intermingled with nature worship and fetishism" (Hulbert).

Today there are few adherents to the Buddhist faith. Ancestor worship and shamanism, the cult of good and evil spirits, are the prevailing religions. In the latter spirits are supposed to people hills, rivers, trees, and air.

Various Buddhist Institutions exist in this country. Among these is the ancient monastery of Hyang-San, in northwestern Korea.

One June day found us on the road leading to this famous

shrine. We traveled as usual in sedan-chairs and on horse-back, alternating from one to the other.

We went north. The valleys grew broader, the scenery wilder as we penetrated into high mountains. We passed paddy-fields where rice was cultivated, the luscious green of young plants enameling the valley. Flocks of white herons flew over these verdant expanses. Once a sacred ibis soared by on pale pink wings.

We traveled all night to avoid the heat, a full moon lighting our way. Fireflies flashed their tiny lanterns and the perfume of wild roses lay on the air. The rush of turbulent streams was the only sound in those long still hours.

Buddhist Monastery Hyang-San
(Photographed by Helen Struve Meserve)

Towards morning we came to a narrow gorge between high mountains, apparently impenetrable. A foot-path led through the gorge and beyond rose the grey roofs of the monastery beside a tempestuous river, shaded by pine and willow trees. About thirty temples composed this monastery. The monks gave us one of these as sleeping quarters. A huge gilt Buddha on the altar seemed surprised at our intrusion. Worn out, we lay down on the floor and slept before the servants could undo our camp beds.

A few hours' rest refreshed us. When we awoke bright sunlight flooded the scene. A feeling of peace pervaded the air and over the grey-roofed temples lay the hush of world-old dreams.

An aged monk in a grey robe guided us about. Some of the temples were quite elaborate with wide projecting roofs of grey tile. Beneath the eaves the rafters were richly decorated in soft colours, a feature in Korean buildings. On the main portal of one temple a white dragon was portrayed. Below was the Buddhist emblem of purity, the immortal lotus flower. On the long black altar within, five gilt images of Buddha reposed.

In the court was a pagoda-shaped monument in stone, symbolical of the learning of the monks. "Line upon line, precept upon precept" till perfection is attained.

Fish are painted and carved in many of the temples. "Fish live in water," our old guide said, "so their likeness in the temples prevents fire."

The monks told us that the oldest temple dated back a thousand years. No date is accurate in Korea but the temple looked very ancient so we choose to believe their tale. Nearby was the burial-ground. The graves were marked by egg-shaped stones five feet high, with inscriptions indistinct and covered with moss.

In the cool recesses of one small temple a huge gilt Buddha sat, the hand raised in blessing, the third finger touching the thumb. At his feet was a brass bowl of water. This we also saw in other temples placed before the idols who, we learned, sometimes needed a drink.

In the same temple were ten wooden statues representing the judges of the dead. All Buddhist believers who die are examined by one of them. Those who can show a good record pass to heaven over a rainbow bridge, but the souls of the wicked are tortured and boil in hell. Each judge controls a period of six years of human life. The man who dies at thirty is therefore not examined by the same judge as the man who dies at forty-five.

We called on the head monk in his dwelling and found him seated on the floor. In one hand he held a paper fan, in the other a rosary. A decoration from the Emperor of Korea was flung over his grasscloth coat. He was about fifty years of age, good-looking with brown eyes and very white teeth. A sparse black beard grew on his chin such as the Orient alone can produce. He offered us sweetened water to drink and green leaves fried in oil.

In one of the temples hung a large gong which is beaten all day and prayers are said for the soul of the Emperor. A young monk sat beside it telling his rosary of a thousand beads, for each bead a stroke of the gong and a prayer. When he finishes another monk takes his place, for the prayers must never cease.

In another temple a ceremony was taking place in memory of some departed brother. Sacrifices of food are made yearly on the anniversary of his death. On the altar were spread mounds of flaky rice in shining brass bowls, dishes of rubbery seaweed, pea-cake, beans, and piles of doughy cakes. Earthenware jars contained "sool" (native whiskey). Dressed in grasscloth coats, the monks chanted and droned their prayers. When the ceremony was over I dare say they ate up the food, which would be perfectly natural.

The sonorous tone of a great bronze bell marks the setting

of the sun and is echoed in all the temples calling the monks to evening prayer. Each time a small brass bell was heard they raised their hands to their heads, then clasped them slowly before the breast and prostrated themselves before the altar where Buddha was enshrined. Again and again they bowed, chanting softly, their grey robes sweeping around them, shaven heads touching the floor. The tasks of the day were finished. In silence night closed in.

A Korean Feast

General Hyen, a Korean friend of my father's, has a beautiful estate near Seoul. One spring day the general's son, graduate of an American college, invited us to spend the day on his father's place. Carried in sedan-chairs by coolies, we passed the fine old East Palace where strange stone beasts guard the entrance. Leaving the city behind, a half hour's ride brought us to the Hyen estate. Here we were greeted by young Mr. Hyen and a friend, Mr. Pak, a former member of the Korean Legation in Washington, both of whom spoke excellent English. Dressed in immaculate white clothes and stiff black hats, they were typical Korean "yang-ban" (nobles), courteous, gentle of face and manner.

It was blossom-time. Everywhere peach, pear, and apple trees were laden with delicate blooms. Now and again a mist of petals fluttered down to earth. Violets grew in profusion in the grass. Scattered here and there were numerous small houses, the dwellings of relations and "hangers-on." The general had one hundred and fifty persons living off his generosity. A well-to-do Korean never refuses this hospitality to relations.

Beyond a ravine the city wall rambled along the hillside. A spring of sparkling water bubbled over rocks. Everywhere dull red flowers drooped on their stems, too weary to hold up their heads. Mr. Pak said the Koreans called these flowers the "Little Old Woman," because they are so bent over.

As we stood admiring the lovely scene before us, we heard a chorus of groans. Looking around we perceived twenty coolies slowly ascending an almost perpendicular hill behind us, carrying on their shoulders a heavy European dining-table, upon which our meal was to be served. Finally they staggered to the top. We soon followed, and saw between two hills a crystal brook spanned by a pleasure-house. Over it the pines leaned caressingly. A light wind stirred the branches and rippled the water. The dining table had been placed here and we sat down to a Korean meal composed of fish-soup, vermicelli heaped in large brass bowls, and "kim-chi," the highly-seasoned cabbage relish the Koreans eat with everything. A black pudding, made of rice, honey, and chopped prunes, decorated with almonds, formed the dessert. There were various delicacies such as fresh pears, peeled, quartered and piled in pyramids, also preserved lotus-root and yellow candies made from the flowers of pine trees. There were other things which I no longer recall. We were content to look at much of the food, but the pudding and lotus-root were good. Throughout the repast claret and champagne were served. Afterwards tea was made with a Russian samovar. At the end of the meal Mr. Pak became communicative and told us of himself and of his fifty "hangers-on." He had a lazy brother who, although forty-five years of age, had never worked in his life but lived off Mr. Pak. No gentleman works in Korea. To see them moving about with slow elegant gestures, fan in hand, is a lesson for Europeans suffering from high blood pressure.

We spoke of the many quaint beliefs of old Korea. Mr. Hyen told us that once when he lay sick unto death at the palace, mudangs (woman witch-doctors) were called in to sit by his side. The music of their drums and cymbals is suposed to drive away sickness, which the natives believe is an evil spirit. As he lay there he heard these witch-doctors talking among themselves. Said one: "This poor man must have buried his father in an unlucky place, else he would not be so sick as he is now."

He told us the Korean legend of the "Magpie Bridge": "A lovely princess lived in a faraway star, once when the world was young, but she was unhappy as her husband, whom she loved dearly, was wild and dissipated. In vain the princess implored him to forsake his evil ways. At last her father grew angry and sent this naughty boy to another planet where he might repent alone. The princess still loved him and begged that he might return. Her father permitted him once a year for a single day to leave his distant home. That day no magpies are seen on earth for they form a bridge from star to star for the meeting of the lovers."

As the sun was sinking we left the pleasure-house. Laden with violets and blossoms we went down into the city.